# THE FRAGMENTARY DEMAND

D0880133

# THE FRAGMENTARY DEMAND

*An Introduction to the Philosophy*
*of Jean-Luc Nancy*

Ian James

DISCARDED

STANFORD UNIVERSITY PRESS

STANFORD, CALIFORNIA

2006

BOWLING GREEN STATE
UNIVERSITY LIBRARIES

Stanford University Press
Stanford, California

© 2006 by the Board of Trustees of the Leland Stanford Junior University.
All rights reserved.

No part of this book may be reproduced or transmitted in any form or by any
means, electronic or mechanical, including photocopying and recording, or in any
information storage or retrieval system without the prior written permission of
Stanford University Press.

Printed in the United States of America on acid-free, archival-quality paper

Library of Congress Cataloging-in-Publication Data

James, Ian (Ian R.)
   The fragmentary demand : an introduction to the philosophy of Jean-Luc
Nancy / Ian James.
      p.   cm.
   Includes bibliographical references and index.
   ISBN 0-8047-5269-9 (cloth : alk. paper)
   ISBN 0-8047-5270-2 (pbk. : alk. paper)
   1. Nancy, Jean-Luc.   I. Title.
B2430.N364J36 2006
194—dc22

2005025802

Original Printing 2006

Last figure below indicates year of this printing:
15   14   13   12   11   10   09   08   07   06

*For Ruth*

# Contents

# Acknowledgments

I would like to offer my warm thanks to all those who have helped with the production of this work, in particular Norris Pope, Angie Michaelis, Tim Roberts, and Andrew Frisardi at Stanford University Press. For the various ways in which they have helped, supported, or inspired I would also like to thank: Howard Caygill, Martin Crowley, Ann Deyermond, Patrick ffrench, Alison Finch, Christopher Fynsk, Kristy Guneratne, Jane Hiddleston, Leslie Hill, Michael Sheringham, Douglas Smith, Simon Sparks, Alistair Swiffen, and Emma Wilson. In particular I would like to thank Jean-Luc Nancy himself for the warm welcome he gave me during my short visit to Strasbourg and for his generosity and openness in responding to my questions. I would like to offer my gratitude to the Arts and Humanities Research Board for funding a period of research leave which allowed me to complete this book, and Downing College, Cambridge, both for the sabbatical leave which allowed me to pursue this research and for the stimulating and supportive working environment that it provides. Thanks are also due to Edinburgh University Press for permission given to reproduce material in Chapter 1 originally published in the review *Paragraph*. Lastly I would like to thank Ruth Deyermond for all the support and intellectual stimulus she has given throughout the writing of this work. To all of the above, many thanks.

# Abbreviations

| | |
|---|---|
| *A and B* | Immanuel Kant. *Kritik der reinen Vernunft.* 2 vols. 1781, 1789. Reprint, London: Routledge, 1994. |
| *AI* | Jean-Luc Nancy. *Au fond des images.* Paris: Galilée, 2003. |
| *As* | G. W. F. Hegel. *Ästhetik.* 2 vols. Frankfurt: Europäische Verlagsanstalt. |
| *BP* | Jean-Luc Nancy. *The Birth to Presence.* Trans. Brian Holmes et al. Stanford, Calif.: Stanford University Press, 1993. Quotations from this source are sometimes modified. |
| *BSP* | Jean-Luc Nancy. *Being Singular Plural.* Trans. Anne E. O'Byrne and Robert D. Richardson. Stanford, Calif.: Stanford University Press, 2000. Quotations from this source are sometimes modified. |
| *BT* | Martin Heidegger. *Being and Time.* Trans. John MacQuarrie. Oxford: Blackwell, 1962. |
| *BW* | Martin Heidegger. *Basic Writings.* Ed. David Farrell Krell. New York: Harper and Row, 1977. |
| *C* | Jean-Luc Nancy. *Corpus.* Paris: Métailé, 1992. |
| *CD* | Jean-Luc Nancy. *La Communauté désœuvrée.* Paris: Christian Bourgois, 1986. |
| *CI* | Maurice Blanchot. *La Communauté inavouable.* Paris: Minuit, 1983. |
| *CM* | Jean-Luc Nancy. *La Création du monde; ou, La Mondialisation.* Paris: Galilée, 2002. |
| *CP* | Martin Heidegger. *Contributions to Philosophy (from Enowning).* Trans. Parvis Emad and Kenneth Maly. Cambridge: Cambridge University Press, 1998. |

CPR       Immanuel Kant. *Critique of Pure Reason*. Trans. Paul Guyer and Alan W. Wood. Cambridge: Cambridge University Press, 1998.

DG        Jacques Derrida. *De la grammatologie*. Paris: Minuit, 1967.

E         "Nietzsche: Mais où sont les yeux pour le voir?" *Esprit* (March 1968): 482–503.

ED        Jacques Derrida. *L'Écriture et la différence*. Paris: Seuil, 1967.

ES        Jean-Luc Nancy. *Ego Sum*. Paris: Flammarion, 1979.

ESP       Jean-Luc Nancy. *Être singulier pluriel*. Paris: Galilée, 1996.

FT        Jean-Luc Nancy. *A Finite Thinking*. Trans. Simon Sparks. Stanford, Calif.: Stanford University Press, 2003.

GA        Martin Heidegger. *Gesamtausgabe*. 102 vols. Frankfurt: Klostermann, 1975–. Volumes are cited by number only, as follows: vol. 2 = *Sein und Zeit*; vol. 3 = *Kant und das Problem der Metaphysik*; vol. 5 = *Holzwege*; vol. 9 = *Wegmarken*; vol. 47 = *Nietzsches Lehre vom Willen zur Macht als Erkenntnis*; vol. 48 = *Nietzsche: Der europäische Nihilismus*; vol. 65 = *Beiträge zur Philosophie (Vom Ereignis)*.

GT        Jean-Luc Nancy. *The Gravity of Thought*. Trans. François Raffoul and Gregory Recco. Atlantic Highlands, N.J.: Humanities Press, 1997. Quotations from this source are sometimes modified.

HUA       Edmund Husserl. *Gesammelte Werke*. 38 vols. The Hague: Nijhoff, 1950–. Volumes are cited by number only, as follows: vol. 3 = *Ideen zu einer reinen Phänomenlogie und phänomenlogischen Philosophie*; vol. 16 = *Ding und Raum*.

I         Jean-Luc Nancy. *L'Intrus*. Paris: Galilée, 2000.

IC        Jean-Luc Nancy. *The Inoperative Community*. Ed. Peter Connor. Trans. Peter Connor et al. Foreword by Christopher Fynsk. Minneapolis: University of Minnesota Press, 1991.

KPM       Martin Heidegger. *Kant and the Problem of Metaphysics*. Trans. Richard Taft. Bloomington: Indiana University Press, 1990.

L         Jean-Luc Nancy. *Logodaedalus: Le Discours de la syncope*. Paris: Aubier-Flammarion, 1976.

LA    G. W. F. Hegel. *Hegel's Introduction to Aesthetics.* Trans. T. M. Knox. Oxford: Clarendon, 1979.

LM    Jean-Luc Nancy. *Les Muses.* Paris: Galilée, 1994. 2nd ed., 2001.

N    Martin Heidegger. *Nietzsche.* 4 vols. Trans. Joan Stambaugh, David Farrell Krell, and Frank A. Kapuzzi. San Francisco: Harper and Row, 1987.

NMT    Jean-Luc Nancy. *Noli me tangere.* Paris: Bayard, 2003.

OG    Jacques Derrida. *Of Grammatology.* Trans. Gayatri Spivak. Baltimore: Johns Hopkins University Press 1998.

OP    Jean-Luc Nancy, *L'Oubli de la philosophie.* Paris: Galilée, 1986.

PD    Jean-Luc Nancy. *La Pensée dérobée.* Paris: Galilée, 2001.

PdP    Jean-Luc Nancy. *Le Poids d'une pensée.* Montréal-Grenoble: Le Griffon d'Argile—Presses Universitaires de Grenoble, 1991.

PF    Jean-Luc Nancy. *Une Pensée finie.* Paris: Galilée, 1990.

PoP    Maurice Merleau-Ponty. *Phenomenology of Perception.* Trans. Colin Smith. London: Routledge and Kegan Paul, 1962. Quotations from this source are sometimes modified.

PP    Maurice Merleau-Ponty. *Phénoménologie de la perception.* Paris: Gallimard, 1945.

RJ    Jean-Luc Nancy. Edited with Philippe Lacoue-Labarthe. *Rejouer le politique.* Paris: Gallimard, 1981.

RP    Jean-Luc Nancy. Edited with Philippe Lacoue-Labarthe. *Le Retrait du politique.* Paris: Gallimard, 1983.

RT    Jean-Luc Nancy, with Philippe Lacoue-Labarthe. Ed. Simon Sparks. *Retreating the Political.* Trans. Céline Surprenant, Richard Stamp, Leslie Hill et al. London: Routledge, 1997.

SM    Jean-Luc Nancy. *Le Sens du monde.* Paris: Galilée, 1993.

SP    Philippe Lacoue-Labarthe. *Le Sujet de la philosophie.* Paris: Aubier-Flammarion, 1979.

SW    Jean-Luc Nancy. *The Sense of the World.* Trans. Jeffrey S. Librett. Minneapolis: University of Minnesota Press, 1997. Quotations from this source are sometimes modified.

*T*    Jacques Derrida. *Le Toucher, Jean-Luc Nancy.* Paris: Galilée, 2000.

*TM*    Jean-Luc Nancy. *The Muses.* Trans. Peggy Kamuf. Stanford, Calif.: Stanford University Press, 1996. Quotations from this source are sometimes modified.

*TS*    Edmund Husserl. *Thing and Space: 1907 Lectures.* Vol. 7 of *Collected Works.* Trans. Richard Rojcewicz. Dordrecht: Kluwer, 1997.

*UC*    Maurice Blanchot. *The Unavowable Community.* Trans. Pierre Joris. New York: Station Hill Press, 1988. Quotations from this source are sometimes modified.

*VaI*    Maurice Merleau-Ponty. *The Visible and the Invisible.* Trans. Alphonso Lingis. Evanston, Ill.: Northwestern University Press, 1968. Quotations from this source are sometimes modified.

*VI*    Maurice Merleau-Ponty. *Le Visible et l'invisible.* Paris: Gallimard, 1964.

*WD*    Jacques Derrida. *Writing and Difference.* Trans. Alan Bass. Chicago: University of Chicago Press, 1978.

THE FRAGMENTARY DEMAND

# Introduction: The Fragmentary Demand

> . . . the opening which represents the fragmentary demand, one which
> does not exclude, but rather exceeds totality.
>
> —MAURICE BLANCHOT, *The Infinite Conversation*[1]

## The Opening

The philosophical writings of Jean-Luc Nancy form a vast and heterogeneous corpus. Dating from the 1960s to the present day this corpus
includes over fifty-three authored or coauthored volumes and over four
hundred published articles in reviews or collected works. These writings
range from important and influential readings of classical philosophers
(for example, Descartes, Kant, Hegel) to decisive engagements with other
figures who have played a key role in the development of twentieth-century French philosophy (principally Nietzsche, Heidegger, Bataille, Merleau-
Ponty, and Derrida). Nancy is an accomplished writer on visual art and on
literature, and is recognized as having made an important philosophical
contribution to debates around the question of community and the nature
of the political. He is also a thinker who has sought, with an insistence and
a persistence that imply the urgency of an imperative, to engage with contemporary questions of technology, war, and global injustice.

Indeed, an initial description such as this barely begins to touch
upon the diversity and heterogeneity of the philosophical corpus signed

with the name Jean-Luc Nancy. Such diversity poses a particular problem for the kind of introductory volume proposed here. On one level this problem is fairly straightforward; namely, it is difficult if not impossible to give an exhaustive account of Nancy's prodigious output or to reduce it to a summary presentation or résumé. Yet on another level the problem posed here necessarily pertains to a certain kind philosophical writing and a certain manner of engaging with thought as such. The diversity and heterogeneous nature of Nancy's corpus is not the product of any lack of discipline or methodological rigor on the part of the philosopher, nor does it result from a rejection of the category of philosophy per se, such that we might take this corpus to be a vast work of antiphilosophy. Rather, and this will be the key argument of the following study, the manner in which Nancy writes philosophy, his multiple and fragmented corpus, itself arises from a thinking of, or an exposure to, multiplicity and fragmentation. This experience of fragmentation not only makes demands on thought and on the writing of philosophy, it also makes ethical and pragmatic demands on us, and calls for a certain kind of decision or response on our part, as readers of philosophy and as participants in a shared worldly existence. Nancy's philosophical corpus does, then, need to be seen as a response to a fragmentary demand, or rather to a demand made by the fragmentary.

"The fragmentary demand": this phrase, quoted above in the epigraph, is from a passage of Maurice Blanchot that describes the imperative underpinning the aphoristic writing of Friedrich Nietzsche.[2] In the long section devoted to Nietzsche in his 1969 work *L'Entretien infini*, Blanchot discusses the abuse of Nietzschean philosophy by the National Socialist regime and in particular the editorially abusive interventions of Elisabeth Förster-Nietzsche and Peter Gast in their systematization of Nietzsche's posthumous fragments into the work *Die Wille zur Macht*.[3] Yet, Blanchot asserts, although Nietzsche might at times have attempted to systematize his thought in order to make it more accessible or digestible, it is a thinking which ultimately refuses all system building or the kind dialectical mediations which would synthesize its fragmented parts into a greater whole or unity.[4] For Blanchot, Nietzsche's fragmentary thought is such that it exceeds all figures of totality and refuses all subsumption of fragmentation into a greater whole. This, again, is not because Nietzsche is simply rejecting philosophical system building in favor of poetic effusion or maxim-like insights. Nietzsche, Blanchot maintains, is responding to a question which makes a necessary and unavoidable demand on the thinking of the transvaluation of values and of the transformation of the human that is proposed in works such as *Also sprach Zarathustra* and *Jenseits von Guten und Bösen*. This question is posed by Blanchot in the following terms:

> What happens to thought when being—the unity and the identity of being—has withdrawn without ceding its place to that all too easy refuge, nothingness? When the Same is not the ultimate sense of the Other and Unity is no longer that in relation to which the multiple can be said? When plurality is said without relating itself to the One? At that moment, perhaps, the demand of fragmentary speech makes itself felt, not as a paradox but as a decision.[5]

This demand, the demand of a fragmentary thought and writing, or of an exposure to fragmentation which *makes* a demand on thought and writing, traverses Nancy's philosophical corpus in its totality. His philosophy unfolds as a decision to respond to the demand imposed by the multiple and the fragmentary. This, at least, is the central claim made by the present study. Immediately, though, such a claim necessarily calls itself into question. For how can a fragmentation that exceeds any figure of totality be said to characterize a body of thought in its totality, since it is precisely the figure of totality itself which has been displaced or erased by the fragmentary demand? Referring to the "whole" of Nietzsche's writing, Blanchot speaks of the need to "never conceive of this whole—the non-unitary whole—as a system, but as a question and as the passion of a pursuit in the impulse of truth."[6] What follows, then, will aim to address Nancy's philosophical corpus in these terms and will do so on the basis that this, precisely, is the manner in which his philosophical corpus addresses us as readers who respond to the demands of thought. Nancy's philosophy, most evidently his thinking of the "singular-plural," turns persistently and insistently around the demand imposed by a thinking of being in which any possibility of unity and identity has withdrawn, and where the multiple demands to be thought without reference to any overarching unity or totality.

The problem posed for an introductory volume dedicated to the work of Jean-Luc Nancy results, then, not just from its vast dimensions and heterogeneous engagements, it arises more decisively from the manner in which this thought unfolds as such. The manner in which he attempts to think in response to a fragmentary demand, to think being outside of unity or identity, means that to read his work in terms of a system, or to offer a summary presentation or résumé of the work in its entirety, would be to miss the way in which it functions as thought. This is true even to the extent that one may miss entirely the force and direction of his thinking when one attempts to write "on" Jean-Luc Nancy or to treat the proper name "Jean-Luc Nancy" as a philosophical subjectivity that might claim ownership over ideas, or to whom a certain specific series of gestures or innovations might be attributed in the mode of "propriety" or individual achievement. This is more than just intellectual pirouetting or playfulness. The first chapter of this study engages in a sustained way with the manner in which Nancy reformulates the whole question of philosophical subjectivity, its identity and propriety, through his important readings of Kant and Descartes. Nancy, it will be argued, aims to think outside or beyond figures of subjectivity and stable or self-same identity formations, and does so on the basis of a fundamental ontological questioning. The discussions of space, body, community, and art which make up the subsequent chapters will highlight the manner in which Nancy's thought unfolds as a ceaseless engagement with, or reworking of, other thinkers or bodies of thought. To this extent philosophy in Nancy emerges as an experience of philosophical community or of a sharing of the sense of philosophy itself, a sharing which can be seen to exceed the propriety or identity of the individual philosopher. The aim of this work, then, is not to promote or otherwise claim any particular fidelity to Nancy's thought, or to enhance a following, or to promote an emergence of "Nancy studies." It is arguable that Nancy's fragmentary philosophical writing is highly resistant to any possible cooption into a school or method. This is either a weakness or a strength depending on one's point of view. Rather this study will aim to address Nancy's philosophical writing as a series of singular instances of exposure to the multiple and the fragmentary per se, or rather, as a series of singular exposures to the demand made by the multiple and the fragmentary. To this extent, while what follows will necessarily and inevitably unfold under the sign of the proper name "Jean-Luc Nancy," it will attend to the manner in which the thinking which bears that name unties all logic of propriety which the proper name might properly be said to bear.

This is not to say, however, that a biographical perspective and a chronological overview of Nancy's philosophical itinerary would be impossible or be entirely invalid for an initial engagement with his work.

On the contrary, a number of biographical facts are of immediate interest. Nancy taught in the Philosophy Institute of the University of Strasbourg from 1968 until his retirement in 2002 and during this time held a number of other secondary posts or visiting professorships: at the École Normale Supérieure in Paris, and in Germany and America. In the 1960s he was involved in the Christian Socialist movement and in particular with the CFDT union and the Catholic review *Esprit* in which he began to publish in the 1960s.[7] Although Nancy's official commitment to and involvement with Christianity ended by the early 1970s, it nevertheless left its mark on the development of his later work, for instance in his philosophical meditation on the Eucharist in *Corpus* (and in his thinking of embodiment more generally), in some of his more recent publications on Christian painting, and more generally speaking in what during the 1990s and early 2000s he has come to call the "deconstruction of Christianity."[8] Perhaps the most important biographical fact pertaining to the last decade and a half of Nancy's life has an intrinsically bodily dimension, namely the heart transplant he received at the beginning of the 1990s. It is an extraordinary fact that many of Nancy's most important works, including *Corpus, Le Sens du monde*, and *Être singulier pluriel*, are written after this transplant and during the period of extended physical suffering and illness (including cancer) caused by the antirejection drug cyclosporin. Although the impact of this experience on the development of Nancy's thinking would be impossible to determine precisely, it directly informs the short work entitled *L'Intrus* (2000). This work is both a moving account of physical suffering and a meditation on the experience of organ transplant that engages some of the key philosophical concerns that dominate Nancy's thinking throughout his career: the propriety and identity of the human subject and body, their intersection with technology, and the originary exposure of each to that which is foreign or heterogeneous to them. One of the most persistent thoughts that inform Nancy's philosophy from the early 1970s to the present day is the thought that "the truth of the subject is its exteriority and its excessiveness: its infinite exposition" (*I*, 42). *L'Intrus*, and the very personal nature of what it describes, suggests more than any other work in Nancy's philosophical corpus that his thinking is intimately and actively engaged with his experience of physical, embodied existence, and with the exposure of that existence to an originary heterogeneity or "exteriority."

By the same token, however, the biographical perspective should not be placed wholly under the sign of identity, in such a way that the chronological development of Nancy's thought is framed in terms which imply the propriety and unity of a philosophical subjectivity. A broadly linear trajectory or story can, of course, be traced: Nancy begins his career in the 1970s, and until the early 1980s publishes philosophical texts that can be situated broadly within the genre of commentary (for instance, commentaries on Lacan, on Kant, Descartes, and German Romanticism). This period is also a period of collaboration with his friend and colleague Philippe Lacoue-Labarthe. In the 1980s and 1990s Nancy shifts away from commentary and begins to write the major works which form the bulk of his philosophical achievement, works on community (e.g., *La Communauté désœuvrée* [1986], *La Comparution* [1991]), on freedom (*L'Expérience de la liberté* [1988]), on embodiment (*Corpus* [1992]) and also major works on ontology and finite, worldly existence (e.g., *Une Pensée finie* [1990], *Le Sens du monde* [1993], *Être singulier pluriel* [1996]). As has already been indicated, the 1990s and the first years of the new millennium have seen an increasing interest on Nancy's part in Christian motifs and an increasing engagement with certain aspects of Christian thought. Throughout this lengthy writing career there are also notable continuities, however, for instance an interest in literature and art, and in aesthetics more generally, as borne out in the publication of important works such as *L'Absolu littéraire* (1978), *Les Muses* (1994), and *Au fond des images* (2003). What the chronological perspective offers, then, is a wider sense that the development of Nancy's thinking follows a trajectory from philosophical commentary to works which engage with more general philosophical concerns or questions. Taken together with the biographical perspective it also indicates the degree to which certain concerns (Christianity, subjectivity, body, art) are sustained throughout Nancy's career. Yet, as has been suggested, such concerns, are sustained on the basis of a multiplicity of engagements with other thinkers, such that Nancy's thinking emerges only in, or as an exposure to, a shared community of thought.

To this extent the invocation of Maurice Blanchot's commentary on Nietzsche at the beginning of this introduction is not fortuitous. The first chapter will show the way in which Nancy begins his career as a philosopher in a specific French milieu dominated by a particular reception of both Nietzsche and Heidegger. From the beginning of his career to the present day the thought-paths Nancy takes are closely bound to those taken by others in his French literary-philosophical community: those taken by Blanchot himself, by Bataille and Levinas, Derrida and Deleuze, to name but the most obvious candidates. In the responses which have been made to Nancy to date, by both literary commentators and philosophers, the influence of Heidegger most often has been seen to dominate the general character and direction of his thinking, to the extent that he has been judged to be a neo-Heideggerian, and a fairly orthodox one at that.[9] Nancy's traversing of Heidegger and the marks which this crossing has left are indeed undeniable. Yet a key claim made by this study is that Nancy is neither more nor less Heideggerian than are Blanchot, Levinas, and Derrida; that is to say, all of these philosophers traverse the Heideggerian thinking of being in one way or another, but all do so in order to critique or otherwise radically transform and exceed that thinking. In this context it is arguable that the predominant focus on Nancy's "Heideggerianism" has obstructed any serious and sustained engagement with the full breadth of Nancy's thinking and has hampered any proper attempt to evaluate his importance as a philosopher.[10] It is here that the figure of Nietzsche, and of Nietzsche as a thinker of the fragmentary such as he is portrayed in *L'Entretien infini*, is decisive. As the first chapter will show, Nancy's early writing around the Nietzschean/Heideggerian affirmation of the "overcoming of metaphysics" reads Nietzsche *against* Heidegger. Likewise subsequent discussions, in particular those of space, body, and of community, will demonstrate the manner in which Nancy unties and reworks Heidegger's thinking of being in the name of a thinking of multiplicity, fragmentation, or what Nancy himself comes to call the singular-plural of being. In this respect it can be argued that Nancy's thought exceeds the Heideggerian frame and yet reminds us that Heidegger himself remains a complex thinker whose vast philosophical corpus still demands to be read. Nancy emerges, then, as a thinker who demonstrates the continued importance of Heidegger for contemporary thought and whose breadth of philosophical engagement is far from reducible to any more or less orthodox "Heideggerianism."

Nancy's philosophical engagements include, for instance, influential readings of speculative idealism and important responses to key twentieth-century French thinkers (most prominently Bataille, Merleau-Ponty, and Derrida). Importantly, Nancy's critical attitude toward Heidegger is underlined also by the way in which he maintains an engagement with philosophy as such and refuses any shift towards a "poetic saying" of being and an affirmation of the end of philosophy.[11] Along with many of his contemporaries in the late 1960s and early 1970s Nancy engages with the question of the "overcoming of metaphysics," yet he does so not to proclaim the end of philosophy as such but rather to insist that philosophy be maintained in the questioning of its end, limit, or point of closure. If, in the wake of Nietzsche and Heidegger, philosophy has come to question the sense of philosophy itself and to think the exhaustion of metaphysical possibilities of signification, then, for Nancy at least, the task of philosophy is to maintain itself in a thinking of the sense of this exhaustion. Throughout his career, and in particular during the 1980s and after, Nancy questions the manner in which much contemporary discourse in France and elsewhere has sought to elide or forget the decisive shifts which have occurred within the European philosophical tradition, in the wake of key thinkers of modernity: Nietzsche and Heidegger, but also Marx and Freud.[12] In this context to ignore or elide these decisive shifts, to think as if a certain end or limit point of philosophy had not occurred, would be to forget, according to Nancy, the very task of philosophy itself, such as it presents itself to us at the beginning of the twenty-first century. This is articulated most clearly in *L'Oubli de la philosophie* (1986), where Nancy's affirms that it is "philosophy itself that has posed the question of its own closure, of its own outer limit at the edge of sense. . . . it is through this obstinate engagement with the very limit of signifying presentation that philosophy properly carries out the philosophical act. The forgetting of philosophy is the forgetting of this obstinacy" (*OP*, 33–34; *GT*, 24). Nancy's thinking, then, enacts itself as a kind of obstinacy or persistence at the limit of philosophy itself. This is a practice of philosophy where the philosophical maintains itself as a demand to think the limit as such, that is to say, the limit of philosophical and metaphysical signification. As Nancy himself puts it: "We have not stepped outside of philosophy: we are within it in the instant and in the gesture where the will to signification knows itself as such, knows itself as insignificant, and delivers from itself a different demand of 'sense'" (*OP*, 74; *GT*, 51). As the following chapters will aim to show, Nancy's thought unfolds in response to this "different demand of 'sense'."

This is also a demand to think "sense" itself differently. "Sense" in

Nancy is untied from an exclusive belonging to a symbolic order or relation of signifier to signified; it exists both as an outer limit and as an excess of signification per se, becoming "*the element in which* signification, interpretations and representations *can occur*" (*OP*, 90; *GT*, 59). In this way Nancy's thinking of the limit, end, or closure of philosophy unfolds as a necessary reinscription of the category of "sense," where sense is not meaning or signification, but rather that which, at the outer limit or in excess of signification, makes meaning and signification possible. Sense, here, is the sense of a shared worldly and material existence which always already makes sense, and thus preexists language or any possibility symbolic determination. The emergence of this "different demand of 'sense'" and of a different thinking of sense will be the dominant concern of the first three chapters of this book. What becomes clear in this context is that sense in Nancy takes on an ontological status. It is that element in which things have their being as such and is thus the "real" of the world.[13] To this extent what follows will also argue that Nancy needs to be viewed, albeit in a rather singular way, as both a materialist and a realist philosopher for whom questions of worldly embodied existence and the truth of that existence are of paramount importance.

Thus the persistence of philosophy in Nancy occurs, in the wake of Nietzsche and Heidegger, as the persistence of a demand, imposed by a necessity and urgency of the present, that an exposure to the limits of philosophical signification be maintained and that this exposure be thought as such. If a certain ontology of sense emerges here as a response to this demand, it does not do so in the guise of a transcendental signifier or unifying principle which can restore both word and world to a full presence or symbolic plenitude. Sense emerges as the multiple, fragmented, and fragmentary real of the world to which thought is ceaselessly exposed at its limit. In Nancy's own words: "sense offered at the limit of signification takes us in the movement of a presentation *to* which is a rupturing of presence itself . . . a rupturing of signification and its order" (*OP*, 99; *GT*, 63). The following presentation of Nancy's philosophy will aim to follow this movement by which philosophy is exposed to an offering of sense at the limit of signification. Rather than a summary account or systematizing exposé, this study is written in the mode of critical exposition. *Exposition* here implies an exposure to, or opening onto Nancy's thought, the tracing of its movement *as* exposure or opening. *Critical* on the other hand implies that careful attention will be given to the determinate contexts in which Nancy writes, his engagements with speculative idealism and existential phenomenology, but also his responses to, or collaborations with, other specific figures (Bataille, Blanchot, Derrida, and Lacoue-Labarthe). The five motifs which give each of the five chapters their name, subjectivity, space, body, community, and art, are intended less as thematic unities and more as a series of singular openings. Each motif is construed as an instance of opening onto, or of exposure to, the sense of Nancy's philosophy, in which philosophy itself is articulated as a series of exposures to the limit of sense. Inevitably there are a number of important omissions, that is to say specific works or philosophical interventions on Nancy's part which cannot be discussed in a short work that is necessarily selective of its chosen material. Yet if the presentation of Nancy's philosophy which this work offers is fragmentary or partial, this at least is a necessary result of the fragmentary demand to which this philosophy, as philosophy, responds.

# CHAPTER ONE

# Subjectivity

## Introduction

> What is an author? What does it mean to think philosophical author-
> ship? And finally, what is philosophy? Does this singularity still allow
> itself to be rigorously thought?
>
> —JEAN-LUC NANCY, "MONOGRAMMES"[1]

*At the beginning . . .*

At the beginning of his famous essay "Structure, Sign, and Play in
the Discourse of the Human Sciences," Jacques Derrida alludes to what
he calls an "event" in the history of the concept of structure and suggests
that this event takes the form of a rupture but also a reintensification of
this concept. Published in 1967, the essays collected in *L'Écriture et la différence*, together with the publication of *De la grammatologie*, mark a turning point in the development of French structuralist theory and signal a
shift toward what later became known as poststructuralism.[2] In alluding
to this "event" Derrida clearly has his sights set on dominant structuralist tendencies within the human sciences and specifically within the area
of contemporary French theoretical activity. "Structure, Sign" and a number of the other essays in *L'Écriture et la différence* are focused on key figures or theoretical problems associated with French structuralism.[3] Yet, as

any reader of this essay will know, the event referred to at the beginning of "Structure, Sign," has, according to Derrida, an epochal significance which extends far beyond the shifting currents of the French intellectual milieu of the 1950s and 1960s. It would be easy, he suggests, to show that the concept, and indeed the word *structure*, are central to the episteme of Western science and philosophy.[4] What is at stake, then, in this epochal event is the whole history of Western thought and knowledge, and specifically the tendency within Western philosophical thinking to center or anchor itself upon a fixed point of origin or moment of presence. According to the account Derrida gives of the Western philosophical tradition, this center or point of origin has always functioned like a transcendental signifier guaranteeing the identity and self-presence of philosophical systems and thus grounding them on a bedrock of certainty or truth. This center has taken on various names throughout the history of European thought: essence, existence, substance, subject, transcendence, consciousness, God, man, and so on. The delineation of this tradition of centering or grounding articulates one of Derrida's most famous theses, namely that the history of European thinking is a history of *logocentrism* and the determination of being as *presence*.[5]

The rupture which Derrida attempts to describe here is posited as a historical moment in which Western thought found itself in the latter half of the twentieth century, a moment which, he suggests, was most radically expressed in the philosophical achievements of three key figures: the Nietzschean critique of Christian-Platonic thought, the Heideggerian destruction of the tradition of onto-theology, and the Freudian critique of the subject. In all these cases what is thought is the loss of any founding or transcendental signifier which centers philosophical or epistemological systems on a point of origin or moment of presence. This triad of thinkers—Nietzsche, Freud, Heidegger—form the philosophical matrix which dominates French philosophical activity in the late 1960s and early 1970s, and together articulate the perspectives Derrida mentions: the displacement of traditional philosophical accounts of subjectivity, and the attempt to overcome or move beyond what, in their different ways, both Nietzsche and Heidegger would term *metaphysics*. Interestingly, Derrida emphasizes that the decentering of the concept of structure, and the loss of origin or foundation this implies, is not a process which can be summed up by any specific event, or within the work of any specific author or school; it belongs "without doubt to the totality of an era which is our own" (*ED*, 411; *WD*, 280). This account of the contemporary that emphasizes the "closure" of metaphysics and the overturning of metaphysical foundations will be well known to those familiar with Nietzsche's or Heidegger's thinking, or with wider critical debates around what one might, rather schematically or reductively, term philosophical postmodernity.

Nancy's early philosophical writing can be explicitly situated within the shared sense of an epochal shift or rupture within the Western philosophical tradition, as it is invoked by Derrida in "Structure, Sign." More specifically, it can be identified with the attempt, undertaken by many French thinkers of this period, to rigorously think through the consequences of this rupture, both for philosophy and more widely for the project of Western culture. Indeed, from the outset Nancy's thinking explicitly identifies itself with such an attempt. As will become clear, his early publications are marked by a complex and sustained engagement with the thought of both Nietzsche and Heidegger, and with the different ways each characterizes the metaphysical tradition and attempts to think its "overcoming." As will also become clear, for Nancy, the attempt to think the overcoming of metaphysics involves a fundamental reworking of the foundations of philosophical thought itself and raises two closely interrelated issues: subjectivity, and the relation of philosophy to literature (or, more precisely, the relation of philosophy to the language of fiction, and aspects of style, form, or exposition and presentation). Throughout the 1970s, and in particular through his collaborations with Philippe Lacoue-Labarthe, Nancy's thinking aims to overturn traditional philosophical accounts of the subject as an autonomous self-grounding entity, and in so doing he questions the possibility of grounding philosophy in such a way that would allow rigid separation between the categories "philosophy" and "literature." In Nancy's early work philosophy becomes subject to a kind of generic indeterminacy. It does not become identical with literature, but at the same time any gesture which would seek to preserve philosophical discourse from those contingencies of language in which literature delights (rhetoric, style, form) is rendered fundamentally problematic. For Nancy, philosophical discourse, both his own and that of the philosophers he reads, can never escape the contingency of language, and style or form becomes the stuff of thought itself. The two is-

sues of subjectivity and the relation of philosophy to the language of literature will form the substance of this first chapter, which will examine them
in the context of Nancy's earliest publications and thereafter in the light of
his readings of Kant and Descartes (published in *Logodaedalus* [1976] and
*Ego Sum* [1979], respectively).

The emphasis placed on a mode of philosophizing which is in some
sense literary, or deeply engaged with the question of literature as such,
is reflected in the forums in which Nancy began to publish his work. Although from 1970 onward he worked in the philosophy department of the
University of Strasbourg, he has often published in literary or literary-the-
oretical/philosophical journals whose aims and intellectual scope exceed
the bounds of purely academic philosophy: for example, *Esprit, Poétique,
Aléa, La Quinzaine Littéraire, Digraphe,* or Anglo-Saxon journals such as
*The Oxford Literary Review* or *Sub-stance.* This literary bent is reflected also
in Nancy's collaboration with Lacoue-Labarthe in important works such
as *L'Absolu littéraire* (1978), and in their work published in the first issues
of the journal *Poétique* in the early 1970s. *Poétique,* a journal set up in 1970
and edited by Hélène Cixous, Gérard Genette, and Tvetan Todorov, aimed
from the outset to carry forward what the editors referred to in the first issue as the "theoretical renewal" that had dominated recent literary study
in France and that consisted principally in "an awakening of theoretical
awareness and activity," expressed most clearly in developments in structuralist poetics and narratology. As one might expect, early issues of *Poétique* included publications by well-known figures such as Roland Barthes,
Jean-Pierre Richard, Jean Ricardou, and Hans-Robert Jauss, to name but
a few of those associated with theoretical trends within literary criticism at
the time. Describing itself as a "review of literary theory and analysis," the
first issue of *Poétique* also makes explicit that the theoretical renewal of literature involves a calling into question and a displacement of traditional
generic limits or categories, including those which seek to define or delimit
"literariness" itself: "literariness exceeds the limits of 'official' literature just
as the poetic function surpasses the field of poetry." *Poétique,* then, was to
be a journal dedicated to theoretical hybridity, "a place of exchange and
cross-fertilization between literary theory and criticism," a journal which
exceeded disciplinary and also national boundaries, "a journal without
borders."[6] It was the ideal forum, then, for Nancy and Lacoue-Labarthe,

who called into question at the beginning of their careers the limits that determine and seek to separate the literary from the philosophical. As will become clear, according to Nancy and Lacoue-Labarthe the distinction between philosophy and literature is itself produced by philosophy, in an attempt to assert the purity of its own discursive form and to preserve the rigor of philosophical truth against the rhetorical embellishments of literary style. The relation of philosophy and literature is also, therefore, very much a question of the relation of philosophy to itself, and it is in this context that the figures of both Nietzsche and Heidegger prove to be decisive in the early collaboration between Nancy and Lacoue-Labarthe.

### Nietzsche, Heidegger, and the Overcoming of Metaphysics

Friedrich Nietzsche is a key figure in the development of French thought throughout the 1960s and into the early 1970s, as is Martin Heidegger.[7] Just as important, perhaps, is how the postwar French reception of Nietzsche is inflected by a reading of Heidegger and vice-versa. The key point of reference here is the series of lectures delivered by Heidegger between 1936 and 1940. Published in 1961 in two volumes these lectures were not translated into French until 1972.[8] Yet in many ways the specific publication dates of these lectures, long after they were first delivered, give a misleading idea of the impact they may have made on the French reception of Nietzsche. As Philippe Lacoue-Labarthe points out in an article published in the review *Critique* in 1973 (a year after the French translation of Heidegger's lectures): "Before being translated in effect, the Nietzsche work, as everyone knows, was practically already 'read'" (*SP*, 114).[9] As he also points out, this is largely because of the way in which the interpretation of Nietzsche permeates a great deal of Heidegger's thinking and is clearly present in other works which were translated into French much earlier during the 1950s. Such is the impact of Heidegger's reading that Lacoue-Labarthe can confidently affirm, "there is no way to approach Nietzsche today which is not constrained to pass along the path of the Heideggerian interpretation" (*SP*, 121). The validity of this assertion becomes apparent if one considers the conference held on Nietzsche at Cérisy-la-salle in 1972. The importance of this conference in the history of the French reception of Nietzsche has been remarked upon by a number of

commentators, and is reflected in the list of participants, including highly influential figures who began writing on Nietzsche in the 1930s, such as
Karl Löwith (Heidegger's former student) and Pierre Klossowski (former
friend of and collaborator with Georges Bataille), as well as key thinkers
who rose to prominence in the 1960s and early 1970s, among others: Gilles
Deleuze, Jean-François Lyotard, Sarah Kofman, Jacques Derrida, and of
course, Nancy and Lacoue-Labarthe. Many of the papers given at the Céri-
sy conference mark a settling of accounts with Heidegger's reading of Nietzsche, or at least emerge from it. These papers clearly indicate the milieu
of Nancy's early thinking.[10]

The substance of Heidegger's interpretation is well known and can
be summed up rather schematically as follows. Nietzsche, in his attempt
to overcome metaphysics, remains hopelessly entangled within it, and is
thus the last great metaphysician of the European tradition. As has been
indicated, this judgment on Nietzsche is dispersed throughout much of
Heidegger's writing but is given its most clear and systematic expression in
the 1936–40 lectures. What, precisely, Heidegger means by "metaphysics"
and the way he situates Nietzsche within its orbit can be seen in the following extract:

Nietzsche stands within a decision, as do all Western thinkers before him. With
them, he affirms the predominance of beings over against Being, without knowing what is involved in such an affirmation. . . . Thought metaphysically, Being is
that which is thought *from* beings as their most universal definition and *to* beings
as their ground and cause. . . . Beings are regarded as that which lays claim to an
explanation. Each time, beings take precedence here as the standard, the goal, and
the actualization of Being. (*N*, 3:6–7; *GA*, 47:5–6)

After the publication of *Being and Time* in 1927, Heidegger is famous for
his attempt to pose the question of being in a more originary manner
than the tradition of metaphysics he describes. Being is not posed in Heidegger's work as that which is thought *from* beings, rather it is thought as
that originary event of unveiling or disclosure which allows beings to appear to humans as such.[11] The primary focus on beings (on the ontic) gives
way to an interrogation the existential structures of human being-there
and being-in-the-world (fundamental ontology). Nietzsche, Heidegger
contends, remains within the orbit of metaphysics insofar as he continues to think being on the basis of beings taken as a totality and then con-

ceives of this totality in terms of becoming. For Heidegger, metaphysical thinking always implies this tendency to conceive of being on the basis of beings. Hence one might think of the totality of beings in terms of some higher being which acts as their ground, first principle, or cause underlying their creation (e.g., the Aristotelian *causa sui* or prime mover, or the Christian creator God). Alternatively one might think the totality of beings in terms of being conceived as a world of suprasensible essences or timeless identities, which underlie or make possible the world of phenomenal appearances (Platonic Ideas, the Kantian a priori categories and synthesis, or the Husserlian *eidos* or essences). In each case, Heidegger would argue, we think of beings and then seek their ground, cause, identity, or essence in a principle outside of or prior to them. For Heidegger the persistence of metaphysical thinking in Nietzsche's thought is a consequence of his inversion of Platonism, where the distinction between a suprasensible real world and a sensible apparent world is abolished.[12] Heidegger recognizes, of course, that for Nietzsche the abolition of this distinction is not a simple inversion where the priority given to the suprasensible real is displaced onto the sensible apparent; he recognizes that Nietzsche seeks to think outside of such an opposition. But, he argues, in thinking the totality of beings as chaos, sensation, and becoming he ultimately remains within the orbit of the Platonic opposition like it or not, since he fails to pose the more originary question of being in the Heideggerian sense and in the Heideggerian manner. So just as Platonism thinks of beings in their totality as Idea, so Nietzsche, in his inversion of Platonism, thinks of that totality as the chaos of sensation, with Nietzschean chaos defined, according to Heidegger, as "the concealed, irreducible richness of becoming and of universal flux."

The problem of metaphysics, its overcoming, and the possibility that philosophy may in some sense remain held within metaphysical limits despite the philosopher's best efforts to exceed them, shape the arguments of Nancy's first published articles, as well as his collaboration with Lacoue-Labarthe around the question of philosophy and literature. Significantly, both argue against Heidegger's judgment on Nietzsche, and take up Nietzsche as a paradigmatic figure in their attempt to question the task of thinking at the end of metaphysics.

One of Nancy's earliest articles, "Nietzsche: Mais où sont les yeux pour le voir?" (Nietzsche: But Do We Have The Eyes To See Him?), published in the journal *Esprit* in 1968, aims to address in general terms the importance of Nietzsche for contemporary thought. In particular it engages with the paradoxes inherent in any attempt to invoke Nietzsche as the founding father of an antimetaphysical tradition, when such a tradition would imply the impossibility of any point of firm foundation (which the invocation of Nietzsche as founding father necessarily implies).[13] If metaphysics is the attempt to think the totality of beings in terms of a founding principle or cause which exists outside of or prior to that totality, and if the overcoming of metaphysics implies the loss or destruction of such foundations, then how can one appeal to Nietzsche as a foundation, as a source who would legitimate antimetaphysical thinking? Would not such an appeal to Nietzsche, as founding father, itself involve a metaphysical gesture? Nancy tackles head on the paradox inherent in invoking Nietzsche as the foundation for an antifoundationalist mode of thought: "No doubt Nietzsche has not been promised to us by anyone as the Father of a tradition. But in a more insistent way, is he not, in a number of respects, a figure who authenticates our own nihilism? A figure who, having already proclaimed this nihilism, allows us to name it again, satisfied to at least perpetuate a fidelity to his words" (*E*, 484). The double bind invoked in these lines is drawn very tightly and seems inescapable; Nietzsche is invoked as an authority for that which would appear to abolish all authority: "[he] arouses the desire for a tradition by overturning traditional exemplarity" (*E*, 485). The question of foundation which is posed most insistently here will be posed with even greater insistence in Nancy's readings of Kant and Descartes. It also formally repeats the argument that Heidegger brings to bear in his judgment of Nietzsche as the last metaphysician. As Heidegger maintained, Nietzsche's attempt to think the totality of beings as a groundless chaos of sensation and becoming, itself implies a grounding of that totality. In the same way an invocation of Nietzsche's authority as an antimetaphysician affirms a foundation and is therefore implicated in the metaphysical moment it seeks to contest. Yet, despite the force of this double bind, Nancy's contention against Heidegger is that "Nietzsche escapes from the theoretical space of metaphysics" (*E*, 500) and offers his readers the means of doing so. But how does Nancy extract Nietzsche and his readers from the seemingly unavoidable double bind he so clearly evokes? The escape from the theoretical space of metaphysics he alludes to is a rather curious one, since it occurs, "in the first instance, in the playing out to the very end the game of this metaphysics. The entirety of metaphysics can be found in Nietzsche" (*E*, 500). Nancy seems to be trying to press beyond Heidegger's interpretation by suggesting that, while remaining ineluctably within the totality of metaphysics, Nietzsche somehow also exceeds or displaces its inner logic. On this reading Heidegger's interpretation regarding the persistence of metaphysical thinking in Nietzschean thought is nothing new, in fact it is preempted by Nietzsche himself and given an outcome or point of issue which is other than the Heideggerian insistence on an originary thinking of being: "Certainly, Nietzsche warns us with the utmost rigor that metaphysics cannot be surpassed, that one cannot leave one's tradition. Heidegger today maintains this warning. But Nietzsche is there to show us another way" (*E*, 500). What emerges most clearly from the argument of "Nietzsche: Mais où sont les yeux pour le voir?" is the insistence that, in the contemporary philosophical debate around the question of metaphysics and its overcoming, Nietzsche is first and foremost the figure who can provide philosophy with a way forward. However dominant a figure Heidegger is, and remains, in Nancy's thinking, from its earliest inception through to its development in the 1980s, 1990s, and beyond, this initial Nietzschean emphasis *against* Heidegger is decisive. It shapes both the style and direction of Nancy's thinking and the manner in which he comes to read other philosophers.

The image of Nietzsche which emerges in this essay is that of the philosopher genealogist, the thinker able to take soundings from the sedimented layers of philosophical systems to reveal their hidden and shifting foundations (thus the metaphorical hammer with which Nietzsche philosophizes in *The Antichrist* would first and foremost be a geologist's hammer). He emerges also as the thinker of interpretation, of truth and knowledge *as* interpretation, and of existence as fable or narrative. These two interrelated elements allow Nancy to position Nietzsche in relation to metaphysics in his characteristic way. On the one hand the philosopher genealogist discovers the obscured metaphysical foundations of philosophical systems to be hidden prejudices, instances of value which are not grounded as such but need rather to be evaluated and subject to *transvaluation*. Nietzsche offers, first and foremost, a way of reading "texts as systems and as symptoms of that which they do not admit" (*E*, 495). He is a thinker of suspicion, whose mistrust is placed above all on language itself, in what Nancy dubs "the Anti-logos of suspicion." Philosophical systems are not read as grounded truths, but as interpretations whose grounding values can be evaluated as such, but whose status is closer to metaphor or rhetorical trope than to pure concept or timeless, abstract reason. In this sense, if Nietzsche does fall back onto an apparent foundation and thus appears also to fall back into the embrace of metaphysical thinking, that foundation, according to the corrosive logic that circulates in the Nietzschean text, is itself a value, a metaphor, an interpretation, which can be subject to further evaluation. Interpretation, figuration, and evaluation always precede and exceed any apparent gesture of foundation in Nietzsche's thinking. Hence metaphysics is everywhere, but also everywhere looped into an infinite movement of genealogical evaluation and interpretation that are necessarily without end and that displace or undermine the metaphysical attempt to lay foundations for the understanding of beings in their totality. Nancy expresses this logic of Nietzsche's text in the following terms: "Perhaps metaphysics, by dint of being infinitely spread out in Nietzsche, of revealing itself as the free circulation of interpretations, . . . perhaps metaphysics has delivered itself from itself. Neither suppressed, nor surpassed: delivered. Freed to occupy its own metaphysical perspective, but also to be put into play against itself" (*E*, 501–2). Central to this logic of infinite interpretation is the affirmation of existence as fable or fiction. Such an affirmation is, as one would expect, itself an interpretation, an instance of the fable or fiction it describes. One might insist that the affirmation of existence as fable or fiction, of truth as metaphor, is the one thing that the Nietzschean hermeneutics of suspicion cannot be suspicious about, and must posit as a ground or foundation (proving Heidegger correct in his view). Yet one can equally insist, as does Nancy here, that while such an affirmation appears to posit a moment of foundation, at the very same time it unleashes a logic which absorbs that moment into the movement of fiction and interpretation it describes. Hence, as Nancy claims, metaphysics is everywhere in Nietzsche's thought and also everywhere displaced into fiction and interpretation. This position is argued out further in Philippe Lacoue-Labarthe's essay entitled "La Fable (philosophie et littérature)," published in the first issue of *Poétique*, and also in a more complex and extended way in Nancy's treatment of Kant and Descartes.[14] What it necessarily implies, though, is the fact that philosophical language, Nietzsche's, or indeed Nancy's, is itself fiction or fable. Philosophical language is subject to the infinite circulation of interpretation which Nietzsche's genealogical thinking embodies. As Nancy makes clear, this represents a rupture with the image of the philosopher as legislator or judge, which, he maintains, has dominated Western thought from Plato to Kant (*E,* 500). It also represents the moment when philosophy becomes inescapably bound up with its own language, with its metaphors, figures, tropes, and style. This is not philosophy in the form of literature, but rather style itself becoming thought. If Nietzsche shows the way in the overcoming of metaphysics, he does so by returning existence to fable, and thought to the figures and tropes of language which give it life. This is the outcome of Nancy's first discussion of Nietzsche. In many ways it is the starting point of a thought-path and a way of thinking that develops throughout his work up to the present day. Lacoue-Labarthe continues along this thought-path in his essay "La Fable" in a manner which will be decisive for the account Nancy gives of philosophy and the subject of philosophy in his first full-length works.

The collaborative dimension of Nancy and Lacoue-Labarthe's contributions to *Poétique* is reflected in the way the articles published by each demonstrate similar approaches, concerns, and points of reference.[15] "La Fable" begins by explicitly linking the attempt to overcome metaphysics with the attempt to think philosophy as literature; it does so once again by invoking Nietzsche: "It is well known how far the struggle against metaphysics, above all since Nietzsche, has been accompanied by a properly literary effort or has been identified with such an effort" (*SP,* 9). One of the central premises of Lacoue-Labarthe's argument is that philosophical discourse, in its metaphysical moment, is itself responsible for the distinction between philosophy and literature. In its attempt to lay firm foundations for the understanding of beings, philosophy, Lacoue-Labarthe suggests, has always entertained the dream of a "pure saying," which would directly present, or have some kind of unmediated access to, the grounding principles of philosophical truth (e.g., the intelligible realm of Ideas or essences, the certitude of mathematics or reason). In this context the category of literature is produced in reference to those forms of representation which are necessarily held at several removes from the world of Ideas or pure reason, and are always embedded in sensible or contingent elements of language (rhetorical tropes, stylistic embellishments, discursive forms).[16] The dream of philosophy, then, would be to exceed the contingency of the sensible form in which it necessarily exists, to be pure intellection or ideation, and to designate as "literature" all those uses of language which fail to achieve such purity. Lacoue-Labarthe begins his discussion with the desire to pose a number of questions to philosophy:

> I want here to pose to philosophy the question of its "form," or more exactly, to cast upon it this suspicion: what if, after all, philosophy was just literature? . . . I want to question whether the dream, the desire maintained by philosophy since its "beginning" of a *pure saying* . . . has not always been compromised by the necessity of passing through a text, a work of writing, and if, for this very reason, philosophy has not always been obliged to use modes of exposition which do not properly belong to it (dialogue, for example, or narrative). . . . It would, in other words, be a question of interrogating this more or less obscure, more or less silent dread of text, which is perhaps one of the deepest dreads of metaphysics, or which in any case reveals one of its most primitive limits. (*SP*, 9)

Lacoue-Labarthe begins by taking an opposition for which, he contends, metaphysical thinking is itself responsible, that is to say, the opposition between philosophy and literature. He then proceeds by asking how far the accusation brought by philosophy against literature, namely that it is entirely embedded in the sensible contingency of language, can be turned back onto philosophy itself, in such a way that philosophy ceases to be radically different from the literary use of language. Posing questions to philosophy in this manner, Lacoue-Labarthe immediately falls within the strictures of the double bind encountered earlier in Nancy's discussion of Nietzsche. One cannot pose *to* philosophy the question of literature from a space which would be "outside of," or exceed, the play of indeterminacy which is being invoked. Should one achieve a clearly grounded statement about the literary status of philosophy, one would clearly have transcended that literary status and would remain firmly within the space of a legislative philosophical discourse, able to decide categorial distinctions on the basis of metaphysical grounds. Such a statement, as a "nonliterary" philosophical affirmation of the "literariness" of philosophy, would appear to be inherently self-refuting. The assimilation of philosophy to literature would not be something that could be exposed or presented without apparently negating itself and reaffirming the traditional privilege of philosophy (*SP*, 10). Yet, as before in Nancy's discussion of Nietzsche, if this double bind cannot be resolved, it can certainly be twisted in a different direction. Rather than pose the inevitability of a return to philosophy, one can equally think a persistence, and a ubiquity of literature within philosophy itself. Thus the thought which assimilates philosophy to literature would itself necessarily be literature. The apparent self-refutation implied by such a thought would necessarily be governed by a logic of generalized fiction rather than by a logic that recuperates it into a metaphysical ground. This would not exceed the strictures of the double bind encountered above, rather it would think them differently. At stake here is an instance where thought comes to think itself as a kind of necessary fiction or fable, where the paradoxes which arise are themselves part of the logic of fable, and where such a logic necessarily outstrips or assimilates all others. This thought, once again, is in accord with Nietzsche's.

In the course of Lacoue-Labarthe's discussion emerges a reading of Nietzsche that is centered on the famous passage from *Twilight of the Idols*: "How the 'Real World' at last became a Fable." Lacoue-Labarthe takes up the account of fable given in *Twilight of the Idols* and, like Nancy before him, directs it against Heidegger's interpretation of Nietzsche. In his account Nietzsche traces the six stages of the world becoming fable (parodying the six days of the world's creation), beginning with the Platonic assertion of the "Real World" as the suprasensible world of Ideas, and continuing through the various idealist, empiricist, and positivist moments of the Western philosophical tradition (including the Kantian reaffirmation of the suprasensible as a priori synthesis), to culminate in the moment of the "death of God," where, for Nietzsche, the whole notion of an ideal, timeless realm of essences is overcome, and with that the distinction between the "real" and "apparent" worlds.[17] Heidegger's assertion, it should be recalled, was that in seemingly abolishing the distinction between the real and apparent and by affirming the totality of beings as a universal flux of becoming, Nietzsche was affirming despite himself the world of appearance over the "Real" and remaining within the orbit of the real/apparent opposition and hence the metaphysical foundation upon which it rests. Lacoue-Labarthe refuses this gesture in explicit terms by suggesting that the thought of the world as fable or fiction has a more radical force than

Heidegger allows: "To think fiction is not to oppose appearance to reality, since appearance is nothing other than the product of reality. It is precisely to think without recourse to this opposition, *outside* of this opposition; it is to think the world as fable" (*SP*, 16).[18] In the world become fable, a world devoid of ideality, of suprasensible essences or identities, the real is not overturned in favor of the apparent, rather any distinction between the two ceases to be operable; they are both assimilated into the logic of fiction, both are equally instances of fable. As before, the logic of fable precedes and exceeds all attempts to place thought on firmer ground. By implication, therefore, philosophy's attempt to think, or present an unmediated relation to a world of truth (be it one of ideas, essences, or reason) is, and has always been, a colossal fiction, played out in various instances of fable, articulated in different ways at different times within the history of the Western philosophical tradition from the Greeks onward. Like Nancy, Lacoue-Labarthe moves through Nietzsche's thinking of the death of God and the overcoming of metaphysics to pose thought itself as a kind of fiction: "we say that the thinkable and the thought (being, the real, truth) are fictive, that they *are* not (real, true, . . . ). What metaphysics designates as being, namely, and definitively, thought itself, is pure fiction. At the very least, metaphysics is not the discourse of truth but a fictive language" (*SP*, 14). This echoes Nancy's affirmation in "Nietzsche: Mais où sont les yeux pour le voir?" that what is at stake in philosophical thinking after Nietzsche is not the presentation of philosophy in the *form* of literature (as if it were a kind of decoration or a means of access to something higher and extraliterary) but rather "style as thought" (*E*, 490). What is at stake is the necessary looping down of the intelligible into the realm of the sensible, or, more precisely, the overcoming of the difference between the two and the mutual implication of the one in the other.

The consequences of this for the project of thought, and for the status and goals of philosophy more generally, are necessarily wide-ranging. One could easily object that the attempt to think beyond metaphysics in the way Nancy, Lacoue-Labarthe, and many other French thinkers of this period do, is to take a hammer to the whole edifice of philosophy (and of knowledge more generally). It opens the way, one could argue, for total incoherence, arbitrariness, obscurantism, and for a relativism within thinking and knowing, whereby there would be no distinction whatsoever between a fact and a falsehood, reason and unreason, an ethical value and a subjective whim. This, however, would be to mistake the force and direction of the kind of thinking which is unfolding here, or at least to mistake the manner in which Lacoue-Labarthe, and Nancy with him, conceive of such thinking. It has been clear from the outset that there is a double bind at work in the overcoming of metaphysics such that, in a certain sense, the antimetaphysical thinker cannot think outside of its orbit. What Lacoue-Labarthe is suggesting is that in the thought of the world as fable, and of thought as fiction, one is stepping back, remaining within metaphysics, to think its inner logic *against* the logic it proposes for itself.[19] This is less a matter of allowing thought to be arbitrary or relativistic, than it is an attempt, within a necessary structure of metaphysical thinking, to rethink its inner logic and to turn it against itself. According to Lacoue-Labarthe the rethinking of the inner logic of metaphysics, and the displacement of the categories "philosophy" and "literature" which this entails, directs thought toward two initial tasks:

1. To turn back against metaphysics (within metaphysics), under the name of literature, that against which metaphysics has itself turned, that from which it has wanted to constitute itself. This is fighting the good fight.

2. To undertake to force its limits, that is to say, if you like, to displace the bar which symbolically separates literature and philosophy . . . in such a way that on either side literature and philosophy will both be barred and cancel each other out in the moment of their communication: ~~literature philosophy~~. (*SP*, 22)

Thinking, as it becomes a twofold task, firstly of displacing the traditional foundations of metaphysics by returning philosophy to literature, and then of rethinking the limits that metaphysics imposes, does not necessarily affirm total arbitrariness. Indeed it might imply a rather different kind of rigor in the writing of philosophy and in the reading of it. Above all it emphasizes that thought and philosophical discourse (the difference between the two itself being suspended) are more processes or pathways than they are the laying of foundations. Lacoue-Labarthe goes on to think through the implications of this, and also to detail Nietzsche's treatment of metaphor and rhetorical trope, in his subsequent contributions to *Poétique*. In Nancy's reading of Kant, "Logodaedalus," published in the twenty-first issue of the journal, itself dedicated to the question of literature and philosophy, Nancy attempts to develop the consequences of the thinking about thinking which emerges from "La Fable." He demonstrates in this essay that the displacement of the inner logic of metaphysics from within metaphysics itself is necessarily bound up with the way in which philosophers come to write philosophy. Nancy's reading of Kant in "Logodaedalus" is developed and expanded in the publication of subsequent full-length works. It is this more developed reading of Kant, such as it emerges in *Logodaedalus* (1976), to which the discussion now turns.

## Kant and the Foundations of Philosophy

Any philosophical treatise may find itself under pressure in particular passages (for it cannot be as fully armored as a mathematical treatise), while the whole structure of the system, considered as a unity, proceeds without the least danger.

—IMMANUEL KANT, *Critique of Pure Reason*[20]

Nancy begins *Logodaedalus* by calling into question the status of contemporary critical discourses which all too easily invoke the theoretical language of rupture, collapse, or lack of order to oppose it to the values of continuity, plenitude, and solidity, which they associate with "traditional" thinking. By organizing their theoretical language around terms prefixed with such negative indicators as *de-*, *in-*, or *dis-*,[21] such discourses may be responding to what Nancy calls "an imprescribable constraint," and perhaps even to a certain kind of necessity (of the epochal kind discussed above), but they nevertheless have become a fashion within criticism and as such tend to reify, and thus lay a substantive ground for, the very thinking of ungrounding they seek to articulate. Playing on the French homonyms *la mode* (fashion) and *le mode* (mode or substance), Nancy suggests that the making fashionable of critical or deconstructive terminology, its invocation as common currency or as a value which can be taken for granted, ineluctably leads to a transformation of such terminology into its opposite: That is, the means for questioning the assumptions and metaphysical grounding of a certain tradition are returned to that grounding or implicated within those assumptions. As Nancy himself puts it:

The effects of this fashion consist precisely in a return to [*renvoi au*] the system of substance. . . . the fashion, today, consists in a transubstantiation, in an entirely new sense, of all that—by necessity—undermines and undoes the system of substance. The indices of the decomposition, of the deconstruction, of the displacement or excess of this system—that is to say of the entire architectonic and history of the West—which are called for example . . . *text, signifier, lack, drift, trace,* and so on, are converted into values and hypostatized into substances. In a certain way, this transubstantiation is inevitable. (*L,* 7)

Nancy situates contemporary theoretical thinking at a point where a necessary rupturing of the tradition has occurred, but where, at the same time, a recuperation or retrieval of that rupturing into the orbit of tradition is also necessary and unavoidable. To a large extent this appears to repeat the problematic of the overcoming of metaphysics discussed above in relation to Heidegger and Nietzsche, but it does so by transposing it onto the wider field of critical and theoretical debate in 1970s France and more specifically within the context of certain fashionable critical or deconstructive gestures. It also recalls the well-known arguments of Derrida's *L'Écriture et la différence* which explicitly engage with the problem facing those thinkers who attempt to speak beyond the Western tradition of philosophical thought while remaining inescapably caught up in the language and perspective proper to that tradition. Whether it be Emmanuel Levinas, seeking to think outside a certain economy of violence he associates with "the Greek domination of the same and the One," yet having to face the "necessity . . . of installing oneself in traditional conceptuality in order to destroy it" (*ED,* 122–23, 165; *WD,* 83, 111), or whether it be Michel Foucault's affirmation of madness, which, according to Derrida, remains fatally implicated in the dominance of reason it seeks to contest (*ED,* 56; *WD,* 34), many of the essays of *L'Écriture et la différence* have as their central focus the problem of the recuperation within metaphysics of those gestures which seek to contest metaphysics. Indeed, it could be argued that the problem of the recuperation of contestatory gestures recurs regularly in much French philosophical thinking in the late 1960s and 1970s.[22]

For Nancy the inevitability of the recuperation of such contestatory or antifoundationalist thinking is to a certain extent a political/institutional problem indicative of the way certain disciplines within the human sciences adopt philosophical vocabularies for their own purposes and, by removing such vocabularies from their original contexts, reify terms and thus betray their strategic force or conceptual ambivalence. Yet insofar as this transformation or transubstantiation of terms into "hypostatized substances" is inevitable, the question of philosophical foundation and of metaphysics per se is also at stake, just as it was in Nancy's earlier writing on Nietzsche. More specifically, for Nancy, what is at issue is the way in which this question of philosophical foundation always also implies or affirms a topology of *substance*. This, it will become clear, is also the central preoccupation of his reading of Descartes in the 1979 work *Ego Sum*. Nancy's response to Kant in *Logodaedalus* offers him a means to return to the question of foundation in philosophy insofar as he returns also to one of the key inaugural moments within the modern tradition of European thought.

Any reader familiar with the scope and ambition of Kant's first *Critique*, the *Critique of Pure Reason*, will know that this immense philosophical treatise is an endeavor to lay a ground or foundation. The task of critical philosophy, as Kant sees it, is to explicate the conditions of possibility of experience, and with this the foundation for knowledge of the objects of experience. This task entails, first and foremost, an explication or uncovering of the possibility of the unity or synthesis of sensible intuition with forms of intelligibility (logical functions, concepts, categories). Or put another way, Kant's critical philosophy aims to describe the pure essence of knowledge, which makes experience of the sensible world possible, and which has its foundation in the principles of a priori structures. By *a priori* Kant means principles or structures which are not derived from experience but exist prior to it as universal and necessary conditions of possibility for experience. To this extent Kantian thought is idealism insofar as experience is seen to be derived from possibilities or structures of the mind rather than vice-versa (that would be empiricism), and it is "transcendental idealism" insofar as it does not view the existence of the objects of experience either as ideal forms or as a *creation* of the mind (that would be Platonism or subjective idealism), but aims to uncover the ways in which both the subject and the objects of experience are *made possible* by a system of concepts or categories not derived from experience.[23]

It is not within the scope of this discussion (or within the competence of the author) to give a full account of Kant's first *Critique* or of the broader dimension of critical philosophy as a whole. What follows, then, will aim to draw attention to those specific aspects of the *Critique of Pure Reason* which interest Nancy in *Logodaedalus*, namely the overall structure or "architectonic" of the work, the question of "presentation" within critical philosophy (of *Darstellung*, a question which Kant himself addresses), and, crucially, the central role played by the "schematism" within transcendental idealism. It will also aim to situate Nancy's reading within a broader history of certain approaches to Kant, not so much to give a justification or seal of approval to this reading, but rather to show what is at stake for Nancy around the question of philosophical foundations. Perhaps this section will also suggest what the foregoing might mean for Nancy's broader understanding of philosophical writing in relation to literature and for his thinking around the nature and role of subject within philosophy.

As critique Kant's philosophy is about foundation but it is also about limitation, that is, it describes the grounds but also the limits of human experience. Thus it delineates the limits of what we can know, on the one hand, and designates, on the other, all that we must place firmly beyond the possibility of human knowledge. As Howard Caygill has noted, this tension between foundation and limitation has marked much of the reception of the first *Critique* since its publication in 1781. On the one hand there have been the constructive interpretations which follow the ambition of grounding the possibility of knowledge, namely the systematic syntheses of German Idealism (Fichte, Hegel), or the philosophical justifications of science undertaken by late nineteenth-century neo-Kantians (Cohen, Rickert). On the other hand there are those philosophers who have pursued the destructive, critical, or more antifoundationalist possibilities offered by transcendental philosophy, namely the Young Hegelians (Bauer, Feuerbach, Marx) and, most famously, Nietzsche.[24] In the twentieth century this more destructive tendency has given rise to readings of Kant which call into question the foundational ambitions of the *Critique of Pure Reason* itself by focusing on its status as discursive edifice and by highlighting the ways in which the foundations of this edifice may, in fact, be far from secure. Such readings include, preeminently, Heidegger's controversial work, *Kant and the Problem of Metaphysics*, and, after Heidegger, a number of texts published in France, by Granel, and more recently, by Derrida and Bennington.[25] Nancy's *Logodaedalus* can be situated explicitly within this trajectory of antifoundationalist responses to Kant that aim to question the discursive edifice of critical philosophy.

In the introduction of the *Critique of Pure Reason*, Kant himself invokes the metaphor of an edifice provided with secure foundations in order to describe the overall structure, architecture, or *architectonic* of his work: "Transcendental philosophy is here the idea of a science, for which the critique of pure reason is to outline the entire plan architectonically, i.e. from first principles, with a full guarantee for the completeness and the certainty of all the components that comprise this edifice" (*CPR*, 150; *A*, 13; *B*, 27). This architectonic could be described, in rather schematic terms, as follows. The *Critique of Pure Reason* is divided initially into the "Transcendental Doctrine of Elements" and the "Transcendental Doctrine of Method," with the bulk and by far the most important part of Kant's treatise being taken up with the elaboration of the former division. The "Transcendental Doctrine of Elements" is in turn divided into two key parts, the "Transcendental Aesthetic" and "Transcendental Logic," this latter itself comprising a number of further layers and subdivisions (principally the "Transcendental Analytic" and "Transcendental Dialectic"). For most anti-foundationalist readings of the first *Critique* it is the manner in which these parts fit together to form the edifice of critical philosophy that is of crucial interest. Specifically for Heidegger, and then for Nancy after him, the relation between the "Transcendental Aesthetic" and the "Transcendental Logic" is of key importance. A summary account of these two sections of the *Critique* and of the relation between them is therefore necessary.

In its two parts the "Transcendental Doctrine of Elements" offers an analysis of the human faculty of knowing, moving from the experience of objects in sensible intuition (the "Aesthetic"), to the faculty of understanding, which uses concepts in order to make judgments about intuited objects, and then to the faculty of reason, which is able to make further interconnected inferences from these judgments, in a logically rigorous and consistent manner (the "Logic"). In each case the possibility of sensible experience, conceptual judgment, or rational inference must be shown to occur in ways which are universal and necessary, and therefore not derived from the contingency or particularity of experience (hence, taken as a whole, what is at stake is what Kant terms the possibility of "synthetic a priori judgements" [*CPR*, 192; *B*, 73]).

In the case of the "Transcendental Aesthetic" Kant aims to show the way in which the experience of sensible objects, or what he comes to call "phenomena," is possible only on the basis of forms of a priori sensible intuition, time and space. In this sense the "Aesthetic" is focused on the coming into appearance or givenness of objects per se, that is, on the phenomenality of the object world, and to this extent has an important ontological dimension which has been brought out only to varying degrees within the history of responses to the *Critique of Pure Reason.*[26] Space, here, is taken to be a necessary a priori representation that grounds the possibility of external intuitions, and not a determination that depends upon those intuitions.[27] This is not to say that Kant in any way denies the empirical reality of space. He is very explicit in his affirmation of this empirical reality, but affirms it only insofar as he affirms also its transcendental ideality, that is space exists for us, for human consciousness and knowledge, to the extent that we are able to represent it a priori and on this basis perceive objects as being spatially extended and related to each other in a spatial manner (*CPR*, 176–77; *A*, 26–27; *B*, 42–43).[28] Time also is shown to be an a priori form of sensible intuition, that is, not an empirical concept derived from a particular experience, but a necessary condition or foundation for all experience per se. Kant describes time as the form of internal sensible intuition, that is, the intuition of our own selves and of our inner state as temporal in nature. The a priori representation of time, therefore, is a general condition for the experience of external phenomena, insofar as phenomena can only be experienced within the mediating frame of temporal succession, but time is also, more specifically, the immediate condition for interior experience (thoughts, feelings, etc.) (*CPR*, 180–81; *A*, 32–36; *B*, 49–52).

In the case of the "Transcendental Logic" Kant is interested in demonstrating how, for knowledge to be possible, it must be constituted in sensible intuition (phenomena) on the one hand and concepts on the other, and, most importantly, in and through a means of uniting sensible intuition with the ideality of concepts. In this sense what Kant calls "pure general logic" refers to those pure a priori principles, which constitute a canon of the understanding and of the faculty of reason. The term *pure* here indicates an essential abstraction from the content of experience. Thus these principles are formal and logical in their usage and do not refer to empirical content as such, but rather to how ways of knowing relate to each other; or more properly speaking, these principles constitute what Kant describes as "the form of thinking in general" (*CPR*, 196; *A*, 55; *B*, 79). Whereas the "Transcendental Aesthetic" offers rules for sensible intuition, the "Transcendental Logic" offers rules for conceptual understanding and rational inference. In the first division of the "Transcendental Logic" Kant seeks to describe the pure nonempirical concepts of the understanding in terms of what he calls judgment. Judgment here refers to the mediated knowledge of an object through the use of concepts. In this sense concepts, for Kant, are always predicates of possible judgments and in the section entitled "Transcendental Analytic" he adumbrates different logical functions of the understanding within judgments (of quantity, quality, relation, and modality), together with the different pure concepts of understanding or categories (again of quantity, quality, relation, and modality). These he refers to respectively as the tables of judgment and those of categories (*CPR*, 206, 212; *A*, 70, 80; *B*, 95, 106). Again we should note that what is important for Kant here is not that these logical functions or concepts have a content but that they have a formal-logical structure that allows for the articulation of possible content (and thus can be said to be a priori conditions of possibility for understanding and knowledge).

What is also essential for Kant, however, and this will be central to Nancy's reading of the *Critique of Pure Reason*, is that these formal logical structures can be united or synthesized with sensible content. The necessity of transcendental philosophy, therefore, is to deal with concepts that are to be related to their objects a priori, and hence to "offer a general but sufficient characterization of the condition under which objects in harmony with those concepts can be given, for otherwise they would be without all content, and thus would be mere logical forms and not pure concepts of the understanding" (*CPR*, 270; *A*, 136; *B*, 175).[29] It could be argued, as Nancy will, that the success and solidity of critical philosophy depends on its ability, on the basis of "a general but sufficient characterization," to present the universal and necessary conditions by which sensible intuition and conceptual forms can be united or synthesized in order to provide the foundation for the "synthetic a priori judgments" that constitute knowledge. The basis for the possibility of such a unity or synthesis of the sensible with the intelligible Kant calls the "schema" of the concept, and the process or method by which concepts are applied to sensible intuitions he calls "schematism." The schema of a concept is a pure, formal condition of the understanding that limits the usage of that concept. Like the *Critique* as a whole, then, the force of the schema is both enabling (it makes knowledge possible by grounding the unity of a sensible intuition with a con-

cept) and limiting (it dictates that concepts cannot be united with intuitions in an arbitrary or variable manner). Kant views the schema in terms
of what he calls a "representation of a general procedure of the imagination," by which a concept procures its corresponding sensible image (*CPR,*
273; *A,* 140; *B,* 179–80). The function of what he calls the "transcendental
synthesis of the imagination" is central to his understanding of the process
by which intuition and concept are united, or as he puts it in the language
of the *Critique*:

> the schematism of the understanding through the transcendental synthesis of
> imagination comes down to nothing other than the unity of all the manifold of
> intuition in inner sense, and thus indirectly to the unity of apperception, as the
> function that corresponds to inner sense (to a receptivity). Thus the schemata of
> the concepts of pure understanding are the true and sole conditions for provid-
> ing them with a relation to objects, thus with **significance**. (*CPR,* 276; *A,* 145–46;
> *B,* 185)

At the center of the *Critique*, then, is this process of the imagination, the
schematism, in which the content of sensible intuition and conceptual
or categorial principles are brought together, to make the experience and
knowledge of the world of objects possible in a unity (referred to here as
the unity of apperception) which Kant designates as the unity of the "I
think" of consciousness.[30] Thus the subject of philosophy in transcendental idealism (the "I think" recalls the Cartesian Cogito) is produced along
with the experience of worldly, sensible objects on the basis of a priori
forms of sensible intuition, conceptual or categorial principles, and the
possibility of their synthesis in the schematism. This underlines a point
already made, that transcendental ideality is not subjectivity (and hence
not subjective idealism) but rather that system of universal and necessary
structures of the mind which make subjectivity, and so objectivity, possible
to begin with.[31]

　　The philosophical, and indeed ontological, status of the schematism
is of central importance for Nancy in *Logodaedalus* in his questioning of
the foundations of the first *Critique*. Kant himself is famously vague about
the exact nature and operation of the schematism: "This schematism of
our understanding with regard to appearances and their form is a hidden art in the depths of the human soul, whose true operations we can
divine from nature and lay unveiled before our eyes only with difficulty"

(*CPR*, 273; *A*, 141; *B*, 180–81). As has been already indicated, Kant is explicit about the necessity for critical philosophy to "offer a general but sufficient characterization" of the conditions under which the objects of sensible intuition may be brought into accordance with concepts. Yet here he suggests that the schematism is not at all straightforwardly "offered," and this difficulty of presentation (which will form the crux of Nancy's reading of Kant) leads to a number of rhetorical moves on the part of the author of the first *Critique* in an attempt stay with that which can be exposed in a clear and distinct manner. For instance, after having elaborated on the role of the schematism and the importance of the schemata of concepts, he immediately avoids pursuing his detailed elaboration any further: "Rather than pausing now for a dry and boring analysis of what is required for transcendental schemata of pure concepts of the understanding in general, we would rather present them according to the order of the categories and in connection with these" (*CPR*, 274; *A*, 142; *B*, 180). In *Kant and the Problem of Metaphysics*, Heidegger questions whether it is simply the dryness or the tediousness of presenting the schemata of concepts that motivates Kant to turn suddenly to an adumbration of the categories (*KPM*, 72–73; *GA*, 3:106). The introduction of the categories into the first *Critique* at this point is somewhat abrupt, and represents a return to familiar philosophical ground, insofar as the notion the categories represents (albeit in modified form) a return to an Aristotelian approach and thus constitutes perhaps one of the least original moments of Kant's treatise. As has been pointed out Kant's detailed adumbration of the categories compresses the rules of a certain method of (scientific) knowledge as they emerge within the history of Western philosophy up until the eighteenth century.[32] One might legitimately question, along with Heidegger, why Kant avoids elaborating further the transcendental schemata of pure concepts in favor of a return to familiar and well-trodden territory, and whether this is solely an attempt to avoid "dry and fastidious exposition."

The answer Heidegger gives to this question sets the terms for Nancy's reading of Kant in *Logodaedalus*. In *Kant and the Problem of Metaphysics* Heidegger reads the foundational ambition of the *Critique of Pure Reason* in ontological rather than epistemological terms. The *Critique* is not, as neo-Kantians of the late nineteenth century such as Cohen or Rickert (one of Heidegger's teachers) would have it, a theory of knowledge, that is, a theory of how our concepts correspond to the given reality of the object world. Rather, in the way in which the "Transcendental Aesthetic" and "Logic" combine, the *Critique* lays the grounds of possibility for subjective experience and phenomenal givenness per se, or as Heidegger puts it in his own terms,

transcendental knowledge does not investigate the being itself, but rather the possibility of the preliminary understanding of Being, i.e., at one and the same time the constitution of the Being of the being. . . . The *Critique of Pure Reason* has nothing to do with a "theory of knowledge." If one generally could allow the interpretation of the *Critique of Pure Reason* as a theory of knowledge, then that would be to say that it is not a theory of ontic knowledge (experience), but rather a theory of ontological knowledge. (*KPM*, 10–11; *GA*, 3:16–17)

This ontological dimension of Heidegger's reading has already been signaled in the above account of the "Transcendental Doctrine of Elements." In reading the *Critique* in this way Heidegger also, and necessarily, confers a key ontological importance on the schematism, and consequently on the "pure productive power of the imagination" in which the schematism is grounded. The "preliminary understanding of Being" is possible a priori only in the ability of the schematism to unite sensible intuitions with the functions and concepts of the understanding, or, as Heidegger puts it, "The Transcendental Schematism is consequently the ground for the inner possibility of ontological knowledge," and later, "The problem of the Schematism of the pure concepts of the understanding is the question concerning the innermost essence of ontological knowledge" (*KPM*, 74, 76; *GA*, 3:108, 111). In this context all conceptual representing per se—whether it be in firsthand worldly experience which allows us to understand phenomena as such (in the unity of intuition and understanding) or in the very act of thinking, reasoning, and philosophizing (e.g., that of Kant's treatise itself)—is, or occurs, on the basis of schematism. Thus, in Heidegger's terms, "The pure productive power of the imagination, free of experience, makes experience possible for the first time" (*KPM*, 91; *GA*, 3:133). It becomes clear, in light of Heidegger's approach, the extent to which the whole edifice of Kant's critical philosophy may largely stand or fall according to the successful exposition or presentation of the schematism. And yet, as has been shown, Kant himself elides his account of the schemata and of the "schematism," that "art hidden in the depths of the human soul," in favor of the more traditional and "accessible" elaboration of the pure concepts of the understanding. And yet again, as has also been shown, these do not, in themselves, offer a foundation for experience and knowledge, since, in and of themselves, they are empty, logical forms and not pure concepts of understanding.[33] That which is given a foundational role in experience, the "schemata" of concepts and the process of the schematism in the pure power of the imagination, is precisely that which appears to elude the "exposition" of the first *Critique*. Heidegger ascribes this to an essential failure of thought on the part of Kant at the crucial moment. Just as he roots experience in a hidden art of the human soul inaccessible to clear presentation, he shrinks back from the implications of this by focusing on the more clearly presentable and reliable categories of transcendental logic: "In the radicalism of his questions, Kant brought the 'possibility' of metaphysics to this abyss. He saw the unknown. He had to shrink back. It was not just that the transcendental power of the imagination frightened him, but rather that in between [the two editions of the *Critique*] pure reason as reason drew him increasingly under its spell" (*KPM*, 115; *GA*, 3:168). It should be noted that this interpretation of Kant's motives would be hotly contested by more orthodox readers of Kant.[34] Yet the essential point, for Heidegger at least, is that the indisputably central and foundational role played by the schematism is rendered highly problematic by its mysterious, hidden, and inaccessible nature, and thus, at the very center of the foundational ambition of transcendental idealism, an abyss opens up, which is never properly accounted for. Thus the moment of grounding within critical philosophy becomes a moment of ungrounding.

It might be recalled at this point that Lacoue-Labarthe's ambition in the *Poétique* article "La Fable" was to address the issue of metaphysical foundation by questioning the relation between philosophy and literature, and more specifically the extent to which the discourse of philosophy is able to abstract itself from the sensible contingency of language in order to present thought as the pure ideality of reason or concept. His conclusion suggested that the inner rethinking of metaphysics entailed a twofold task of thought: to return metaphysical thinking to its embeddedness in the sensible contingency of language and with this to force the limits of demarcation between philosophy and literature. Nancy takes up this twofold task, and develops Heidegger's reading along more Nietzschean lines, by focusing on the problem of the style in Kant's first *Critique* and by posing the question of "presentation" (*Darstellung*).

He begins by drawing attention to Kant's own repeated, and rather defensive, comments on this issue in the prefaces to the first and second editions. In the preface to the first edition Kant comments on the clarity or accessibility of his treatise (defending against accusations of obscurity and inaccessibility): "Finally, as regards **clarity**, the reader has the right to demand first **discursive** (logical) **clarity, through concepts**, but then also **intuitive** (aesthetic) clarity, through **intuitions**, that is, through examples or other illustrations *in concreto*" (*CPR*, 103; *A*, xvii–xviii). The clarity of the work, then, will rest entirely on the clarity of its presentation of concepts and on concrete examples of intuition (and it should be borne in mind that this clarity will only be possible on the basis of the schematism that Kant himself will determine). This is qualified by the assertion that, at times, adding excess material in order to clarify specific points further may itself be an impediment to the clarity of the whole and the ability of the reader to grasp the overall structure and coherence of the *Critique* (*CPR*, 104; *A*, xix). Thus, at times, further elaboration or clarifying embellishments in relation to specifics may be sacrificed in favor of the accessibility of the whole (this might be an allusion to the curtailment of the account of the schemata of concepts that precedes the presentation of the categories in the "Transcendental Analytic"). In the Preface to the second edition of the *Critique* Kant goes further, invoking not just the clarity of concepts and intuitions but suggesting that the presentational style of his work must take as its example the clarity of demonstration achieved by scientific treatises, the idealist philosopher Wolff being his model in this respect: "Wolff . . . gave us the first example . . . of the way in which the secure course of a science is to be taken, through the regular ascertainment of principles, the clear determination of concepts, the attempt at strictness in proofs, and the prevention of audacious leaps in inferences" (*CPR*, 119–20, *B*, xxx-vi). The clarity and logical necessity of the scientific method is an ideal to which the style of the *Critique of Pure Reason* appears to aspire. Yet Kant once again goes on to qualify his assertion in a famous comment which is of key interest for Nancy and which was cited above as the epigraph to this discussion: "Any philosophical treatise may find itself under pressure in particular passages (for it cannot be as fully armored as a mathematical treatise), while the whole structure of the system, considered as a unity, proceeds without the least danger" (*CPR*, 123; *B*, xliv). However much philosophical language may aspire to the rigor and exactitude of scientific methodology, it will always fall short of the specific rigor and exactitude proper to mathematics, but, Kant adds, this failing does not undermine the overall structure and integrity of his system as a whole. For Nancy, it is precisely the structural integrity of the system as a whole which is called into question in the problems of philosophical style or presentation that Kant himself poses in the two prefaces to the *Critique*. Indeed Nancy detects in these assertions and qualifications a defensiveness which arises both from the necessity of transcendental idealism to pose such questions and an unresolved philosophical question within Kantian thought about the status of presentation itself.

In *Kant and the Problem of Metaphysics*, Heidegger was not interested in posing the question of presentation per se. Rather, seeking to follow the path of Kant's thinking, he traced Kant's attempt to lay the ground for metaphysics by demonstrating the possibility of synthesis of sensible intuition and intelligible forms in the schematism, but then tried to show how Kant recoils at a key moment when confronted with the groundlessness, the "abyss," of the pure power of the imagination. Nancy develops Heidegger's account by addressing more specifically the way in which the obscurity of the schematism resists presentation and the way in which this impacts on the overall solidity of the first *Critique* as a foundational project. In so doing Nancy is responding to the clear necessity, within critical philosophy, not only to describe the a priori forms of sensible intuition and logical/conceptual function as well as their possibility of synthesis, but also to give an adequate presentation of these in order to fulfill its foundational ambition. This necessity arises because Kant's treatise, as the foundation for transcendental idealism, is both the description of that foundation and the very enactment of it in and through its own discursive presentation of the a priori principles of reason. In Kant's own terms, it is not sufficient for these conditions simply to be described or alluded to, they must be presented or exposed in "the secure course of a science" and with "a general but sufficient characterization" (*in allgemeinen aber hinreichenden Kennzeichen*).

The assertions and qualifications in the comments from the two prefaces cited above thus perform a crucial function insofar as they explicitly address the question of presentation, or as Nancy puts it: "it was necessary that philosophy pose to itself the question of style or of philosophical genre, the question of the manner of presenting or exposing philosophy, or, absolutely, of philosophical exposition" (*L*, 26). His point is that this question needs to be explicitly addressed by Kant because, as Kant himself admits, philosophical argumentation can in fact never fully match the discursive rigor or exactitude of mathematics. Thus, for Kant, philosophical language has its strength insofar as it aspires to scientific or mathematical rigor, but falls short of such rigor insofar as it is language. According to Nancy this vulnerability of philosophical exposition has a threefold consequence:

Exposition is vulnerable because it is philosophical. This implies three things:

firstly, that exposition is not entirely independent, nor even heterogeneous in relation to "contents";

then, that philosophy presents a particular fragility insofar as it exposes itself [*s'expose*];

finally, and at the same time as the principle and consequence of these two findings [*constats*], that philosophy as such cannot avoid passing through this vulnerable exposition and exposing itself to its effects. (*L*, 41)

Carrying forward the implications of Lacoue-Labarthe's arguments in "La Fable," Nancy refuses to take for granted that the language of critical philosophy can abstract itself from its own contingent discursivity in order to attain, or even approach, the status of pure thought or mathematical abstraction. Crucially he refuses also to accept Kant's view that the vulnerability proper to discursive exposition does not affect the structural unity of the system as a whole. In the formal-logical language of mathematics there is an exact equivalence or *adequation* between the presentation of the respective concept or intuition and the concept/intuition itself. A mathematical proof needs nothing other than its presentation as proof, using mathematical signs for it to be grounded as such. In this sense mathematics is the only space of presentation proper, and its very exactitude or adequation marks philosophical presentation as something different. Mathematics, Nancy writes, "is thus the site of *presentation*—of *Darstellung*—in the proper and full sense of the term. . . . the division of mathematics and philosophy opens the division of Darstellung itself, the *crisis* which separates Darstellung *stricto sensu* from another mode of 'presentation,' the philosophical mode, that for which Kant precisely chooses the name *Exposition*" (*L*, 42). This gap that opens up between mathematical presentation and philosophical presentation or exposition is exactly what interests Nancy. It signifies that, however much Kant may aspire to make philosophy, if not identical to mathematics, then akin to it—that is, to make of philosophy a movement and self-grounding of pure reason in and through the faculty of pure reason itself—its embeddedness in the sensible contingency of language may have more profound consequences than Kant is willing or able to allow. This is because, for Nancy, exposition is not and cannot be presentation in the mathematical sense; it cannot unfold in the manner of a proof or equation, rather it must always necessarily be rooted in *discourse*. This, perhaps, is stating no more than the obvious, yet for Nancy it is vitally important to the extent that Kant's whole philosophical method depends, as has been shown, on philosophical language achieving a status superior to that of nonphilosophical language, that is, on its ability to transcend the limitations of nonphilosophical language. Here, according to Nancy, is where the question of separation between philosophy and literature is posed within critical philosophy.

The potentially defensive tone of the comments about style and presentation in Kant's two prefaces has, Nancy contends, a certain necessity within the overall scope of critical philosophy. In order to be properly philosophical, to expose its concepts in a clear and distinct manner, and in order, above all, to approach the determination of the faculties of understanding and reason in the sure way of a science, critical philosophy must differentiate itself from the arbitrary and contingent embellishments or inventions of literature. Throughout his argument Nancy is careful to draw out the semantic resonance of the key German terms under discussion, namely *Darstellung* and *Dichtung*. The former, which has been translated as "presentation," means literally, "placing-there," "placing-in-front-of," "showing," or "exposition." The emphasis of *Darstellung*, therefore, lies specifically on the act of bringing into presence or into view the determinations and deductions of pure reason. The use of the term *Dichtung* in German is distinct from *Poesie* and implies more generally an invention or creation which would include all novels and literary forms as well as verse. According to Nancy, Kant's critical philosophy finds itself in a curious double bind. It must, as philosophy, be the clear and distinct presentation

(*Darstellung*) of forms, concepts, categories, and so on, and yet, by its own admission, it cannot achieve the (mathematical) exactitude or adequation of presentation proper, and so, as presentation, it also demands or is necessarily rooted in invention (*Dichtung*). This necessary relation of simultaneous distance and proximity that subsists between *Darstellung* and *Dichtung* leads to a structural ambivalence or equivocation in Kant's treatise which goes to the very foundation of the system as a whole.[35] In the first instance this ambivalence within critical philosophy demands resolution in the attempt to rigorously separate philosophy and literature:

Defending philosophical language consists in defending a *Dichtung* which, in itself, has nothing to do with poetry—but which derives from *Darstellung* itself. *Darstellung* demands a *Dichtung*, because, as *exposition*, it has already been deprived of pure and direct *Darstellung*. It is therefore exposition which demands, for its *Darstellung* or by way of its *Darstellung*, a *Dichtung*. The latter must be the palliative, the cloak of a naked and mutilated presentation. (*L*, 94)

Philosophical prose, deprived of the purity of mathematical presentation, must present itself both as the work of pure a priori reason, abstracted from all sensible contingencies *and* as discursive exposition, that is, as contingent language or discourse which cannot ever attain the purity it necessarily desires. It is this very double bind that, according to Nancy, necessitates the distinction between philosophy—that is to say, sober prose, or that by means of which "a general but sufficient characterization" is a *sufficient* (but not entirely pure) presentation of the work of reason—and "literature," that is to say, all other creative use of language which remains more thoroughly embedded in its sensible contingency. Nancy describes this act of delimitation in the following terms:

Prose guarantees the discourse of all literature—that is to say that it guarantees, by closing the eyes, ears, and even the mouth of the thinker, the unblemished purity of reason. The institution of *pure* reason—or the critical gesture itself—that is to say, ontology as the legislative autonomy of reason, demanded the preservation of this purity, that is, the production of the *impure* mode of production, of *Dichtung*, in order to distance and banish its dangerous taint. It was necessary for it to name tainted *Darstellung Dichtung* . . . and to name *literature* all that it kept at a distance from its autology: the rest, all the rest. (*L*, 90)

Taken in this light Kant's comments about style in the prefaces to the *Cri-*

*tique* can be interpreted, not just as defensive gestures, but more specifically as attempts to preserve a privileged space for philosophical presentation (the *Darstellung souillé* which falls short of pure presentation as such), by instantiating itself as *Dichtung* or invention but only to the extent that this specific mode of invention is rigorously separated from literary or poetic invention, which is then held at a distance, marginalized, or put into a position of secondary importance. Thus literature is produced by philosophy itself as philosophy's excess or remainder, that is, all that is left over once the language of philosophy has established the autonomy and self-grounding nature of reason in sober and rigorous prose.

The consequences of this are, according to Nancy, far-reaching both for Kant's transcendental idealism and for philosophical discourse per se. This is because philosophical discourse here only succeeds in founding itself as such in and through a legislative gesture, which separates philosophical and literary invention but does so by necessarily presupposing the very separation upon which it relies in order to perform the legislative gesture in the first instance. Thus it tries to attain a specificity for itself which it needs already to have taken for granted in order to attain that specificity. In this sense the initial double bind which dictated the necessity of separating philosophy from literature, namely that philosophy must be the pure presentation of reason (*Darstellung*) but at the same time the mediation of that presentation through discursive invention (*Dichtung*), is tightened even further in the attempt to produce literature as a category clearly demarcated from the work of philosophical presentation. In order to separate philosophy from literature in a clearly delimited and conceptually rigorous manner, philosophy must already be philosophy and this it cannot yet be. This, at least, is the train of Nancy's argument in *Logodaedalus*. As has already been suggested, in pursuing this argument in this way Nancy is responding directly to Lacoue-Labarthe, who described the twofold task of rethinking the inner essence of metaphysics as, first, "to turn back against metaphysics (within metaphysics), under the name of literature, that against which metaphysics has itself turned," and second, to "to displace the bar which symbolically separates literature and philosophy" (*SP*, 22). The result of this is that philosophical presentation necessarily maintains an uncertain, or what Nancy calls "undecidable," relation with the very category of literary invention it seeks to distance itself from.

The term *undecidable,* or *indécidable* in French, is precisely one of those terms about which Nancy speaks at the beginning of *Logodaedalus,* that is, a deconstructive term, which, when used freely and without due contextualization in the "fashion" of critical language, is deprived of its strategic ambivalence and transformed into a substantive and meaningful ground. As Nancy takes pains to point out: "It is not enough to say that there is undecidability within a discourse. It is not enough to say it in order to have decided the fate, the structure, or the power of that discourse" (*L,* 5). In order to highlight the specific rigor of this term Nancy draws attention to its origin within the context of mathematics. An undecidable proposition, he recalls, is a mathematical proposition which cannot be the object of a demonstration, that is, a proposition produced within and by a theorem, but which that theorem cannot account for, or which is not deducible from within the bounds of its system. An undecidable proposition, then, is not just something which could loosely be "this or that"; rather, it can be neither proved nor refuted by the specific logic of the theorem or system which produces it, while at the same time it does not oppose that logic in any direct way (*L,* 11).[36] It is not sufficient, Nancy asserts, simply to say that a discourse produces undecidability. What is important is that the production of such undecidability be exactly and rigorously accounted for. This is precisely Nancy's aim in working through the implications of the relation between *Darstellung* and *Dichtung* in Kant's *Critique of Pure Reason.* The logic of critical philosophy necessarily requires a distinction between pure presentation (*Darstellung*) and philosophical presentation (*Darstellung,* supplemented with the necessary blemish of *Dichtung* or invention), but this requires a further distinction between philosophical and literary invention. Yet is the language which makes or legislates for such distinctions itself philosophical or literary invention? Prior to the making of the distinction it is both or neither, and therefore not in a position *as* philosophy to make such a distinction. It is in this sense that the discourse of Kant's treatise maintains an undecidable relation between philosophy and literature, since the very language which would distinguish between them is necessarily implicated in an uncertain play between one and the other. The undecidable status of Kant's discourse implies an ineluctable persistence of the literary within the philosophical insofar as the boundaries between the two are subject to this necessary undecidability, and thus gives rise to what Nancy calls "the multiple and insidious insistence of literature within philosophy" (*L*, 117).

In *Logodaedalus* Nancy argues that the Kantian system produces itself as fatally contaminated by, or implicated in, the very literary invention it would seek to exclude from its own constitution as system. This has further implications for the entire architectonic of the first *Critique*. Kant wants to give a clear and logically necessary presentation of the grounding principles of knowledge in the faculties of understanding and pure reason—effectively the autofoundation of reason itself. Yet the embeddedness of the language of the *Critique* in literary-philosophical invention means that presentational gaps or elisions, obscurities or inconsistencies, cannot be dismissed as contingent moments which do not affect the integrity of the system as whole. Such elisions and gaps will always be of decisive importance for that integrity. More serious still, this embeddedness of thinking in discourse also implies an essential and necessary *dislocation* of the whole, since thought finds itself dismembered into discursive parts which resist simultaneous and unified articulation. As literary-philosophical invention, thought can never gather itself up into a simultaneous instance of the autofoundation of reason: "Philosophical poetry, philosophy contaminated by poetry, against its will, means this: the system, insofar as it includes presentation—and it necessarily includes it—brings with it dislocation" (*L*, 118). The unity or synthesis of the various parts of the critique, a unity which the success of the Kantian account of phenomenality and knowledge requires, is called into question in the very moment of its presentation or exposition within the discursive edifice of the *Critique* itself. Nancy is alluding to the way in which Kant wants his reader both to be able to follow the logical necessity of his demonstrations as they unfold *and* to step back, in order to "attain a survey of the whole" and to view "the articulation or structure of the system, which yet matters most when it comes to judging its unity and soundness" (*CPR*, 104; *A*, xix). Rather than the various parts or divisions of the *Critique* being able to abstract themselves from the contingency of their exposition to be an instance of pure, unified thought, demonstrating its own conditions of possibility and grounding itself as such, these parts and divisions remain dislocated, embedded, dispersed within the language of their own discursive exposition: "the system itself, to the extent that it is constructed or presents itself, carries with it among [*au nombre de*] its fundamental rules the disjunction of its places, dislocation. Kantian unity is always posed in plurality, and in this discourse always in principle forbids the simple reabsorption into pure self-presence" (*L*, 118). It could be argued that, ultimately, such a reading of the *Critique of Pure Reason* relies on a refusal of the distinction between the sensible and the intelligible. If such a distinction were maintained it would be possible to assert that, although a logical deduction presented in linguistic signs needs to be carefully and rigorously presented with those signs, it is not dependent upon them for its ultimate logical truth or consistency (which would be nonlinguistic in nature). By maintaining this distinction one could also argue that what is important about the first *Critique* is far more its overall logical conceptual structure than its specific discursive architecture, important though this will be. If the distinction between the sensible and the intelligible is suspended, however, such arguments become much more problematic.

It might be recalled at this point that Kant, in presenting the a priori forms of sensible intuition on the one hand, and the a priori forms of intelligibility or understanding on the other (logical functions, categories, etc.), also required the operation of the schematism to unite or synthesize the two. The schematism, as Heidegger remarked, made possible all phenomenal or conceptual presentation per se. Indeed the operation of the schematism, grounded in the pure power of the imagination, was shown to be the bedrock upon which the whole edifice of critical philosophy was built. It appeared also, by Kant's own admission, to be inaccessible to presentation as such, to be that "art hidden in the depths of the human soul." Within the context of Nancy's argument, turning as it does around the whole issue of philosophical presentation and the undecidable status of literary-philosophical invention, the inaccessibility of the schematism has the most far-reaching consequences, or as Nancy himself puts it, "it is not possible to present [*prélever*] the 'schema' object, it carries away with it Kant's entire discourse" (*L*, 8). As the a priori condition of possibility par excellence, the schematism should be presentable or demonstrable a priori. Without the possibility of demonstrating it in the clarity of presentation (*Darstellung*), the possibility of grounding any synthesis between sensible intuition and conceptual form is suspended. At this point the entire edifice of transcendental idealism, its foundations, and with this its ability to properly delineate and delimit a priori conditions of possibility, begin to shake, or in Nancy's terms to *syncopate*. Its critical, legislative powers of demonstration and presentation stand or fall on the basis of the schematism: "what is at stake with [Kant's work], and with the schematism . . . is precisely the demonstration of the 'face-to-face encounter' of theory with itself, and the exhausting, disequilibriating question of the standing of his discourse" (*L*, 8). Without its foundation in the schematism, the ability of critical philosophy to be the work of pure reason, to make conceptual distinctions or demarcate conceptual limits, indeed its whole function *as* critique, is suspended also.

In the syncopation of Kant's discourse, philosophy, in the very moment of its self-grounding, encounters an absence of firm ground. In the very act of presentation or self-demonstration by which pure reason seeks to establish its identity, and with that the self-identity of its concepts and judgments, that identity is ruptured or syncopated. For Nancy the term *syncopation* describes a movement of presentation and withdrawal which governs any philosophical gesture seeking to present or posit in a direct and unmediated fashion the purity, self-identity, and self-groundedness of thought. As the purity of reason presents itself, it does so necessarily in the absence of pure presentation, in an undecidable relation of *Darstellung* and *Dichtung* (*Dardichtung*, as Nancy calls it), and therefore vanishes in the very instant of its disclosure. What is presented therefore is not a pure instance of self-legislating reason, but rather a syncopated beat in which consciousness, the "I think" of the transcendental unity of apperception, occurs only in the rupturing of self-identity, and the simultaneous presentation and withdrawal of a secure ground:

In this way that which is called a consciousness without doubt only ever lets itself be apprehended as an identity when it disappears: this is syncopation. Syncopation decides self-identity: it marks it, irrefutably, in the gesture and in the instant which withdraws it from all demonstration, and above all from all autodemonstration, from all autopresentation or presentification. (*L*, 13)

This play between grounding and groundlessness, between presentation and withdrawal, to a certain extent repeats Heidegger's reading of Kant. Heidegger argued that Kant established the transcendental unity of apperception and the foundation of ontological knowledge in the pure power of the imagination, and then recoiled at the very inaccessibility and abyssal obscurity of that faculty. But for Nancy the absence of foundation within philosophy is encountered not simply in the moment Kant hesitates or recoils from the implications of his own thinking. The exposure to the groundlessness of thought is constitutive of philosophical discourse per se, it exists or is held by this groundlessness in its very enunciation *as* discourse. In the structure of presentation and withdrawal which governs it, "philosophical discourse is articulated on a syncopation or by a syncopation. It is 'held' by an undecidable moment of syncopation" (*L*, 17–18).

This then, according to Nancy, is the fate of metaphysics and of metaphysical foundations within philosophical discourse. His reading of Kant in *Logodaedalus* responds to the problem of the overcoming of metaphysics which, it was shown, informed his collaboration with Lacoue-Labarthe in the early issues of *Poétique*. What emerges from this reading is the thought that, however inevitable it may be that philosophical gestures which contest metaphysical foundations will be recuperated into the language of metaphysics (Heidegger's judgment on Nietzsche, Derrida's deconstructions of Levinas, Foucault, and others in *L'Écriture et la différence*), the very language of metaphysics, as language or discourse, can never, in fact, establish for itself the foundation or ground which it desires. The inevitability of recuperation into metaphysics is also, at the same time, the inevitable recuperation of metaphysics into the contingency of discursive presentation, into an undecidable relation of philosophy to literature, whereby "pure reason opens vertiginously onto the exclusivity of its own ground: in this *dichten* and *darstellen* become indistinct" (*L*, 83). In "Nietzsche: Mais où sont les yeux pour le voir?" Nancy had argued, against Heidegger's reading, that interpretation, evaluation, and figuration in Nietzsche's philosophical writing always preceded and exceeded their recuperation into the orbit of metaphysics. His account of the relation between *Darstellung* and *Dichtung* in Kantian discourse, and his affirmation of the inevitable syncopation of critical philosophy, extend and develop this reading. Syncopation, Nancy writes, is that which "metaphysical discourse cannot withstand, that which makes it sick to its core" (*L*, 16), but at the same time, it necessarily governs any attempt by metaphysical discourse to lay a foundation or ground.

As should by now be clear, the context for Nancy's reading of Kant is multiple, responding as it does to a certain tradition of antifoundationalist approaches to the first *Critique* and to the more contemporary "epochal" question of the overcoming or closure of metaphysics. Yet, as was indicated at the outset of this discussion, Nancy is concerned also with the politics of contemporary critical or theoretical discourse, which, according to the dictates of fashion, appropriates philosophical terminology as a ground of signification, but in so doing becomes fatally implicated within a topology of substance. As will become clear in the discussion of Descartes which follows, substance, for Nancy, always also implies subjectivity and the reliance of critical discourse on a metaphysical logic of subjectivity which remains largely unthought and unacknowledged. The importance of Kant in *Logodaedalus* lies not just in the problematic foundational ambition of the first *Critique*, but also in its attempt to think that foundation on the basis of a synthesis which would be the transcendental unity of apperception. Even though it is not subjectivity, or subjective idealism, transcendental idealism lays the ground for the subject, for its autonomy and self-identity in the unity of the "I think." Nancy is not interested simply in exposing an absence of foundation within thought in some philosophical wrecking exercise. Rather he is attempting to think that foundation otherwise, and outside any logic of substance or subjectivity, and this is why he talks principally in terms of the syncopation of the Kantian system rather than using Heidegger's term *abyss* (*Abgrund*). Ultimately what is at stake in Nancy's reading of foundation in Kant is the status of philosophical discourse (its status as *Dardichtung*), but with this also the status of the subject of philosophy and of subjectivity per se. Nancy underlines this by relating syncopation and the "I think" of the transcendental unity of apperception to the Cartesian Cogito: "Syncopation is not the negative passage of one moment to another, it is not a gap which would serve as a footbridge. It has, very exactly, the instantaneous, punctual and discrete nature . . . of the *cogito*: and one understands besides this that if it *is* not the *cogito*, then nor is there any *cogito* without it" (*L*, 13). The syncopation of critical philosophy is not simply its negation or destruction, rather it is an interruption of the self-identity and substance of the thinking subject. The undecidable relation between philosophy and literature, here, has as its consequence the modification or transformation of metaphysical ground. By questioning the foundation of transcendental idealism in this way, Nancy ultimately calls into question the ground of subjectivity, and this brings him in *Ego Sum* to a more extended reading of the Cartesian Cogito.

## The Persistence of the Subject: On Descartes and the Cogito

Returning, one might say, after having been exiled or eclipsed for a number of years—in Structure, Text, Process—the Subject is once again occupying contemporary discourses.

—JEAN-LUC NANCY, *Ego Sum*[37]

Writing at the very beginning of *Ego Sum* (1979), Jean-Luc Nancy's sense of a contemporary "return" of the subject echoes the concern expressed in the opening pages of *Logodaedalus* about the transubstantiation or transformation of philosophical terms in the critical fashions of the 1970s. This return of the subject in theoretical discourse is signaled, Nancy believes, most clearly in the language and terminology of Lacanian psychoanalysis.[38] Indeed much of the force of the argument of *Ego Sum* is aimed at undoing the Lacanian account of the subject, and to this extent it continues the reading of Lacan that Nancy gives in 1972 with Lacoue-Labarthe.

Published under the title *Le Titre de la lettre*, Nancy and Lacoue-Labarthe stress that their work is by no means a definitive account or systematic critique of Lacanian psychoanalysis, but is rather simply a "lecture," a reading, and a provisional one at that. Nevertheless *Le Titre de la lettre* was critical enough for Lacan himself to dismiss both as simply being, and I quote, Derrida's "underlings."[39] The substance of this earlier reading can be summed up in two main criticisms. First, Nancy and Lacoue-Labarthe note the way in which Lacan is engaged in a discourse of theoretical mastery: the splitting of the subject comes to it from the big Other, from the law of the symbolic which constitutes it, by dividing it and thus inscribing it within an economy of lack. In this way the true subject of subjectivity is identified as Other and at the same time the discourse of psychoanalysis which masters and theorizes this negative identity is authenticated and given its authority. Thus, according to *Le Titre de la lettre*, the alterity which constitutes and alienates subjectivity is subordinated to and mastered by the discourse of psychoanalytic theory.[40] Following on from, and closely related to, this first criticism Nancy and Lacoue-Labarthe insist that, by inscribing the subject within a dialectic of recognition with the Other, Lacan, influenced by Alexandre Kojève, is offering a reinscription and *détournement* of Hegel's dialectic. Lacan's is seen as a negative discourse of the dialectic of desire as it is outlined by Hegel in the *Phenomenology of Spirit*, one which, though emphasizing a constant dis-appropriation or dispossession of the subject by the Other, ultimately and necessarily affirms an outcome of *réintegration et d'accord* (reintegration and agreement).[41] Negative dialectics, then, like negative theology, are always subsumed back into their opposite.

An evaluation of the merits and demerits of these two criticisms is not directly the aim here. What is significant is that, for Nancy, the Lacanian account of the Subject is crucial to what he comes to see in *Ego Sum* as a persistence of the traditional Subject of metaphysics within contemporary theoretical discourse. Specifically Nancy is concerned about what he calls the anthropologization or re-anthropologization of the subject. The Lacanian symbolic order, it should be noted, owes its formulation, at least in part, to the influence of Lévi-Strauss's structuralist anthropology. In this context, the return or persistence of the subject, Nancy will argue, both repeats and conceals an anthropological perspective, a traditional metaphysics, or indeed an onto-theology:

Our contemporaneity consists of, and insists within, a prolix expansion of the anthropological subject—as a necessary consequence, indeed more than a consequence—as an effectuation of a metaphysics of the Subject, but, at the same time, as a *forgetting* of the metaphysical provenance and nature of this subject, a forgetting, mis-recognition or denegation of the metaphysics (or onto-theology) which it perpetuates. (*ES*, 13)

And so Nancy identifies a return or persistence of metaphysical thinking within the return of the subject and specifically with the institution of the Lacanian "subject of the enunciation." The instance of recuperation he is responding to here occurs not simply because of the reification or "transubstantiation" of terms within the fashions of critical discourse such as it was addressed in *Logodaedalus*. Rather what is at stake here is a more fundamental persistence of traditional modes of subjectivity within the structure of theoretical thought itself.

What follows, then, will offer a partial account of Nancy's engagement with Descartes in *Ego Sum*, specifically addressing four issues: first, the manner in which Nancy, through his reading of Descartes's *Discours de la méthode*, seeks to counter or interrupt the persistence of the metaphysical subject within the contemporary discourses alluded to above; second, the way in which Nancy's critique of the Cartesian Cogito seeks to displace and overturn Lacan's account of subjectivity;[42] and third, it will be suggested that Nancy's untying of the Lacanian "subject of the unconscious" entails the affirmation of an instance that would be prior to any inscription within a symbolic order or any dialectic of desire/recognition. This prior instance, in excess of any symbolic order or any possibility of figuration, is at once a radical exteriority but as such it is also a spacing, a temporalizing/spatializing *espacement*, which is both the condition of possibility for any everyday experience of time and space, but also for any experience of thought, symbolization, and figuration.[43] To this extent *Ego Sum* gives a clear indication of the trajectory of Nancy's thought after the antifoundationalist reading of Kant in *Logodaedalus*, and the manner in which the syncopation of philosophical foundations in his work leads to a rethinking of philosophical subjectivity, and of being per se. Nancy, as we shall see, moves from what one might call an "exteriorization" of subjectivity to a thinking of space and spatiality. In so doing he both repeats and transforms a Heideggerian thinking of being in a way which both recalls and exceeds Derrida's thinking of *différance*.[44] Finally, this chapter will be brought to a close with a discussion of the status of Nancy's own philosophical discourse, that is, his own way of writing and thinking such as it emerges in his readings of Kant and Descartes. His thought, I will suggest, is itself governed by a literary-philosophical logic and an encounter with a certain aporia. This logic of aporia governing Nancy's text engenders a discourse which is not quite philosophy and not quite theory, but which is figural and affirms itself as a certain kind of fictionality or ficticity. In this sense then, Nancy's thinking about the relation of *Darstellung* and *Dichtung* in Kant, when taken together with his reading of the Cogito in *Ego Sum*, has implications for the status of his own philosophical writing and the way in which we may more broadly think the relation between philosophy and literature within the "closure" of metaphysics.

In his lectures on Nietzsche in the late 1930s Martin Heidegger underlines the extent to which the dominance of the subjective underpins modern humanity's experience and understanding of existence. Heidegger's critique of the subjective in modernity from Descartes onward needs to be placed within his wider understanding of metaphysical thinking and his understanding of the tradition of onto-theology.[45] For a great deal of modern philosophy, Heidegger argues, to be or to exist is either to be an object present in space and time as measured by the mathematical projections of quantitative natural science, or to be is to be a subject, a self-conscious, self-present mind. Throughout the manifold phases and multiple thought-paths of Heidegger's philosophical career, his rejection of this ontology of presence remains constant. Heidegger is interested in the way in which our experience of being unfolds or gives itself temporally as an event; we experience a meaningful world because we are rooted in the past and thrust into a future: all experience of and possibilities of action within the present arise therefore out of temporal projections both forward and backward. Our being as humans, Heidegger insists from the start, has to be grasped in terms of temporality, thanks to our temporality we reach out into a meaningful world and to an experience of being, and thereby make possible an experience of individual beings.[46] Being, then, for Heidegger, is that temporalizing event against which beings or entities show themselves and become intelligible as such.[47] Through our insistence on presence, he argues, and through the dominance we give to the subjective, our culture has become obsessed with theoretical propositions about things, with measuring, quantifying, and thereby violently mastering and exploiting existence. In so doing, according to Heidegger at least, we turn humans and the object world into exploitable commodities and become dangerously alienated from the richness and multiplicity of our pretheoretical, prescientific experience. We think only about beings to be controlled and theoretically mastered, and perhaps even catastrophically, send the question of being into oblivion.

Now, this dominance of the subjective, for Heidegger, comes to its most specific and foundational formulation in the thinking of Descartes, who in the famous Cogito, *I think therefore I am*, offers the subject that thinks as the solid ground for the basis of a knowledge of beings, beings themselves being considered as so many other objects or things and human being being thought of as a thing that thinks, *res cogitans*. In its strictest sense, therefore, the metaphysical subject is conceived of as a substance, as a grounding or foundation.[48] The term Heidegger uses here is the Latin *subiectum*. He writes, "According to the concept of its essence, *subiectum* is in a distinctive sense that which always lies before and so lies at the basis of something else whose ground it therefore is" (*N*, 1:96–97; *GA*, 48:181). When we experience, represent, know, or measure something, a subject, substance, or ground is always affirmed; the subject which knows and measures, as well as the subject which is known. Both are seen in terms of substances or a kind of foundation. In the Cartesian ontology, then, where beings are either objects present in the world or are the thinking thing, the subject immediately self-present to itself, the subject is always the ultimate ground or *subiectum* on the basis of which existence can be known, calculated, and mastered.

This is the distinctly Heideggerian frame of reference in which Nancy is working when he identifies the return of the subject in the 1970s as a return of metaphysics, and as a forgetting and perpetuation of onto-theology. For all the ways in which theoretical thinking has displaced or sought to overturn the traditional notion of the subject, as a stable, self-same, self-legislating identity, it has, Nancy argues, regrounded the subject insofar as it persists in referring to a ground, to a substance which can be identified, circumscribed, talked about, and subjected to the mastery of theoretical thinking. Much postwar theoretical discourse—for instance structuralism, psychoanalysis, anthropology—far from overturning the metaphysical Subject, has, in Nancy's view, constantly reposited and reaffirmed it in one form or another:

So it is that, in all quarters, the subject of the unconscious, the subject of history, the language-subject, the machine-subject, the text-subject, the body-subject, the subject of desire (and everywhere the subject declared to be the simple-effect-of-the-subject), have produced thus far only the aggravation, or even, to put it more simply and more imposingly, the exacerbation of the *status* of the Subject. (*ES*, 30)

It seems that every time a certain kind of theoretical thinking proclaims the displacement, decentering or overturning of the subject, it does so in relation to a ground, a substance, or at least an *instance*, on the basis of which it is possible to figure or represent a new identity (be it unconscious, textual, corporeal, or what have you), and to take it as the object of theoretical knowledge.

The subject, it seems, persists, despite the attempt by theoretical discourse to speak outside or beyond its traditional conception. It persists as the substratum, as the ground or foundation of theoretical discourse and does so in a way which seems impossible to circumvent: as much as one seeks to place oneself outside of the conscious subject, the subject of reason and mastery, one falls back onto a ground or grounding, a positing of a *subiectum* or substance. This point remains a constant throughout Nancy's later writing. In *La Communauté désœuvrée* Nancy remarks, "The subject cannot be outside of itself: this is even what ultimately defines it—that its outside and all its 'alienations' or 'extraneousness' should in the end be suppressed by and *sublated* in it."[49] In this context Nancy talks in *Ego Sum* of an "infinite substratification of the subject," in which the identification of any subject, even if it leads to an identity which is negative, critical, dissociated, or chaotic, is itself definitively the Subject—the substratum, the grounding of a metaphysical subjectivity. It may seem then that all theoretical, critical, and philosophical discourse is caught up within the closure of the Subject and of an economy of subjectivity. This may indeed lead us to think of the subject as both inevitable and in a real sense foundational, and so we might proclaim that, as Nancy puts it, "nothing escapes from the Subject, it governs the world" (*ES*, 30).

This persistence and dominance of the subject within theoretical discourse leads Nancy, just as it led Heidegger over forty years earlier, to return to Descartes. Descartes, who in the extreme moment of methodical doubting, identifies the Cogito as the self-positing and self-grounding of the subject of thought and knowledge, thus marking, for Heidegger at least, an inaugural moment in the development of modern metaphysics.

In his famous essay on the Cogito and Foucault's *Histoire de la folie*, published in *L'Écriture et la différence*, Derrida remarks that although it may be foundational for Descartes, "nothing is less assuring than the Cogito at its proper and inaugural moment" (*ED*, 87; *WD*, 56). In this context Derrida remarks that the inaugural moment of the Cartesian Cogito cannot be made part of a totalizing story or history of the exclusion of madness, as is Foucault's aim in the *Histoire de la folie*. Rather the Cogito is something which, from the outset, must necessarily recount itself, turn itself into a story in order to be. According to Derrida the Cogito, *I think therefore I am*, is a process of thought whereby thought appropriates itself as its own ground, as its own self-grounding. In this sense, if it occurs at all, it occurs as an event in time, within temporality or a movement of temporalization.

It should be noted here that, for Derrida, thought, meaning, and any experience of space and time are possible only because of the prior opening of *différance*, which in a sense is prior to and in excess of all these instances as their condition or possibility. Reworking and displacing Heidegger, *différance*, for Derrida, is in excess of all conceptuality or ontological disclosure, and is both a spacing and a temporalizing which allows us to experience space and time as such, but which at the same time means that space and time are never self-same or self-identical, but are always imbricated within the movement of *différance*, which opens them up and acts therefore as a kind of paradoxical and quasi-transcendental condition of possibility and impossibility.[50] So, when Derrida talks of temporalization here, we should note that it is his own thinking of *différance* which is at stake. This reading, it will become clear, will be decisive for Nancy's analysis of Descartes in *Ego Sum*.

Descartes, Derrida asserts, "must temporalize the Cogito, which itself is valid only in the instant of intuition, the instant of thought being attentive to itself, at the point, at the sharpest point of the instant. And here one should be attentive to this link between the Cogito and the movement of temporalization" (*ED*, 89; *WD*, 58). A gap or disparity opens up, therefore, between the foundational event or instant of the Cogito and its representation in language or discourse. Throughout his account Derrida underlines this disparity and points out that from the moment that Descartes utters "I think therefore I am" within his own philosophical writing, he necessarily inscribes it within "a system of deductions and protections that betray its wellspring" (*ED*, 91; *WD*, 58–59). The act or event of the Cogito must be distinguished from the language or deductive system in which Descartes must inscribe it in order to make it intelligible and communicable as such. To a large extent then, it is clear that Derrida's reading of Descartes prefigures the problem of philosophical presentation that Nancy will address in his reading of Kant a number of years later.

This disparity between the event of thought and the representation of that thought within language provides the focus for Nancy in his reading of the *Discours*. In *Ego Sum* he highlights the way in which Descartes states that the *Discours de la méthode* is a narrative; it must be seen, in Descartes own words, as a "story" or "if you prefer, . . . as a fable."[51] Nancy focuses in particular on the way Descartes presents the *Discours* as a portrait or picture; "I shall be very anxious," writes Descartes, "to indicate, in this discourse, the paths that I have followed, and to represent my life as if it were a painting."[52] Descartes gives us a method, a founding of the subject of knowledge, but only insofar as he gives us a self-portrait, and with that the story of the method, the story of the path he has taken to become who he is. The story in question will be familiar to all those who have read the *Discours*. It's a story of foundations. Descartes recounts how he has discovered the ground upon which the philosophies and sciences of his time are built to be unstable and unreliable. He tells us the story of how he himself set out to seek a method that would allow him to know the things that presented themselves to his mind with the level of certitude offered by arithmetic or mathematics. The story, then, is one of a search for a foundation of solid rock, rather than one of moving earth or sand, upon which to erect the edifice of knowledge. The rock is the Cogito, *I think therefore I am*, that of which one can still be certain when everything else has been methodically doubted.

What one finds in the *Discours de la méthode*, the story of the Cogito, is a portrait of the author of the Cogito, a "picture" which reveals the truth of Descartes and which seeks to narrate the possibility of grounding truth itself. Yet the status of the *Discours* as painting or fable carries with it, for Nancy, a fundamental ambivalence or equivocation. Descartes wants his fable to be simultaneously a portrait of Descartes *and* the presentation of the truth of Descartes himself—that is the truth of the Cartesian method. Put another way, it offers a narrative of the self-grounding of thought, and thus the placing of knowledge on firm foundations, but at the same time seeks to perform or enact that self-grounding in its unfolding as narrative. As Nancy puts it: "The author of the method can only present himself in a picture—and this picture is at once its own original, and the mask of the original which dissimulates itself, at a second remove, behind its own portrait" (*ES*, 68–69). Yet this supposed identity between the self-grounding movement of thought and its representation as portrait or fable is impossible within the context of the discrepancy identified above, the discrepancy Derrida highlights between the temporalizing movement of thought and the representation of thought in language. We might note here again that thought is being posed as a temporalizing and, we will increasingly see, spatializing movement which opens the possibility of conscious thought as represented in language. Thought is not being posed as that of a conscious individual or identity, nor as that of any unconscious subject, inscribed within a symbolic order or otherwise. For Nancy, building on Derrida's argument, there lies, at the heart of the *Discours*, an impossibility of positing an identity between the pictorial or narrative representation of thought, as self-grounding certainty, and the movement of thought itself, which would seek to posit a ground. As readers we view the portrait of René Descartes which emerges throughout the *Discours*, but, Nancy argues, the process of thought which it narrates is unsituatable and unverifiable, never presented or made present within the narrative as such: "It will never therefore be possible to do away with or remove the veil or the picture, for one would no longer see anything at all, only darkness—a darkness which no light has yet separated it from itself, and which cannot even take the figure of a shadow" (*ES*, 83). We may see the representation or the picture of a subject, which comes to ground itself, in a moment of self-apprehension or self-seizure, *I think therefore I am*, but this is not the same as the movement of the thought itself, which figures, represents, paints its own portrait. What then, Nancy asks, might lie behind the portrait of Descartes and his Cogito? As has been indicated Nancy is trying to interrogate a movement of temporalization, of thought in excess of any subject, which figures itself as Subject in the Cogito as it is narrated, but which lies somewhere prior to the Cogito as its condition of possibility. This movement of thought that figures itself but that is not itself figured, insofar as it lies before the Cogito which posits a subject, also lies before the enunciation of the subject, before the subject of both the *énoncé* and the *énonciation*. What kind of instance would this prior movement resemble, Nancy asks, what kind of Cogito, or, he continues, punning badly, what kind of "chaogito," the formless chaos which is the prior possibility of representing the Cogito itself? Nancy's conclusion is as direct as it is disarming; this prior instance is unrepresentable, unverifiable, without figure: "If the chaogito paints itself, this means at the same time that it *cannot* paint itself, and that it can only show itself as a picture; the reason for this remains the same: it resembles nothing" (*ES*, 83). Nancy's reading of the *Discours de la méthode* as portrait, picture, or fable is charged with a heavy philosophical outcome. Representation cannot coincide, become identical, or copresent with the instance of thought it seeks to represent. Thought figures a subject, but the subject of thought is itself unfigurable: "There is nobody behind the mask, thought is without figure" (*ES*, 93).

The subject which founds itself as a "thinking substance" in the Cartesian Cogito is, for Nancy, a strange and paradoxical subject, one which, as will become clear, both founds and unfounds itself in the very same moment. This is because "the *cogito* has the exact structure of the fable of its exposition" (*ES*, 114). *I think therefore I am* offers a figure or an image of a self-grounding subject, but not being coincident or copresent with the movement of thought it figures, it does not in any way ground itself; the Cogito gives an image of a subject and nothing more: "The subject does not imagine itself, but because it can only be the subject of its own representation, it *images itself* in each instance, it *figures* itself" (*ES*, 89). On one level then, the subject is only ever a figure, a mask; it is itself only ever a fable or representation.[53] As mask, image, or figure the subject for Nancy can never operate as a stable ground or substance. In Heidegger's terminology it is never a *subiectum* because in the moment thought tries to seize itself in the self-certainty of the Cogito, it seizes nothing at all; it is unable to figure or grasp thought itself, it only produces fabulous images. Or as Nancy puts it: "In the very instant of appropriation, the subject appropriates *only the groundlessness of a substance still without surface, or the formlessness of the a medium which has not yet taken pictural form*" (*ES*, 88). In the moment of grounding, the Cogito encounters only an absence of ground. The Cogito remains the crucial point of reference for Nancy as it is for Descartes. In Descartes's text it founds the subject after everything has been doubted, in Nancy's it un-founds the subject in the very moment of its foundation.

In *Ego Sum* the Cogito marks an extreme point where the Subject of metaphysics announces itself but in the very same gesture denounces itself and, with that, all possibility of posing a substance or ground. In the Cogito substance is not something which *is*, which underlies and acts as foundation, but something which, like the subject, announces or performs itself in a movement of figuration: "Substance is not something underlying [*sous-jacent*], it enunciates itself" (*ES*, 121). Prior to the subject of both the *énoncé* and of the *énonciation* is the temporalization of thought itself, ungraspable, unfigurable, and irreducible to any mode of substance or ground. Nancy substantivizes the infinitive of the French verb *énoncer* and speaks of *l'énoncer* (translated here as the English present participle). The use of the infinitive in French seeks to address this prior instance of thought in terms of movement, in terms of temporalization: "Enunciating: the enunciating [*Énoncer: l'énoncer*] consists in substantivizing the infinitive. This might also be the same as, in spite of everything, and at least provisionally, a way of infinitizing substance, a way of removing its completion and foundation" (*ES*, 124). In the verb-become-noun *énoncer* Nancy is attempting to speak of or theorize an instance which is not a substance, which is prior to figuration, and which, ultimately is not an *instance* that can in any way be theorized. It is here that one begins to encounter the resolutely paradoxical status of Nancy's writing of the Subject: "In the enunciating [*l'énoncer*], the subject loses all that is finite, all the completion of a figure [*tout fini, toute finition de figure*]: it is not, above all not, infinite, nor is it any longer finite. Infinite, it is not. And in the end, I must renounce any attempt to define it. The enunciating carries with it this renunciation" (*ES*, 124). Nancy theorizes the subject as in excess of theory. This seems like a theoretical implosion, a moment where a philosophical discourse undermines itself in a self-destructive or suicidal gesture. Nancy renounces any possibility of figuring or grounding a subject; the subject of thought to which Descartes appeals in order to place knowledge generally on firm foundations.

Yet the moment of paradox is what's important here. The juncture at which the subject gives itself in the "enunciation" of the Cogito is the exact point at which it is simultaneously withdrawn, unfounded in the movement of "enunciating" (*l'énoncer*); or as Nancy puts it: "In enunciating the thought of man as subject withdraws in the very moment of its exposition" (*ES*, 154). This is a paradoxical gesture of presentation and withdrawal, of which Derrida wrote in his discourse on the gift or the double bind. For Nancy, this gesture of presentation and withdrawal is an encounter with a violent aporia (which recalls his use of the term *syncopation* in *Logodaedalus*). It is a convulsion or a spasm. He refers to this as the "structure of extreme withdrawal" that governs the Cogito, a structure that is always in place whenever a subject tries to pose itself, announce itself, or appropriate its own self as ground. The "I" of the subject only ever appears insofar as it simultaneously disappears, it is posed only as an "punctual identity" (*identité ponctuelle*) which is without identity, since it exists "in a spasm which articulates and dismembers it, and only articulates it by dismembering it" (*ES*, 152). All that presents itself in representation is a residue, a fable, a mask, a fake that can never coincide with that convulsive instance that fakes, masks, is imaged itself in fable.

It should perhaps be clear how this paradoxical structure of the subject is, in part at least, a response to Lacanian theory, according to which, as Lacan asserts in his second seminar, "the subject poses itself as operating, as human, as I, from the moment when the symbolic system appears."[54] Nancy is identifying, however paradoxically, a movement of thought prior to any inscription within the symbolic, prior to any dialectic of desire or recognition, and prior to any "'stage'" (*stade*). Such a movement cannot be subject to the mastery of a psychoanalytic discourse; in Nancy's words "it surges inexorably outside, in excess of all psychoanalysis" (*ES*, 161). Indeed, taken in this light, Nancy's impossible subject appears far less like the suicide of philosophy than it does a modification of philosophy's foundation. This modification of foundation manifests itself in the figural dimension of Nancy's writing and is most evident in his use of the figure of *la bouche*, the speaking mouth. The operation of this figure in Nancy's text shows how he begins to rethink space and spatiality, not as the objective measurable and three-dimensional space of science, but rather as exteriority and as non-mathematizable "extension," in which distinctions such as mind/body, sensible/intelligible, transcendent/immanent cannot properly operate. At the same time the figure of *la bouche* sheds light on the status of Nancy's own writing, its ficticity and the relation between philosophy and literature which this implies.

In the first instance we might think of Nancy's focus on the figure of *la bouche* as a response to and displacement of Lacan's privileging of the eyes and ears in his meditation on the symbolic subject in the second seminar. Where, for Lacan, eyes and ears are sites of reflection which offer a perfect figure for his emphasis on the specular quality of the imaginary order and the dialectic of desire and recognition instituted by the symbolic, for Nancy, *la bouche* figures this instance of thought, of presentation and withdrawal of an I which surges forth in a spasm of "extreme withdrawal" prior to any economy of exchange or of recognition. "Imagine,"

Nancy tells us "a mouth without a face . . . a mouth without a face then, making a ring from its contraction around the noise: *I*" (ES, 157). The mouth here is not the mouth that we represent and place within an identifiable face. Rather it is that opening or *béance* around which the mouth that we know forms itself. On one level Nancy here is trying to rethink the two Cartesian modes of extension or space, the extension of the objective space of the world and that of thought, of the *res cogitans*. At some point, Descartes has to think of the way in which, given the split of body and mind, these two forms of extension are nevertheless conjoined. For Nancy *la bouche* seems to figure a movement which opens up an incommensurable extension of thought, one which has so far been called a temporalizing movement, which is prior to conscious thought and any intersubjective symbolic unconsciousness; he writes, "The incommensurable extension of thought, is the opening of the mouth" (*ES*, 161). The opening of the mouth, in the sense that Nancy develops here, is exactly that singular point of spasm, that "punctual identity" in which the subject both presents itself and is withdrawn in a violent convulsion—this, he says, is *ego*, the I governed by the "structure of extreme withdrawal" alluded to above. But, as the whole of Nancy's reinscription of Descartes indicates, this *Ego*, formed in an opening to which the figure of *la bouche* is given, is not in any way interior to any process of representation or symbolization. It is an exteriority and a spacing of space: "Ego makes, or makes itself, *exteriority*, the spacing out of places, the distancing and unfamiliarity which makes a place, and thus space itself, the primary spatiality of a veritable tracing in which, and in which alone, ego can spring forth, trace itself, and think itself" (*ES*, 163). And he adds, "The mouth is the opening of *Ego*, *Ego* is the opening of the mouth. What happens there, is that the there spaces itself [*Ce qui s'y passe, c'est qu'il s'y espace*]" (*ES*, 162). By ejecting subjectivity into an exteriority in excess of any subject, one could argue that Nancy is reinscribing existence, each irreplaceable human existence, in terms of a singularity that is not subject to the law of the symbolic, the bar of castration, and an economy of lack. Nancy allows us to think of space, of, if you like, the giving of being, in a way which builds on but is crucially different from Heidegger, and perhaps even from Derrida. A singularity, it should be noted, exists as such in relation to other singularities—thus we come to think space not as an objectifiable, mathematizable extension or presence, but as a temporal unfolding in which singularities, prior to any logic of a subject, expose themselves to each other.[55] This, indeed, is the sense of *la bouche* as Nancy develops it in relation to his thinking of community in *La Communauté désœuvrée:* "The speaking mouth is . . . the beating of a singular site against other singular sites" (*CD*, 77; *IC*, 31). It should be emphasized here that Nancy's critique of the persistence of the subject and of Lacan is not a negative or destructive gesture. Rather it is an attempt at untying the various topologies of substance which traverse modern theory, perhaps to promulgate more traditional metaphysical structures of thought, in order to rethink the giving of being in terms of singularity, spacing, and what Nancy comes to call *comparution*. In this context the importance of Nancy's work lies in how it allows us to think of the, perhaps inevitable, persistence of the subject, not as the persistence of a metaphysical substance or ground, but as an instance which is constantly ungrounded and exposed to an unmasterable excess. This instance would be the temporalizing, singular, and plural giving of being itself which would be irreducible to any concept or figure and any possibility of ontological disclosure.[56]

To understand this better we need to address Nancy's use of the term *la bouche*, which figures, as has been indicated, an instance that, as exteriority, is without figure. As such this term seems to be governed itself by a logic of presentation and withdrawal: that instance which it gives us is immediately taken away. Put in another manner the *bouche* as figure occupies an uncertain place at the limit of representation. It figures an unfigurable instance and as such internalizes a difference with itself. As the key term around which the text of *Ego Sum* comes to organize itself, it doesn't function as a concept or idea; rather it traces a limit of thought and figuration which, in a sense, cannot be encountered or mastered as such. The *ego* or opening of *la bouche* about which Nancy talks is itself affirmed as exteriority; as such it is subject to a movement of "exscription" which Nancy goes on to develop in much of his later writing.[57] As Nancy's text affirms an opening or an *espacement*, which it immediately exteriorizes, it obeys a complex relation to the limit of representation. This can best be described in his own words in the later text *Une Pensée finie:* "it is a question of that movement through which, incessantly, the unlimited [*l'illimité*] raises itself [*s'enlève*], unlimits itself [*se délimite*], along the limit which delimits and presents itself [*qui se délimite et se présente*]. This movement would trace in a certain way the external border of the limit" (*PF*, 168; *FT*, 225).

This, precisely, is the logic which governs the term *la bouche* and indeed the movement of Nancy's text as a whole. It is also the logic which Nancy uncovered in Descartes's text and in the Cogito. As such, Nancy's text, like that of Descartes, becomes not theory or concept, but fable, mask, fiction of an always already exteriorized moment. In the exscription of the sense of his own text Nancy affirms both the singularity of his own writing and the ficticity which makes of writing a tracing or spacing (*espacement*) where philosophy and literature come together in their very difference from themselves.

## Conclusion: Philosophy as Figural Praxis

Nancy's engagement with the question of metaphysical ground or foundation throughout the 1970s led him to a thinking of a philosophical subject which persists, yet which persists only in its exposure to an absence of ground. The subject, as Nancy comes to think it, persists only in its being-outside-of-itself, its exteriority, irreducible to any order of the symbolic, or logic of *subiectum* (i.e., that which lies beneath, which supports or grounds) such as it is described by Heidegger in his lectures on Nietzsche. Yet in describing this instance, an instance which one might call the persistence of a subject ceaselessly and infinitely exposed to its own excess, Nancy is also attempting to describe or theorize that which necessarily exceeds the possibility of description or theoretical disclosure. His thought is held, syncopated, within a repetition of this paradoxical moment. His thought, as the thought of a thinking subject, exposes thought to an exteriority or excess. Thought, for Nancy, is not the work of concepts since it does not "conceive" of a presence or identity which it re-presents. Terms such as *la bouche*, or the speaking mouth, operate as figures rather than concepts, precisely insofar as they do not coincide or have any identity with what they speak about. As has been indicated, the logic of the figure, here, is one of nonidentity whereby a difference with what is figured is internalized within the figure itself. The figure figures the unfigurable. Since it operates in excess of the ideality proper to concepts, the figure is also very much embedded within the contingency, the historicity, and the temporality of writing.

This figural quality of Nancy's thought emerges as one of the most distinctive aspects of his early works in the 1970s and arguably persists throughout his career. Any reader familiar with Nancy's works will be aware of the very particular style or idiom in which they are written. The style of Nancy's writing can be difficult to engage with and even, at times, painful to read. Yet it can also give rise to moments of lyrical beauty or affective intensity which can leave the reader genuinely moved (as is the case, for instance, with the work *L'Intrus*, published in 2000). More importantly it must be borne in mind that the figural status of Nancy's philosophical writing means that certain key terms which dominate much of his later thought must not be taken at face value. Terms such as *sense, community, corpus,* and *being* do not signify an identity or mark a presence or substance. Rather they always mark, or *exscribe,* a certain excess of signification and thus obey the paradoxical logic of presentation and withdrawal that Nancy elaborates in his early commentaries on Kant and Descartes.

At the same time, *as* resolutely figural, as a movement of exscription or exposure to its own excess, Nancy's practice of philosophical writing clearly articulates a shifting relation between philosophy and literature. When thought becomes a figural writing rather than the work of the concept, the relation between philosophy and literature becomes undecidable. This undecidability does not mean that philosophical and literary writing are the same. The indecisive relation of the one to the other means rather that one cannot be hierarchized over the other on the basis of any privileged access to a pregiven ideality or truth. Both philosophy and literature, in their different ways, might be said to operate figurally in relation to an unfigurable real.

In a later work, *Le Sens du monde,* Nancy affirms clearly his sense that philosophical writing, as a figuration where sense is in excess of signification, exists as responsibility toward what he calls "the excess of sense":

Once the possibility of signifying truth is a thing of the past, another style is necessary. . . . It is not a matter of stylistic effects or ornaments of discourse, but of what sense does to discourse if sense exceeds significations. It is a matter of the *praxis* of thought, its *writing* in the sense of the assumption of a responsibility for and to this excess. (*SM,* 37; *SW,* 19)

The implications of this affirmation of philosophy both as figural praxis and as responsibility will be explored throughout the remaining chapters of this study.

# CHAPTER TWO

# Space

Spatialization—space and time—first of all makes or opens up existence
as the possibility of sense.

—JEAN-LUC NANCY, *The Sense of the World*[1]

## Introduction

Nancy's account of subjectivity, then, is intimately bound up with an
account of space and spatiality. Implied also is a certain understanding of
the body and of embodiment as a fundamental aspect of any experience
of space. It will have become abundantly clear that space, in this context,
is not the three-dimensional extension as measured by geometry. Rather,
in Nancy's terms, it is an exteriority, a spacing or *espacement*, which is at
the same time also a temporalizing movement, an opening up of spatiality
prior to space as we might traditionally think it. This conception of space
as a spatial-temporal unfolding, or opening of an intelligible world, owes
much, as the previous discussion has implied, to Heidegger's account of
primary spatiality in *Being and Time* and to its development in Heidegger's
later thinking. Yet more generally, Nancy's thinking of space should be situated in relation to the wider context of the German phenomenological
tradition (a tradition in which Heidegger occupies a rather singular position), and specifically its reception within the French philosophical community during the period immediately following the Second World War.
Of particular significance in this respect is the account of space given by

the founding father of German phenomenology, Edmund Husserl (1859–1938), in his 1907 lecture series entitled *Thing and Space,* and the development of Husserl's thought by Maurice Merleau-Ponty in key works such as *Phénomenologie de la perception* (1945) and *Le Visible et l'invisible* (1964).

As is the case with Derrida's work, Nancy's thinking moves decisively beyond the ambit of the phenomenological approach yet at the same time, I would argue, it cannot be understood without reference to it.[2] This becomes clear if one considers the extent to which the phenomenological understanding diverges significantly from classical debates about the existence of space. Developments within the phenomenological tradition (such as one might find in Merleau-Ponty's work), or within critiques of phenomenology (such as are articulated in different ways by both Derrida and Nancy) serve to intensify or heighten the initial divergences, which Husserl's writing originally articulates, from the classical paradigm of thinking about space. If these initial divergences are not taken into account what one might call a "postphenomenological" thinking of space, its significance, its terminology, and its relation to issues of being or existence are likely to remain rather opaque and inaccessible.

What follows, then, will give a brief account of the classical debate about the nature and substantive existence of space, and then a fuller account of Husserl's treatment of this issue in the 1907 lectures *Thing and Space.* The discussion will highlight the way in which Husserl's account decisively breaks from the concerns and terms of reference which inform the classical debate. It will then examine Heidegger's account of primary spatiality in both *Being and Time* and his later thought. In this way it can be seen that Nancy's thinking of space, such as it develops across a number of important texts written throughout his career, emerges both as a reinscription, but also as a radical critique, of the phenomenological account. Finally, Nancy's complex and seemingly more tangential relation to Merleau-Ponty's philosophy will be examined, particularly in terms of the relation between the experience of space and of embodiment, which is posed in the writing of both thinkers.

## Space: Classical and Phenomenological

### *The Classical Debate*

The classical debate relating to space is essentially ontological, and could be summed up, rather schematically perhaps, in the question: does space exist? We experience things in the world as spatially extended and as separated from each other by distances or volumes of emptiness, but does this mean that space is an entity in its own right, that it is a thing, albeit a thing very different in nature from entities we can see and touch? According to Heidegger's account of European philosophical modernity discussed in the previous chapter, our dominant understanding of space would be broadly Cartesian: space is an extension in which extended things are placed and encountered by an autonomous self-grounding subjectivity in a moment of presence. Yet Heidegger's account of modernity in the Nietzsche lectures, focusing as it does on what he sees as the dominant subjectivism of the modern era, does not address or take into account key aspects of the broader debate which turns on the objective existence or otherwise of space.

The choice of Descartes as a foundational figure for a modern conception of space would have its justification in the Cartesian rejection of Aristotelian and neoscholastic thought, which viewed both space and time as a function of the categories. In Aristotelian ontology the categories of space and time allow us to name and classify sensory experience, but their status is somewhat ambiguous insofar as they can be considered either as straightforward empirical ways of grouping sensible facts together or as more abstract generalities which have a status far superior to empirical or sensory experience. In Cartesian thought space ceases to have a categorial status and becomes the absolute of extension where objects are extended things (*res extensa*) and the human subject is the thinking thing (*res cogitans*).[3] As was indicated in the last chapter this shift lays the ground for the mathematization of space in modern science and for the foundation of the subject of scientific knowledge. It also lays the ground for subsequent philosophical disputes which Heidegger's account passes over.

Within the Cartesian notion of space as extension the question arises as to whether space exists as a substance or an attribute of being (or of *the*

Divine Being), or whether it is simply an order which is in some way immanent to the totality of existing things. Descartes himself does not entirely resolve or give a clear answer to this question, and after Descartes it
subsequently forms the basis of two opposing views about the ontological status of space, known as *substantivalism* and *relationalism*. The two
key figures in this well-known classical debate are Newton and Leibniz. As
Newton's presence here suggests, this is a question which is tied up with
the wider corpus of scientific knowledge, and, as an interrogation of the
objective properties of the physical world, developments within this debate have always been closely related to scientific theories and observations.[4] As this discussion progresses it will become evident why Heidegger
might have little interest in the debates around substantivalism and relationalism. The phenomenological approach, we shall see, changes in key
ways the terms of reference relating to the ontological status of space.

By way of summary one could characterize substantivalism and relationalism and the differences between them in the following ways. Substantivalists claim that the physical world consists of material objects but
also of a further substantive entity, space. Relationalists deny the objective
existence of space as a separate entity; they argue that objects existing in
the world are directly related to each other by spatial relations. According to the relational view space does not exist as such, rather it needs to be
thought of in terms of spatial relations which would be distinctive properties of material objects. In this sense substantivalists would think of the
world in terms of space-object relations (objects being intrinsically related
to space as such and having some of their properties defined by these relations), while relationalists would think primarily in terms of (spatial) object-object relations. Such theoretical differences may not seem to be of
much importance to our everyday engagements with our spatial world,
but, as has been indicated, they have been of central concern to scientific
considerations. They have also had, historically at least, a substantial theological importance.

Indeed, the initial taking of positions and subsequent dispute about
this issue between Newton and Leibniz had an important theological dimension. Newton's substantivalism, his belief in the existence of an absolute space in which material bodies are positioned, was closely tied to his
religious convictions and his desire to incorporate his scientific insights

into a wider vision of absolute space as a divine attribute (the "sensorium" of God). Likewise Leibniz's polemic against Newton, his rejection of absolute space and assertion of the relationalist position stemmed, in part at least, from what he took to be the theologically unacceptable implications of Newton's views.[5] The details of the debate between these two figures are beyond the scope of this discussion, as is its wider historical and scientific legacy. In this context it is important to highlight two key points. First, the specific way that this debate focuses on an ontological question (does space exist?), and does so in highly theoretical terms, should be noted once again. As has been indicated, there is no attention paid to our everyday, pretheoretical experience of spatiality; attention is paid to its objective existence or otherwise and to the relation of space to material objects. Second, one might note the extent to which the primary ontological dimension of this question has wider implications, which historically were largely theological in nature, but are also necessarily of epistemological importance. The conditions under which we know objects would be very different if space is a property of object-object relations rather than an independent entity that would allow us to think in terms of object-space relations.

In view of this one might be tempted to assimilate the substantivalist position to an empiricist approach and the relationalist perspective to a broadly idealist outlook. If space is a substance or thing then it is an entity whose attributes and qualities can be observed from experience in the same way as other things or entities placed within space. If it is nothing in itself but only a function of the relational properties of material objects, then the apprehension of space could be considered to be a function of the mind which perceives those relational properties rather than observation of those properties as they are in themselves. The respective cases of Newton, the empirical scientist, and Leibniz the idealist philosopher might seem to justify such an assimilation. In reality, though, relationalism is a doctrine that comes in a variety of guises: some have a more empiricist bent (*realist relationalism*), others focus more on the activity of the mind (*idealist relationism*). Where the former would view knowledge of spatial relations on the basis of the observable properties of things, the latter would place a key emphasis on the activity of the mind and its ability to construct spatial patterns out of the sensory experience of objects. At the same time Kantian idealism, with its construal of space and time as a priori sensible intuitions and its (modified) reintroduction of the Aristotelian categories, might not appear to be compatible with a substantivalist account. Yet Kant explicitly sought to refute any relationalist understanding of space, conceiving it in what one might call *idealist substantivalist* terms. In this context space is an absolute entity, existing independently of other entities, but it is a *conceptual* entity, an ideal thing which exists as a component of our mental experience.[6]

Different forms of both substantivalism and relationalism can, therefore, be situated on either side of the empiricist/idealist divide. In view of this, it could also be argued that the substantivalist and relationalist debate as a whole, taken together with the range of epistemological possibilities the two alternatives imply, is subordinated to the polar opposites of idealism and empiricism, and by implication to a range of dependent dichotomies which these opposites articulate: mind and body, the sensible and the intelligible, subjectivism and objectivism, relative and absolute truth, and so on. The specific way in which one answers the ontological question of *whether* space has an absolute or substantive existence would also, and perhaps necessarily, entail or affirm an implicit epistemological understanding of *how* we know space and things in space, that is to say, an affirmation of a knowing subject and known object, conceived of as separate entities, one of which can be given priority over the other in the constitution of spatial experience.

### Phenomenological Space

Insofar as Nancy's account of space and spatiality is deeply rooted in the phenomenological account (and might be described as a "postphenomenological" thinking of space), the work of Edmund Husserl is of key importance. The phenomenological account of space is developed in a number of different contexts by a wide range thinkers with a variety of concerns.[7] From its foundational moment in the work of Husserl the phenomenological thinking about space breaks from the terms of the classical debate insofar as it does not give primacy to the ontological question about the objective existence of space as an entity independent of other entities. Neither does it rely on a clear or straightforward opposition between subject and object, the ideal and the empirical. In the very broadest terms, phenomenology could be described as a philosophical project which aims to describe the character of consciousness in the most clear and systematic way, and which concerns itself only with that which presents itself to consciousness. Its exclusive concern, therefore, is with things such as they appear in subjective experience; the question of the existence of things independent of experience is not posed, nor, indeed, is it considered to be a viable philosophical question. In this context it could be argued that the most distinctive contribution made by phenomenology to the European philosophical tradition consists in the way in which it plots a path between the alternatives of idealism and empiricism in a manner which is not strictly reducible to either.

Husserl's most comprehensive account of space is given in the 1907 lecture series entitled *Thing and Space*, and occurs at a point in his thinking which marks a key shift from his early thought, most comprehensively articulated in the *Logical Investigations*, to his later work, whose most significant expression can be found *Ideas I* (1913), *Ideas II* (published posthumously in 1952), and the very late *Crisis of European Sciences and Transcendental Phenomenology* (1937).[8] Although Husserl's project undergoes all sorts of shifts in the decades which separate *Thing and Space* from the *Crisis*, the earlier text is written after his discovery of the phenomenological reduction (in 1905), a discovery which decisively marks the entirety of his subsequent career and crucially his thinking about space and spatiality.

Husserl begins the lectures on *Thing and Space* by emphasizing the extent to which he is aiming to focus his phenomenological analyses on a level of experience which would be prescientific and therefore in a decisive sense pretheoretical. His argument is based on the understanding that science abstracts from the immediate givenness of experience, and thus, in determining the objectivity of its observations via theoretical and mathematical frames, deviates from the essential character of immediate experience upon which it nevertheless relies in order to constitute itself as science. In this sense Husserl distinguishes between a natural apprehension of the world, a world which we encounter in perception, which is familiar and always already there for us, and a scientific apprehension of the world, which is rooted in or necessarily dependent upon the natural world:

The scientific grasp of the world may be very far removed from that of pre-scientific experience, and science may indeed teach that the sense qualities have no immediate Objective reference such as natural experience attributes to them. Yet the fact remains that straightforward experience, immediate perception, memory, etc., give to the sciences the things which they determine theoretically—merely by deviating from the ordinary modes of thought. (*TS*, 3; *HUA*, 16:6)

The emphasis placed here on the pretheoretical immediacy of given experience necessarily changes the manner in which one considers the existence of space and spatiality. The classical debate, it should be recalled, turned essentially on the question of the objective existence of space as a substantive entity and was closely bound to the sphere of scientific observation and theory. From the outset Husserl appears to ground questions of objective reality within the sphere of more immediate perception:

All the reality judgements grounded by the natural scientist lead back to straightforward perceptions and memories, and they relate to the world which receives its first givenness in this straightforward experience. All mediate grounding, as carried out by science, rests precisely on immediate givenness, and the lived experiences in which reality comes to be given immediately are perception, memory, and, taken in a certain immediacy, also expectation and other acts similar to it. (*TS*, 3; *HUA*, 16:7)

This distinction between natural, immediate, and prescientific experience on the one hand and the mediate scientific apprehension of the world on the other is a fundamental aspect of Husserl's thought. The logical priority Husserl gives to the former over the latter is carried forward into the broader phenomenological tradition in decisive ways: in, for example, Heidegger's account of being-in-the-world and his subsequent critique of technology; in Sartre's relative disdain for all things scientific; and in Merleau-Ponty's account of perception.

Such a grounding of scientific objectivity and of reality judgments within the sphere of straightforward perception may appear to lead Husserl's thought ineluctably into the domain of subjectivism or idealism. If phenomenology aims solely to describe the character of consciousness and to ground all human realities solely in relation to consciousness, then it may necessarily be at best a form of subjective idealism and at worst an extreme form of solipsism. Although there is unmistakably a neo-Kantian dimension to his thought, Husserl always denied that his phenomenology was reducible to idealism.[9] In his phenomenological descriptions Husserl is interested exclusively in the "self-constitution—the self-mani-

festation . . . of experiential objectivity at the lowest level of experience .
. . . the lived experience of straightforward intuition or intuitive grasping,
upon which the higher acts of the specifically logical sphere are first built
and thereby bring about" (*TS*, 7; *HUA*, 16:8). Yet he does not argue, as
subjective idealism would, that consciousness *creates* the world in any ontological sense. Rather he argues (and this will be a key point which will
be developed in the ensuing discussion of Heidegger and Nancy) that consciousness is the ground of all objective reality only insofar as it opens up
or renders intelligible a meaningful world, which would imply that nothing we can know or posit can be thought of as separate from consciousness.[10] In this sense, consciousness and the immediacy of perceptual intuition, has for, Husserl a fundamental disclosive role in the constitution or
manifestation of a meaningful or intelligible world. "Consciousness," Husserl writes, "is absolute Being. . . . The world is born, as it were, by consciousness" (*TS*, 34; *HUA*, 16:40). This must seem to some an unasham-
edly ontological claim, making a philosophical statement which would be
undeniably idealist in character. Yet, as always in Husserl, the word being
here does not refer to any being-in-itself, rather it refers to being-for-consciousness, or more properly, a being-intelligible-for-consciousness, which,
he would argue, is the only form of being we can posit. As one commenta-
tor has recently remarked, if this is idealism, then it is far more a form of
epistemic idealism than a form of ontological idealism.[11]

While it is true (as will become increasingly clear) that Husserl wish-
es to preserve a sphere of *ideality*, which would be the realm of meaning
or sense as an intentional structure, it would, nevertheless, still be possible
to argue that any dichotomy between the empirical and the ideal, the objective and the subjective, does not hold within the context of phenomenological analysis, where objectivity is always necessarily subjectively constituted, and where the two poles of subjectivity and objectivity are never
separated such that the former might be the cause of the latter (idealism)
or the latter the cause of the former (empiricism). Of crucial importance
here is Husserl's discovery of the phenomenological reduction. The phenomenological reduction can best be described as the attempt by Husserl to bracket off all experience except that which is given immediately
to consciousness (and thus closely resembles the methodological doubt of
Descartes). This, precisely, is what allows him to focus his analysis on that

which is most essential to what he calls above "absolute being," that is, the world-disclosing, meaning-constituting sphere of that which is given immediately in perception. For Husserl the emphasis, within the reduction, on the givenness of objects in the perceptual immediacy of experience does not imply that things exist with an identity which is then "presented" to perception, but rather, as has been emphasized, that perception constitutes the identity of things as such: "the essence of a type of lived experience in the phenomenological reduction and in intuitive abstraction does not merely present itself, but instead it is an absolute givenness in rigorous 'immanent' abstraction and not merely a 'presentation of'" (*TS*, 20; *HUA*, 16:23). The reduction allows Husserl to focus his thinking on that which is immanent to perception, or put another way, on that which presents itself to "consciousness of something within the flesh" (*TS*, 33; *HUA*, 16:39).[12] Along with the charge of idealism, Husserl would reject also the accusation that his use of the reduction in this way entails a form of solipsism. The isolation of "pure consciousness" which the reduction allows is, he would argue, an appeal to a moment of meaning constitution which precedes individual self-consciousness as such (and which would be its condition of possibility in the Kantian sense). What matters is the way in which the reduction allows the phenomenologist to isolate and describe in a rigorous and clear manner the form and disclosive role of meaning-constituting structures.

It should be clear at this point the extent to which the ontological debate about whether space is, or is not, a substantive entity in its own right has become redundant within the framework of Husserl's phenomenological considerations. The argument of the *Thing and Space* lectures is necessarily focused on the constitution of the objective sense-identity of things within the pretheoretical and prescientific perceptual sphere. Within this context space is not an entity "in-itself," such that we must think in terms of object-space relations, nor is it merely a relationality of things "in-themselves," allowing us to pose only object-object relations. Rather the identity of space is *constituted*. At its most fundamental level it is constituted as a form of the thing, and as a unity produced by the co-constitution of things within the sphere of perceptual immanence. Despite the neo-Kantian dimension of Husserl's thought, he does, in fact, explicitly reject Kant's claim that space is a form of a priori intuition. "Space," he writes, "is a necessary form of things and is not a form of lived experience, specifically not of 'sensuous' lived experiences. 'Form of intuition' is a fundamentally false expression and implies, even in Kant, a fatally erroneous position" (*TS*, 37; *HUA*, 16:43). This position is reflected in the overall structure of the *Thing and Space* lectures, which begin with an account of the way in which perceptions stand in what Husserl calls a "unity of identity-consciousness" or a "synthesis of identification," such that the thing is perceived as a thing. Only after Husserl has accounted for the phenomenological constitution of things and the spatiality proper to them can he then account for space as that which is constituted through the unity of ordered contexts within which things are placed. Rather, within phenomenological intuition every appearance of a thing necessarily contains a stratum, a schema of the thing which is itself spatial and upon which all other forms of spatiality depend.

For Husserl the manner in which things are disclosed or made manifest within consciousness cannot be abstracted from their spatiality. As a perceiving entity I necessarily encounter things as spatially extended such that the constitution of things as self-identical entities within my visual field is necessarily also and simultaneously the constitution of a primary spatial extension. According to Husserl, then, the appearance of the thing always contains a spatial element, a layer or stratum, which in *Ideas I* he comes to call the "schema of the thing": "It becomes apparent (always in eidetic-phenomenological intuition) that every appearance of a thing necessarily contains a stratum which we call the schema of the thing: that is the spatial structure merely filled with 'sensuous' qualities" (*Ideas I*, 361; *HUA*, 3:370). The thing is a spatial structure or a "spatial schema" with a sensuous filling. In phenomenological terms the experience of space needs, therefore, to be understood through the way in which streams of sense data, both visual and tactile, are structured into self-identical entities or logical unities which are perceivable as such despite changes which might occur within the flux or stream sensory data. This process of structuration is complex; its description makes up the lengthy phenomenological analyses of the *Thing and Space* lectures as a whole.

Within these phenomenological descriptions of the constitution of space the concept of perceptual "field" plays a key role. Husserl is interested in the way the perception of an object is, as it were, "built up" from a manifold of sensations within the visual and tactile fields of the perceiver. "Spatiality," he writes, "is doubly constituted, once with visual and another time with tactile determinations" (*TS*, 132; *HUA*, 16:156). The concept of field here is difficult. It refers to a form of apprehended extension which is logically prior to the extension of space as such and which would act as its ground or foundation. In this sense a field, for Husserl, is "prephenomenal" or "preempirical," insofar as it consists of extended manifold sensory impressions from which phenomena and all empirical entities will be derived. The preempirical extension of the visual field could not yet be regarded as a plane in space but rather that two-dimensional manifold from which space is first constituted: "The field is a pre-empirical expanse, and has these or those determinate visual fillings. All visual pre-empirical expanses, which in every case provide the presentational foundation for all things given in the same total perception, fit within this field as pieces" (*TS*, 68; *HUA*, 16:83). In this sense the visual field is essentially fragmented and heterogeneous, offering a multiplicity of "pre-empirical matter, pre-empirical places, shapes, sizes etc." (*TS*, 141; *HUA*, 16:166). The visual field is a "system of places," which together with tactile determinations provide the raw material for the appearance of things and space.

According to Husserl the process by which the heterogeneity of the sensory fields becomes the consciousness of things is inseparable from the fact that perception is always *embodied* perception (an immanence "within the flesh"), and from the fact that the perceiving body is always positioned and always moving in some way, even if this movement is merely the movement of the eye which sees or the hand which touches. The perception of a thing, therefore, and the spatial extension of a thing, are inseparable from the variation within the stream of data constituting the perceptual fields, this variation having its roots in the inherent mobility or motility of the body: "the constitution of the Objective location and of the Objective spatiality, is essentially mediated by the movement of the Body, or, in phenomenological terms, by the kinaesthetic sensations, whether this be constant or changing kinaesthetic sequences" (*TS*, 148; *HUA*, 16:176). Husserl's use of the term *kinaesthetic* to describe the nature of sensory content within the visual field reflects the fundamental importance he gives to movement in the constitution of perceived things by consciousness. The changing manifold of "kinaesthetic sensations" forms "kinaesthetic sequences" and then "kinaesthetic systems" as the body, or parts of the body (initially the eyes or the "oculomotor field"), move forward or backward, or turn to the left or right. What interests Husserl is that within this constant flux, this mass of heterogeneous data which makes up the preempirical expanse or diffusion of the senses, an order and a unity occurs, which means that we perceive things, things which have their own self-same identity and remain positioned within determinate contexts or locations and places. This order or unity of perception which underpins the identity and location of things is also that which, for Husserl, constitutes space. In this sense the "thing" or object is nothing other than a unity within the stream of sense data contained in the preempirical expanse of the sensory fields. "The object," Husserl writes "is what is unitary in the kinaesthetically motivated manifold of appearances" (*TS*, 164; *HUA*, 16:196). Only in the ability of consciousness to unify or order modifications within the manifold of "kinaesthetic" sensory data into sequences and systems can the perception of things and therefore of space occur:

The "motivated unity" of the modifications belongs essentially to the constitution of something identical, and it is a unity of modification that concerns the ordered contexts, or constellations of places which are found by means of the images and which allow them to be grasped as unitary complexes. . . . In the consciousness of unity that penetrates these modifications of the ordered contexts, the order of space is constituted. (*TS*, 183; *HUA*, 16:217)

The ability of consciousness to provide this "motivated unity" is what makes it foundational for Husserl within the overall structure of his phenomenological thinking. Consciousness is always an "identity-consciousness," that is, something which orders the mass of sensory data into something which is intelligible and which has meaning within fixed determinate order. Only on the basis of such a determinate order can space be experienced as such. Husserl describes this "identity-consciousness" as a "peculiar phenomenon" insofar as it is able to form the unity of a perception and to bind perceptions together in a synthesis of identification. This synthesis of identification is inseparable from Husserl's belief in the essentially intentional structure of consciousness and from the *temporal* nature of intentionality. In this sense the perception of things and of space is, therefore, intimately bound up with Husserl's thinking of temporality.

The stream of sensory impressions which form the basis of perception have, for Husserl, a tenseless ordering that becomes tensed only through the temporal intentionality of conscious experience. In this context every moment of sensation within the flux or stream of sensory data represents itself as present but does so by incorporating past and futural elements. Sensations of the immediate past are retained in the present sense data just as possible future sensations are anticipated (or as Husserl says *protended*). It is this temporal structure of retentions and protentions or anticipations which form the basis of the human experience of time and of temporal passage. Husserl would argue that our idea of *objective* time, and of physical time in particular, is necessarily secondary in nature, since it depends for its existence on the experience of this primary temporal flux of retentions and protentions from which all other theoretical understanding of time must derive and upon which it must rely in order to be. Just as any abstract or scientific understanding of space must be grounded in a primary phenomenological spatiality, so must all understanding of time be grounded in phenomenological temporality.[13] The process by which things, and hence the system of ordered contexts that make up space, are constituted from kinaesthetic sensations, sequences, and systems (indeed the ability to form sequences and systems from kinaesthetic sensations) is temporal at its most fundamental level. The "synthesis of identification" or identity consciousness which binds sense data together relies on the retentive and protentive intentionality of consciousness in its ability to form unity out of multiplicity, a unity which remains constant and self-identical across the flux of sensation. In this sense the formation of the thing within perception is always as much a temporal process as it is spatial; or as Husserl puts it, "Temporal extension is a sibling of the spatial. We wish to cast a glance at the latter as well. Like temporality, spatiality pertains to the essence of the appearing thing" ( *TS*, 55; *HUA*, 16:65–66). The appearance of things and of space is therefore, according to Husserl's account, a spatializing-temporalizing process or event of "pure consciousness" whereby an identity and fixity of sense is conferred upon a manifold of appearance.

It has been suggested that Husserl, through his use of the phenomenological reduction and his isolation of a sphere of pure, intentional consciousness, aims to trace a philosophical path between the alternatives of empiricism and idealism which would not be reducible to either. It is not that we structure our experience of the world from patterns of experience or the inherent self-identity of observable things, or that consciousness creates the world, or that things exist absolutely as ideal forms. As has been indicated Husserl believes that being as we know it is only ever being-for-consciousness, and that consciousness discloses the world as meaningful or intelligible by ordering the flux of sensory data into perceptions which exist in and are bound together by an identity of sense. Despite his refusal to be assimilated to either empiricism or idealism, there is an indisputable idealizing turn in Husserl's thought after his discovery of the reduction. He is interested not in empirical realities but rather the isolation of those logical essences or what he comes to call "eidetic" structures which consciousness intends in order to constitute any experience of things and of space. It is only on the basis of these essences or structures, upon what one might term the *ideality of sense* within the phenomenological reduction, that the spatializing-temporalizing intentionality of consciousness can apprehend or bring into appearance a spatial world of things from within the flux of sensory data.

What emerges, then, from this brief summary of Husserl's phenomenological account of space is his consistent refusal to talk about "things-in-themselves." In Husserlian phenomenology being is only ever possible in its groundedness within or mediation through intentional consciousness. At the same time space can no longer be reduced to an entity or a series of relations between entities. Rather space is constituted in the event of consciousness by which things are made manifest or come into appearance. Space, as a three-dimensional field of extension which can be determined according to geometrical relations, only exists for us on the basis of the prior spatial-temporal unfolding immanent to perception. What is most important for phenomenological description in Husserl's writing is the ability of the philosopher to isolate, by way of the reduction, those logical essences or idealities of sense, which allow consciousness to intend objects and relations and thus to constitute an empirical world from the flux of the senses.

In the context of this discussion, which argues that Nancy's thinking rewrites or reinscribes the phenomenological account of space in an important way, what is important is the way in which Heidegger comes to criticize Husserl's conception of the reduction and, more specifically, the way in which he offers a critique of the idealizing tendency within Hus-

serl's thought. The "ideality of sense" upon which the Husserlian constitution of thing and space relies becomes subject to an essential finitude in
Heidegger's thought in a manner which will be decisive for Nancy's understanding of spatiality as it develops from some of the earliest moments
of his career.

## Heidegger and Existential Spatiality

As was shown in the preceding chapter, Heidegger's critique of subjectivism in the Nietzsche lectures of the late 1930s took Descartes, and the
Cartesian understanding of the subject, as a foundational moment within
his account of philosophical modernity. In *Being and Time* and later texts
such as *Contributions to Philosophy* and "On Time and Being," Heidegger's
account of space also takes the Cartesian position to be paradigmatic of
the dominant understanding of being within the recent history of European "onto-theology."[14] As some commentators have argued, when Heidegger refers to Descartes he may well be seeking to identify a foundational figure within the tradition of modern subjectivism, but he is also
using Descartes as a means of criticizing his erstwhile mentor Husserl.[15]
The extent to which Husserl's adoption of the phenomenological reduction and his grounding of phenomenology within the immanence of mental states echoes Descartes's use of methodological doubt and his isolation
of the Cogito has already been noted. Heidegger's attempt to overturn the
Cartesian understanding of space is intimately linked to his rejection of
the implicit Cartesianism of Husserl's solipsistic method. Where Husserl
thinks the constitution of space from within a sphere of immanence and
on the basis of eidetic structures or essences, Heidegger aims to think phenomenological spatiality through the *transcendence* of understanding toward the world (or what he terms Dasein, the being-there of being-in-the
world which is our own distinctive mode of existence or being). The decisive manner in which Heidegger breaks from Husserl is crucial for Nancy's
understanding of space and for the way in which he then comes to rethink
Heidegger.

Husserl began his account in *Thing and Space* by emphasizing that
the physical or scientific understanding of space was a secondary phenomenon or more precisely an abstract theoretical construct which presup-

posed a prior encounter with the world, itself founded in the immediacy of perception. The aim of his phenomenology was to return to a pretheoretical sphere, to isolate perception in the immediacy of immanent mental states and describe their intentional structure. For Heidegger, though, Husserl's approach remains highly abstract and secondary in relation to the more primary engagement of what, in *Being and Time*, he calls "being-in-the-world." To interpret something as if it were in the first instance a perceptual object, and more specifically an abstract identity or logical essence, is, according to Heidegger, to interpret it theoretically in just the way that Husserl was seeking to avoid. Crudely put, Husserl views the disclosure of an intelligible world as founded in perception, while Heidegger would claim that something like perception can only occur on the basis of interested and purposeful engagements which themselves disclose a world.

Rejecting the Cartesian account of space as extension and of objects as *res extensa*, Heidegger argues in *Being and Time* that we can think space and extended objects theoretically in this way because we first encounter them pretheoretically within a certain context of involvement, or what he calls "world-hood": "The 'environment' does not arrange itself in a space which has been given in advance; but its specific world-hood, in its significance, articulates the context of involvement which belongs to some current totality of circumspectively allotted places. The world at such a time reveals the spatiality of the space which belongs to it" (*BT*, 138; *GA*, 2:104). Heidegger repeats Husserl's insistence, foundational for the phenomenological approach, that space be understood as constituted on the basis of a prior "spatiality." Things or objects are first encountered in a certain purposeful manner, and within a complex of assignments, references, and meaning, or what Heidegger refers to as "significance" (*Bedeutung*). "Circumspection" (*Umsicht*) indicates the way in which we always encounter things with a view to something, a relation, a "for-the-sake-of-which," an "in-order-to" or a "with-which." The use of the words *current totality* underlines the way in which "significance" and "circumspection" combine to make of world-hood a system or whole: "The context of assignments or references, which as significance, is constitutive for world-hood, can be taken formally in the sense of a system of relations" (*BT*, 121; *GA*, 2:88). It will become clear that Heidegger's understanding of world-hood, and of world-hood as significance, is decisive for the account Nancy gives of space

and for his use of the French term *sens* (sense or meaning).

In this context Heidegger builds his account of spatiality, just as Husserl did before him, by describing the way we first encounter things, but he diverges from Husserl in his insistence that we (as Dasein, or being-there) first encounter things in a purposeful manner as "ready-to-hand" in the world. "Ready-to-hand" implies that as we encounter a thing "for-the-sake-of-which" we wish to do something, or in order to do something we maintain with that thing a certain relation of closeness or proximity: "Every entity that is 'to hand' has a different closeness, which is not to be ascertained by measuring distances. This closeness regulates itself in terms of circumspectively 'calculative' manipulating and using" (*BT*, 135; *GA*, 2:102). According to Heidegger, as we circumspectively encounter things "for-the-sake-of-which" or "in-order-to" within the context of a frame-work of significance or a system of relations, we do so through bringing them into a closeness which reveals things, and with that the world, to us as things or world. This "bringing-close" through which we encounter things in the world Heidegger calls *de-severence* (*Entfernung*):

"De-severing" amounts to making the farness vanish—that is, making the remoteness of something disappear, bringing it close. Dasein is essentially de-severent: it lets any entity be encountered close by as the entity which it is. . . . Only to the extent that entities are revealed for Dasein in their deseveredness, do they "remoteness" and distances become accessible in entities within the world themselves. (*BT*, 139; *GA*, 2:105)

Heidegger takes pains to emphasize the fundamental existential structure of what he calls de-severence. It is not that things exist within a framework of near and far and are then brought close into the immediate field within which we encounter them. Rather it is only on the basis of this prior, and fundamental, bringing-close which is de-severence that such things as near and far can be conceived as characteristics of things (i.e., as a relative po-sitioning with the de-severence which brings all things close in order that they be intelligible as such). In this sense the primary-spatiality of our ex-perience in the world is based, for Heidegger, on the essentially de-severent manner in which things are encountered and upon which such relations as near and far, here and there, leftward and rightward can be established: "*Dasein is essentially de-severence—that is, it is spatial.* It cannot wander about within the current range of its de-severences; it can never do more

than change them. Dasein is spatial in that it discovers space circumspectively, so that it indeed constantly comports itself de-severently towards
the entities thus spatially encountered" (*BT*, 143; *GA*, 2:108). So rather
than founding the experience of the world and of spatiality within the immanence of perceptual states, Heidegger sees space as constituted in the
transcendence of understanding toward the world in the bringing close of
entities through de-severence. Transcendence here refers to a reaching out
for or a passing over into a world through which an experience of being occurs as Dasein. Husserl's sphere of immanence as the constitutive field for
any experience of space (or of any experience per se) has been replaced by
what one might call the exteriority of being-in-the-world as the disclosive
bringing-near of entities and spatializing of space.

Throughout *Being and Time* Heidegger maintains this emphasis on
closeness or proximity in his account of the constitution of space and of
being-in-the-world. "*In Dasein*," he writes, "*there lies an essential tendency
toward closeness*" (*BT*, 140; *GA*, 2:105). This tendency toward closeness is a
key aspect of his attempt to think being anew and beyond its traditional
conceptions. Although Heidegger has abandoned the more abstract sphere
of Husserlian essence in favor of the worldly contingency of significance
and circumspectful engagement, he still remains attached to the notion of
the "essential," in the sense of that which most fundamentally belongs to
or is "proper to" being-in-the-world such as he elaborates it throughout his
lengthy treatise. Indeed *Being and Time* as a whole could be said to be concerned with the adumbration of those essential structures of being-in-the-
world, or existentials, that is, the constitutive features of human existence,
which function, as it were, as conditions of possibility of any experience
at all.[16] These features would be, amongst others, deseverence, spatiality,
anxiety, care, death and above all temporality.[17] For Heidegger the world
is disclosed to us as intelligible because it is encountered de-severently as
essentially spatial, but also because our circumspective relation to things
disclosed in this spatiality is inflected by our emotional concerns, moods,
and other fundamental interests. Heidegger aims to show that the ultimate horizon for this is temporality, and in this sense he repeats Husserl's
insistence that the constitution of spatiality within phenomenological description cannot be isolated from the fundamentally temporal nature of
experience.

Heidegger takes over Husserl's conception of temporality as a structure of retentions and protentions which constitute a moment of presence, although once again this structure has been transposed from the "internal" sphere of reduced experience to the sphere of interested engagements "in-the-world." In this respect he describes the structure of temporality as "ecstatic" or "ecstatico-horizonal," meaning, according to the etymological roots at least, "standing outside of." This term describes the way in which the circumspectful engagements through which we experience a meaningful world arise from temporal projections both forward and backward. The significant and circumspectful engagement which allows us to encounter an entity "for-the-sake-of-which" can only occur because we are rooted into the past and thrust into a future. This means that world-hood, de-severence, and spatiality are all temporal in nature, they are not entities but rather an event of disclosure which allows entities to be encountered as such. It also means that experience is without any interiority (such as one might ascribe to a traditional notion of the subject), it is only ever an exteriority, a standing outside of itself or "ek-stasis." Only on this basis is an experience of "spatiality" and a spatial world possible for Heidegger: "*Only on the basis of its ecstatico-temporality is it possible for Dasein to break into space.* The world is not present-at-hand in space; yet only within a world does space let itself be discovered" (*BT,* 421; *GA,* 2:369; Heidegger's emphasis). The spatiality of our experience is, therefore, more fundamentally rooted in the distinctive temporality of our experience, the taking up of a past and projection into a future in order to constitute a present, or as Heidegger puts it: "Dasein's specific spatiality must be grounded in temporality" (*BT,* 418; *GA,* 2:367). Temporality emerges as the most fundamental of all the existentials in *Being and Time;* deseverence, anxiety, care, and death all have a temporal structure which is constitutive of our being-in-the-world at its most fundamental level.

The overall trajectory of *Being and Time,* then, with its attempt to pose the question of being not on the basis of beings (which for Heidegger would be metaphysics), but rather in a more fundamental manner as a temporal event in which a spatial world is disclosed, is heavily indebted to Husserl's thinking but at the same time makes a decisive break from it. Heidegger's insistence that the constitutive features of experience cannot be reduced to mental states, but must be seen in terms of pragmatic worldly engagements, transforms the phenomenological project from a search for atemporal, logical, and meaning-constituting essences to an attempt to describe an event of being which would, in essence, be historical and subject to a certain fundamental historicity. At the same time the irreducibility of the phenomenological thinking of space to any form of idealism or empiricism becomes more decisively marked in Heidegger's thinking. It has been noted that, despite Husserl's protestations, the Cartesianism of his approach after the discovery of the reduction was considered by some to be a form of idealism and that there might be a good case for considering Husserlian phenomenology to be an epistemic idealism. Interestingly, however, Heidegger's rejection of his former mentor's Cartesianism does not, of course, transform his thinking into anything like empiricism or pragmatism in the traditional sense. By transposing the primary disclosure of the world from the sphere of perceptual immanence to the transcendence of understanding toward a world (in ecstatico-temporality), being, and the being-in-the-world of Dasein, are thought here as neither subject nor object. Dasein is neither a subjective inside which encounters an objective outside, nor an outside which determines an inside. All residual traces of this dichotomy, which arguably persist in Husserl's thinking, Heidegger would argue, have been overcome. This point is given particular emphasis his account of the spatiality of Dasein:

*Space is not in the subject, nor is the world in space.* Space is rather "in" the world in so far as space has been disclosed by that being-in-the-world which is constitutive for Dasein. Space is not to be found in the subject, nor does the subject observe the world "as if" that world were in a space; but the "subject" (Dasein), if well understood ontologically, is spatial. (*BT*, 146; *GA*, 2:111; Heidegger's emphasis)

This is a perfect evocation of the manner in which phenomenological understanding aims to situate itself in between the poles of the empirical and the ideal. For understanding to be able to empirically observe an object within space, or for an object to be thought of as a concept or ideal entity, it must first be disclosed through a prior and more basic encounter that is the essential spatiality of Dasein and the temporal-spatial disclosure of being-in-the-world.[18] According to Heidegger, then, this primary disclosure or spatializing of space is pre-predicative, preconceptual, and pretheoretical. As was the case with Husserl's account, the classical debate around space and the disputes around substantivalism and relationalism do not seem to have any place within the Heideggerian problematic of being. This point is foregrounded in *Being and Time*: "The Interpretation of the Being of space has hitherto been a matter of perplexity, not because we have been insufficiently acquainted with the content of space itself as a thing . . . , but because the possibilities of Being in general have not been in principle transparent, and an Interpretation of them in terms of ontological concepts has been lacking" (*BT* 147–48; *GA*, 2:113). Within the overall conceptual structure of *Being and Time* the ontological question "does space exist," such as it has been posed within the classical debate, lacks a sufficient clarification of the "being" of existence. When the meaning of the being of existence is posed more fundamentally (in, of course, the Heideggerian manner) space *is* neither an entity nor a relationality, its being is neither empirical nor ideal; primary spatiality unfolds, or is given, as that temporalizing-spatializing event, which discloses a world in which beings can be intelligible as such for Dasein.

In *Being and Time* Heidegger offers an account of primary or existential spatiality which, although subject to certain key changes of emphasis as his thinking develops, will remain roughly the same for the rest of his career. Within the context of this discussion a number of points should be highlighted that will be of key significance for the manner in which Nancy comes to think space. First, in his rewriting or rethinking of Husserlian phenomenology, Heidegger has subjected being, and with that the signifying spatiality of being-in-the-world, to an essential finitude. The idealities or logical essences of Husserl's thought have become worldly, temporally contingent, signifying structures determined by an essential historicity of being. Second, Heidegger seeks to think the unfolding or disclosure of existential spatiality in terms of a prior instance, site, or place. In *Being and Time* this site or place is the spatiality of Dasein as being-in-the-world within the horizon of an ecstatic temporality. At this stage in his career Dasein still has a personalized quality for Heidegger. It is always an individualized or singularized Dasein with its sphere of "ownness" (*Jemeinigkiet*) whose "ownmost" possibility is death (thus Dasein here is "being-toward-death"). As his career progresses the nature of the site of the unfolding or giving of being will change for Heidegger. The famous *Kehre* or turn within his work marks a shift from the personalized or singularized Dasein to a more impersonal conception of being.[19] The language of being that the later Heidegger adopts is notoriously opaque and difficult to grasp. It moves increasingly toward a kind of poetic saying, a saying that would have as its task the announcing of being (which is covered up in ordinary language). Being, however, becomes an event of appropriation or "enowning" (what Heidegger will call *Ereignis*) that discloses a world and spatializes space but is not an event of a personalized singular entity. It occurs as an originary giving of being from other places or sites by which each singular existence or experience is then itself appropriated.

In the early 1930s this site becomes the historical-destinal sending of the being of a *Volk*. Soon after that it is art, poetry, in particular the poetry of Friedrich Hölderlin, which will become the site from which the being of beings and the spatiality of space is given and must be thought. There will be other formulations in the decades which follow. In each case, though, Heidegger thinks the unfolding of space or the historical-destinal sending of being in terms of a privileged site or place. As a number of commentators have remarked, the instances that Heidegger identifies as the site of an originary giving of being always articulate a closeness, nearness, or domesticity.[20] While it is true that the unfamiliar, uncanny, or alienating aspect of being-in-the-world is always considered to be a fundamental existential, the emphasis placed on closeness and the familiarity of the everyday dominate Heidegger's phenomenological descriptions of experience. This is reflected in a number of motifs which recur in his thinking, centering on notions of the proper, the originary, and the primordial in terms of certain belonging which is rural, domestic, and indeed German in nature: the Rhine, Hölderlin, Swabian peasants, the family table, the hearth.

The fundamental importance given in *Being and Time* to nearness in the constitution of space is carried over into the later philosophy of being in the language of belonging, of propriety and appropriation, which informs Heidegger's use of the term *Ereignis*.[21] With this term he is seeking to think the temporalizing-spatializing event of being in terms of a gathering, conjoining, or event of binding together or appropriation. The most extended elaboration of this thinking emerges in the series of private reflections *Beiträge zur Philosophie* (*Contributions to Philosophy*) written between 1936 and 1938 and published posthumously in 1989. This is a difficult work, the scope and complexity of which will be impossible to summarize here. However, the question of time and space is central to the meditations of the *Contributions* and it is worth remarking on a number of points in it. In this text Heidegger carries forward the central tenet of *Being and Time*, namely that both being and time need to be thought together such that neither can ever be thought without the other. It is the belonging of the one with the other that motivates Heidegger's adoption of the term *Ereignis* to describe the event of being. He emphasizes this point himself in another late essay, "On Time and Being" (which in many ways can be thought of as a summary of *Contributions*): "What determines both time and being in their belonging together, we shall call *Ereignis*, the event of Appropriation. . . . One should bear in mind, however, that 'event' is not simply an occurrence, but that which makes any occurrence possible."[22] In *Being and Time* Heidegger sought to derive spatiality from temporality in such a manner that the latter operated as a quasi-Kantian condition of possibility for the former. In the *Contributions* the Kantian "residue" of the earlier work has been abandoned and Heidegger thinks in terms of "time-space," indicating that although temporality is still in a sense primary it is no longer a horizon from which spatiality is derived; rather, time and space, or more properly speaking temporalizing and spatializing, are simultaneous within the event of appropriation, enowning or *Ereignis*:

> Time as what removes-unto and opens up is thus simultaneously what *spatializes*, it provides "space." What is ownmost to space is not what is ownmost to time—as time belongs to space.
>
> But *space* here must also be grasped originarily as spacing (as can be *shown* in the spatiality of Dasein, even if not fully and originarily grasped . . . ). (*CP*, 134, *GA*, 65:192)

In the later thought, then, the ecstatic horizon of temporality which allows Dasein to "break into" space becomes the more originary "time-space," the temporalizing-spatializing opening or disclosure of a world as the event of being (*Ereignis*). The "bringing-near" of de-severance in *Being and Time* has become a movement of gathering through which being is given: "Timing spacing—spacing timing . . . as the nearest region of joining for the truth of being" (*CP*, 184, *GA*, 65:261), or as Heidegger puts it elsewhere: "*Time-space* is to be unfolded in its essential sway as *site for the moment of* enowning" (*CP*, 227, *GA*, 65:323). Crucially, in *Contributions to Philosophy* this event of appropriation or enowning is not something thinking can appropriate or conceptualize; rather, and this is key for Heidegger, insofar as this event is originary *it* appropriates thought and thus makes all thought, events, all action, and so on possible in the first instance (as is indicated in the comment for "On Time and Being," cited above).

It is for this reason that the language of Heidegger's later thought is so strange and often impenetrable. It does not seek to bring being into the light of clear and distinct conceptuality, rather it attempts to "say" being, not to grasp or appropriate it, but to be appropriated by the essential movement which is proper to it. In this sense Heidegger is seeking a language which would be "proper-to" the event of being, not one which would seek to represent that event as such. This is why his philosophical language becomes increasingly poeticized as he comes to see poetry itself as a key site for the disclosure of being. At the center of this thinking, though, is the thought of time-space as the "site" for an originary opening which gathers, binds, appropriates. This language of oneness is perhaps the dominant key of Heidegger's later poetic "saying" of being. As he puts it in *Contributions*: "Oneness makes up beingness. And oneness here means: unifying, originary gathering unto sameness of what presences together-along-with and of what is constant" (*CP*, 138, *GA*, 65:197). In later Heidegger, time-space is always a site of oneness or belonging-together in the event of appropriation. As indicated above this site recurs in Heidegger's thought as a series of places, all of which indicate a moment of historical, finite belonging: the Rhein, Hölderlin, and so forth. What Nancy's thinking of the "sense of space" offers is a radical critique of this tendency within Heidegger to think the temporalizing-spatializing of space, and the "ownness" of the event of appropriation, in such domestic and parochial terms. More broadly Nancy's rethinking of existential spatiality articulates a radical critique of "propriety" within Heideggerian thought. In so doing it makes an original contribution to the wider phenomenological tradition of thinking about space.

## The Sense of Space: Nancy's Thinking of Spatiality

Like Heidegger, Nancy insists that we take seriously the relationship between sense and our experience of space. Yet the manner in which he aims to think the temporal-spatial disclosure of an intelligible world and the site from which such an experience of world-hood unfolds is in certain key respects quite different. For Heidegger the notion of world-hood as a context of assignments and references, as a signifying totality or system of relations, was crucial to Dasein in its spatiality. For Nancy also the experience of a spatial world is possible because of the existence of sense or meaning (what he calls in French *sens*), or, more precisely, because existence *is* sense or meaning. The summary accounts of Husserl and Heidegger given above show the extent to which the category of sense is central also to the phenomenological account of space. Building on this account, sense, for Nancy, takes on a key ontological importance, as he puts it in the essay "Une Pensée finie": "Of course, by 'sense' I mean sense, taken absolutely: the sense of life, the sense of man, of the world, of history, the sense of existence; the sense of existence which is or makes sense, which without sense would not exist. And the sense which exists, or which produces existing, without which there would be no sense" (*PF*, 10–11; *FT*, 3). Nancy's use of the term *sense*, then, is not only decisive for his thinking of space but is decisive also for his rethinking of ontology in the wake of Heidegger and the phenomenological account of space. Despite his obvious indebtedness to the Heideggerian understanding of being, Nancy's thinking of the sense of space leads him to formulate a materialist, or more properly speaking, a *bodily* ontology, whose specific emphasis on singularity and plurality leads the overall trajectory of his thought in a very different direction from that of Heidegger. This rethinking of ontology is dispersed throughout the corpus of Nancy's writing and, as the last chapter indicated, is already implied in his published work of the 1970s. It finds its most developed expression, however, in a number major works published in the 1990s, first and foremost *Une Pensée finie* (1990), *Corpus* (1992), *Le Sens du monde* (1993) and *Être singulier pluriel* (1996). Although Nancy never thinks in systematic or systematizing terms, these works taken together offer the fullest and most coherent account to date of Nancy's mature thought and most clearly mark his proximity to and radical divergence from existential phenomenology.

According to the phenomenological account of space, spatiality, world-hood, and being per se cannot be understood in terms of any substance, or in terms of beings or entities. Rather the experience of space and world is seen to unfold as a spatial-temporal event of being, of being understood as a clearing of space or an opening of a world in which beings could be intelligible as such. To this extent Husserlian phenomenology gives consciousness and perception, insofar as it is grounded in the bodily sense organs, a key role in the constitution of spatial experience, and, in Heidegger's case, while references to the body are almost entirely absent in *Being and Time*, a strong emphasis is placed on the situated facticity of Dasein.[23] Nancy follows this account in arguing that space and things, as extended entities which can be placed or situated in space, exist through a spacing (*espacement*) which is also temporal in nature and which must therefore be thought of as prior to time and space proper: "*There* is a measure of space, of spacing, that gives time its origin, *before* time. Movements, histories, processes, all times of succession, of loss, of discovery, of return, of recovery, of anticipation—all this time essentially depends on the space opened up at the heart of things, of this spacing that *is* the heart of things" (*PF*, 203; *BP*, 172). In this respect Nancy's understanding of space remains intimately bound up with Heidegger's thinking of *Ereignis* or the event of appropriation. In order to determine the extent to which Nancy's thinking of space, and with this his rethinking of ontology, is indebted to Heidegger, what follows will highlight the way he combines diverse elements from Heidegger's earlier and later thinking, that is, elements from *Being and Time* and from *Contributions to Philosophy*, the two Heideggerian texts which are most frequently referred to in Nancy's writing. Fundamental to this is Nancy's reinscription of being-in the-world as a sharing, or division (*partage*), of sense.

### Sense and Existential Phenomenology

In *Being and Time* world-hood was thought in terms of a totality of signifying relations or a context of involvement in which things and spatial relations were encountered circumspectively with a view to something, a "for-the-sake-of-which," an "in-order-to" or a "with-which." Heidegger called this context of assignments and references constitutive of world-hood "significance," "meaningfulness," or in German, *Bedeutsamkeit*. In addition to *Bedeutsamkeit* Heidegger also uses the words *Bedeutung* (significance) and *Sinn* (meaning/sense). The use and interrelation of these terms in the text of *Being and Time* is rather complex, and it varies according to the specific context. Broadly speaking though, both *Bedeutsamkeit* and *Bedeutung* can be translated as "significance," but the latter tends to be used to refer to individual meanings or moments of signification (and hence can be used in the plural) while the former tends to refer to the whole of meaningfulness or intelligibility as such (and hence only occurs in the singular). *Sinn* (meaning/sense), like *Bedeutsamkeit*, has a more diffuse sense, referring, in *Being and Time* at least, to a general understanding which is prior to words, a projection allowing particular entities to be intelligible as such. Heidegger is interested in the way in which the being-there of Dasein encounters the world as always already meaningful in some way, that is to say, in the way in which we can assign a signification to something or ascribe attributes or predicates to it because we have a prior or pre-predicative understanding of it as meaningful within an overarching context of sense, or as Heidegger puts it: "*Meaning* [Sinn] *is the "upon-which" of a projection in terms of which something becomes intelligible as something; it gets its structure from a fore-having, a fore-sight, and a fore-conception,*" or, "Meaning is that wherein the intelligibility of something maintains itself" (*BT*, 193, *GA*, 2:151; Heidegger's emphasis). In this sense both *Bedeutsamkeit* and *Sinn* function as *existentials* of Dasein, that is, they play a fundamental and constitutive role in the disclosure of an intelligible world to which linguistic signification or predicative attributes can be given.[24] To this extent, both are also, and crucially, prior to language as such and act as its condition of possibility. Although the issue is not entirely clarified in *Being and Time*, Heidegger appears to give a logical priority to *Bedeutsamkeit* in relation to *Sinn*:

Entities-within-the-world generally are projected upon the world——, that is, upon a whole of significance [*Bedeutsamkeit*], to whose reference-relations concern, as Being-in-the-world, has been tied up in advance. When entities within-the-world are discovered along with the Being of Dasein—that is, when they have come to be understood—we say they have *meaning* [*Sinn*]. (*BT*, 192, *GA*, 2:151)

There appears, then, to be a hierarchy of logical priority in *Being and Time*, where meaningfulness as a totality of assignments and references (*Bedeutsamkeit*) allows for the disclosure of a world which is meaningful or has sense (*Sinn*), and where this then allows meanings to be ascribed to things in a more secondary manner (*Bedeutungen*) and this, in turn, lays the ground for linguistic signification as such (where words embody the *Bedeutungen* disclosed by the initial meaningful engagement of being-in-the-world). Heidegger makes explicit the priority of a level of sense or meaning over language proper, arguing that "in significance [*Bedeutsamkeit*] itself, with which Dasein is always familiar, there lurks the ontological condition which makes it possible for Dasein, as something which understands and interprets, to disclose such things as 'significations' [*Bedeutungen*]; upon these, in turn, is founded the being of words and of language" (*BT*, 121, *GA*, 2:87). Although the later Heidegger will endow language itself with a fundamental, ontological role in the disclosure of being, in the main text of *Being and Time* he insists on thinking significance and meaning as prior to words, such that language and discourse (*Rede*) maintain a derivative and secondary status. To this extent meaningfulness and sense are situated here firmly within the realm of worldly contingency and denied any abstract status either through their inscription within the symbolic dimension of language (itself an abstraction of sense [*Sinn*]) or within any idealized essence. Against Husserl's use of both *Bedeutung* and *Sinn* to denote logical essences which are both universal and timeless, the Heidegger of *Being and Time* aims to think meaningfulness and sense as existentials (of our being-in-the-world, of being-there), and to think them as prelinguistic, as contingent, historical, and finite.[25]

As has been indicated, Nancy follows Heidegger in *Une Pensée finie* insofar as he confers an ontological status on the term *sens*, and thinks the being of a spatial world as an event of disclosure, which is logically prior to time and space as such, and which occurs as an opening or spacing of space. Nancy, like Heidegger, thinks *sens* as constitutive of the existence of the world, conferring upon this term a fundamental ontological status which, once again, situates it prior to the existence of language. Thus it is not that our human world has a meaning or *makes* sense, since for Nancy it only ever exists *as* sense; this is the defining characteristic of what he calls "being-toward-the world" (*être-au-monde*):

Thus, "being-*toward*-the-world," if it takes place (and it does take place), is caught up in sense well before all signification. It makes, demands, or proposes sense this side of or beyond all signification. If we are *toward* the world, if there is being-toward-the-world in general, that is, if there is a world, there is sense. . . . Thus, *world* is not merely the correlative of *sense*, it is structured as *sense*, and reciprocally, *sense* is structured as *world*. (*SM*, 17–18; *SW*, 7–8)

To this extent Nancy's use of the French term *sens* appears to conflate Heidegger's usage of the German terms *Bedeutsamkeit* and *Sinn*, where *sens* is the element or "stuff" of being, both a totality of meaningful relations constitutive of world-hood and the precondition for linguistic meanings and signification in general. This conflation of *Bedeutsamkeit* and *Sinn* may well be justified on the basis that the distinction between the two is itself somewhat vague in *Being and Time* and that both function as existentials. Most importantly, however, sense is prior to or in excess of any relation between signifier and signified, and thus it is in excess also of any fixed linguistic signification. The fact that Nancy bases his understanding of sense and of being-in-the-world upon the categories and distinctions of *Being and Time*, thus avoiding Heidegger's later emphasis on language as the "home of being," means that his thinking situates itself clearly within the realm of factical and pragmatic worldly engagements and aims to think the world in terms of a "concrete" multiplicity of sense. As will become clear, Nancy sets his reading and reworking of the thinking of being against certain tendencies which become more marked in Heideggerian thought from the 1930s onward. These tendencies, already alluded to in the previous section, manifest themselves in Heidegger's penchant for pastoral or national motifs, but also in his later thinking of space and world-hood in terms of a gathering of multiplicity into oneness (e.g. the "fourfold" of earth, sky, gods, and mortals in *Building Dwelling Thinking* or other post–Second World War texts).

If this account of sense is set within the context of the wider field of phenomenological thought as inaugurated by Husserl, it could be argued that what interests Nancy most about Heidegger's account of meaning and of being-in-the-world is the essential emphasis that is placed, within *Being and Time*, on the finitude of Dasein. In thinking sense as constitutive for world-hood, Nancy is interested in affirming what he calls in *Une Pensée finie* "an essential finitude of sense, insofar as this would demand in its turn an essential finitude of thought" (*PF*, 13; *FT*, 4). In this respect his thinking of sense is decisive for the manner in which he conceives of thinking per se, and for the way in which he comes to address certain philosophical problems or issues (most importantly, in the overall context of this study, the issue of the body, of community and the political, and of art, all of which will provide the focus for discussion in the following chapters). The finitude of Dasein in *Being and Time* was, for Heidegger, first and foremost articulated in Dasein's being-toward-death, that is, an existential-temporal structure which placed death as the ownmost possibility of Dasein as an ungraspable horizon of futurity toward which "being-there" projects itself in its "ecstatic" standing outside of itself (its "ek-sistence," in Heidegger's terms). Nancy is less interested in the existential pathos surrounding the theme of death in *Being and Time* and less interested in the language of own-ness which attaches to it, that is to say, the language of the *eigentlich* and of *Eigentlichkeit*, terms which have often been translated, rather mis-leadingly, as the "authentic" and "authenticity." The essential finitude of sense in Nancy needs to be situated in the context of his rejection of any logic of transcendence or immanence within being and his refusal to think in terms of any "ideality" of sense in the way that Husserl does. In the previous discussions of Husserl's account of spatiality it was emphasized that his use of the phenomenological or "eidetic" reductions aimed to isolate a sphere of meaning constituting essences which were abstract and time-less in nature. The phenomenological reduction isolated a sphere of im-manence within consciousness that, in its intentional structure, worked as a transcendence toward a world of objects and things. In different ways, therefore, sense, according to Husserl's account, always has an ideal status, which in turn is governed by a logic of transcendence and immanence, and this arguably places transcendental phenomenology within a trajectory of philosophical idealism, despite its attempt to refuse or move beyond such a categorization. Heidegger, in contrast, by situating both *Bedeutsamkeit* and *Sinn* as existentials of our being-in-the-world, placed meaning within a more contingent and temporally finite sphere. Nancy's thinking of sense both continues and, indeed, radicalizes this tendency within Heidegger. Phenomenology, he argues, insofar as it thinks the disclosure of phenom-ena on the basis of sense or meaning, needs to think the arrival or the event of sense not as something that can be reduced (Husserl) or that can be grasped as an existential within the discourse of fundamental ontology (Heidegger), but rather as that which is always presupposed in the disclo-sure of a world but which is, by the same token, ungraspable, irreducible to any mode of discourse or signification: "all types of phenomenology, in-deed all types of beyond phenomenology, do not open sufficiently to the coming of sense, to sense as a coming that is *neither immanent nor tran-scendent*. This *coming* is infinitely presupposed: one does not let oneself be taken in, carried away, or put out of sorts by it" (*SM*, 34; *SW*, 17). Here the Heidegger of *Being and Time* is judged to be too wedded to the phenomenological method insofar as he conceives his existentials as isolatable (albeit worldly) conditions of possibility of the appearance of phenomena, and insofar as he remains too confident that anything like a fundamental ontology can master the excessive multiplicity of sense which is the very stuff of our being in the world.[26] Sense, for Nancy, is that which the world always already *is*, but it is always also an ungraspable excess, it is that which "exceeds the phenomenon in the phenomenon itself" (*SM*, 35; *SW*, 17). The thinking of sense here, of the sense of the world and of space, exceeds the phenomenological account from which it derives. As Nancy puts it: "*world* invites us to no longer think on the level of the phenomenon, however it may be understood (as surging forth, appearing, becoming visible, brilliance, occurrence, event), but on the level, let us say for the moment, of disposition (spacing, touching, contact, crossing)" (*SM*, 34, note 19; *SW*, 176). This is the point in Nancy's thinking at which a decisive break from phenomenology can be identified. It occurs, perhaps, at a moment of greatest proximity or closeness to the phenomenological account,[27] and it marks the point at which thinking, beyond phenomenology, moves away from all philosophical language based upon visual metaphors, upon any notion of phenomenological seeing, upon motifs of appearance, "lighting," clearing, and so forth. It also necessarily marks the point, already partially present in Heidegger, at which the thinking of sense and of being-in-the-world can no longer take consciousness as its focal point. At the same time this thinking, as it diverges from the phenomenological account, cannot use a language of transcendence and immanence in relation to consciousness (allowing Nancy to speak of a "trans-immanence" of sense).

The site of the passage of sense in Nancy's thought is other than or in excess of consciousness. Insofar as sense, here, is neither ideal nor empirical, neither transcendent nor immanent, it is characterized by a certain kind of materiality or "concretion" (*concrétude*), which is not a materiality in the conventional meaning of the term, but which implies a relation to the bodily and determines a whole range of philosophical terms which Nancy uses to think sense and the sense of space, terms alluded to in the above citation: *position, disposition, spacing, touch, tact,* and *contact.* As he puts it in *Le Sens du monde*: "It is not a matter of signification, but of the sense of the world as its very *concreteness*, that on which our existence *touches* and by which it is *touched*, in all possible senses" (*SM*, 22; *SW*, 10). In order to understand more fully what is at stake in this "concrete" thinking of sense, and in the "spacing" of sense, the relation of Nancy's thought to, and its decisive divergence from, Heidegger's later thinking needs now to be considered more closely.

### Spacing and the Event of Appropriation

The sense *of* space in Nancy should be understood, not as the meaning of the word *space*, but rather in terms of space and spatiality belonging to, or being constituted in, sense. Space exists or unfolds as an opening of sense, or in Nancy's words as "an originary spatiality of sense that is a spatiality or spaciousness before any distinction between space and time" (*SM*, 29; *SW*, 14). Here Nancy's language is reminiscent of Heidegger's later thinking of being, and recalls, more specifically, the thinking of space-time in *Contributions to Philosophy*, where space-time is invoked always as an originary spatializing-temporalizing event of appropriation (*Ereignis*). In the *Contributions*, it should be recalled, space is not derived from a horizon of temporal retentions and protentions, as it is in *Being and Time*; rather, the spatial and temporal elements of space-time are thought of as co-originary. What Nancy refers to as the "archi-spatiality" of sense, a spatializing and temporalizing anterior to space or time as we might traditionally conceive them, repeats, to a certain extent, the Heideggerian thinking of *Ereignis* but also, as elsewhere, decisively moves beyond or radically transforms the nature of that thinking. Heidegger in the *Contributions* does not, for instance, use the terms *Bedeutsamkeit*, *Bedeutung*, or *Sinn*, as he did in the earlier *Being and Time*. In this respect Nancy's account of spatiality emerges as a mixing of the register or lexicon of the earlier and the later Heideggerian texts in order to perform a modification within the thinking of being, whose logic will emphasize far more the singular plurality of sense, rather than a pathos of originary gathering or giving.

At the heart of this modification is a questioning of the political dimension of Heidegger's thought and a rigorous refusal or rejection of his party political commitments during the 1930s, never properly renounced or subject to critique in the decades following the Second World War. A key point of reference in this context is the so-called "Heidegger Affair" of the late 1980s precipitated by the publication of Victor Farias's *Heidegger and Nazism* in 1987, which exposed the extent of Heidegger's commitment to, and involvement with, the National Socialist regime as well as details of his more unworthy dealings as rector of Freiburg University between 1933 and 1934.[28] The public debate that followed the publication of Farias's book and further details that emerged from the work of other biographers did some considerable damage to Heidegger's reputation both as a man and as a philosopher, and, for some, placed a question mark over all those forms of thought which took his thinking as a starting point or a source of inspiration (most notably deconstruction). The debate also led to the publication of important texts by Derrida and Lyotard that addressed Heidegger's text, in strictly philosophical terms, in the broader context of his political commitment and, in Derrida's case, with specific reference to the language used in the now infamous rectoral address of April–May 1933.[29] Significantly though, as Lyotard himself points out in *Heidegger et les "juifs,"* the "revelations" contained in Farias's book surrounding Heidegger's political commitments and activities were not new to philosophers in France at the time.[30] Lyotard's book is itself, in large part, both inspired by and forms a dialogue with Philippe Lacoue-Labarthe's work *La Fiction du politique*, which was published at the same time as Farias's *Heidegger and Nazism* but, as the culmination of research and writing dating back a number of years, was not written with it in mind.[31] In *La Fiction du politique* Lacoue-Labarthe (Nancy's friend and collaborator, it should be recalled) becomes the first French philosopher closely associated with Heidegger's thought to engage with its political dimension *as* thought and to seek to think, tentatively at least, the threads which might connect the man and his political commitments with the man and his thinking. The attempt by the Nazis to exterminate European Jewry in the Holocaust becomes for Lacoue-Labarthe a caesura or interruption within the history of Western culture and thought, one which Heidegger's postwar work singularly fails to take into account, or represses and forgets in some way.[32] At the root of this failure of thought, Lacoue-Labarthe detects an archaic attempt, on Heidegger's part, to associate or conflate a certain thinking of the aesthetic with the political. According to this account Heidegger's attempt to associate art and philosophy in his writings of the 1930s in order to speak the heroic singularity of a people, polis, or site of political self-affirmation is fatally implicated in the language and genocidal desire of National Socialism.[33]

Lacoue-Labarthe's treatment of Heidegger's thinking in its specifically political dimension can be linked to Nancy's work via their collaboration with each other in the Centre de recherches philosophiques sur le politique, founded in 1981. The work of the Center will be discussed more fully in Chapter 4 in the context of Nancy's thinking of community. At this point it is important only to note that the engagement of both Nancy and Lacoue-Labarthe's work with thinking of being throughout the first years of the 1980s is inseparable from a questioning of Heidegger's political affiliations. Thus Lacoue-Labarthe's untying in *La Fiction du politique* of what he calls Heidegger's "national aesthetism," or Nancy's rereading in *La Communauté désœuvrée* of Heideggerian *Mitsein* or "being-with," cannot be separated from an attempt to respond to the erstwhile Rector of Freiburg's National Socialist affiliation.[34]

All this by way of suggesting, in preliminary fashion at least, that Nancy's rethinking of the Heideggerian event of appropriation or *Ereignis* must be understood against the backdrop of this broader political dimension. As has been suggested this is most clearly indicated in Nancy's writing on community as exposed in *La Communauté désœuvrée*, where he reworks the way Heidegger thinks the being of others in *Being and Time* as *Mitsein*. As was indicated in the previous chapter, Nancy affirms Heidegger's dismantling of the logic of the subject together with the project of thinking being and being-in-the-world beyond or outside of any logic of subjectivity. Yet, when it comes to the question of community and specifically of political community, Nancy sees the reemergence of a thinking of the subject in Heidegger: "Although . . . the same Heidegger also went astray with his vision of a people and a destiny conceived at least in part as a subject, which proves no doubt that Dasein's 'being-toward-death' was never radically implicated with its being-with—*Mitsein*" (*CD*, 40–41; *IC*, 14). For Nancy, it is not the overall project of ontology that is compromised by Heidegger's politics or by the crimes associated with that politics. Rather, Nancy's view is that Heidegger's unthought lapses into a traditional metaphysics of the subject allow his thinking and his philosophical language to slip into a thought and language appropriable by National Socialism. This rejection of a latent and unthought legacy of subjectivity within Heidegger's thought lies at the heart of the work that emerges from Nancy's involvement with the Centre de recherches philosophiques sur le politique but arguably informs all aspects of his relation to and reworking of the thinking of being.

In a more recent text, the essay "Heidegger's Originary Ethics," printed in *La Pensée dérobée* (2001), Nancy identifies two opposing tendencies within Heidegger's philosophical thought and language, movements of opening and closing. Opening, here, is the opening of being itself, the spatializing-temporalizing event of disclosure, which opens a world, which spaces space and allows things to be intelligible as such. In this sense, the open, or opening, is always an opening onto, a clearing of space, which would imply a radical exteriority, an ex-centric or centrifugal movement outward, in the unfolding of being. Closing, however, characterizes those moments where Heidegger's thinking slips back into a philosophical language marked by this unthought legacy of subjectivity alluded to above. Nancy specifically identifies the pastoral motifs in Heidegger which cluster around the notion of sheltering being:

Being is properly the bestowal to Dasein of the "keeping" of its truth. It is in this sense that man is said to be "the shepherd of being". . . . Certainly, the terms *shepherd, keeping, watching over* are not exempt from an evangelical and backward-looking connotation. They evoke a preservation, a conservation of that which should only be opening and risk. A reactive tone shows itself here. . . . It is as if the inaugural dignity, exposed in the absence of any acquired protection, of any assurance of a given sense, must itself be protected, sheltered. Yet what is to be "kept," is the open—that which "keeping" itself risks closing. (*PD*, 99)

Nancy also detects this language of opening and closing in the theme of dwelling in Heidegger's later texts:

It would be necessary to analyze at length that which separates and that which binds together in the theme of "dwelling," "Black Forest" conservatism (and first and foremost "conservative revolution") often and justly imputed to Heidegger, and the theme of an "open" conduct of being in the world: the entire essay *Building Dwelling Thinking* can be read in both these directions. (*PD*, 105)

What is a stake here is what Lacoue-Labarthe in *La Fiction du politique* has called the idea of "organicity" in Heidegger's thought, and behind that the idea of "propriety" or ownness. It is within this language of propriety and ownness that Nancy sees the slippage of Heidegger's thinking back into a

traditional metaphysics of the subject. This language is reflected in the domestic and distinctly Germanic motifs, alluded to above, which recur in
Heidegger (the Rhine, Swabian peasants, the family hearth, and so on),
but also in the language of the proper or the "ownmost" which informs the
thinking of being as *Ereignis* or event of appropriation. According to Nancy this language of owness, which is used to talk about the opening of the
event of being, always risks closure and recuperation into a logic of oneness
and identity. Examples of this abound throughout Heidegger's writing of
the late 1930s and the postwar decades. Witness here an example not cited
by Nancy from *Contributions to Philosophy*: "Oneness" Heidegger writes,
"makes up beingness. And oneness here means: unifying, originary gathering unto sameness of what presences together-along-with and of what is
constant" (*CP*, 138; *GA*, 65:197).

This language of organicity, of gathering, sheltering, binding together, and the notion of propriety that lies behind it, represents for Nancy the
tendency toward closing in Heidegger's thinking, which reaffirms subjectivity and allows for the identification of the German people and the native
soil as privileged sites for the thinking of being and political self-affirmation. Nancy's response is to read and rethink Heidegger in the direction of
a radical opening and the exteriority of an existence which is always outside of itself. "Existence," he writes is "ek-sistence," a manner or conduct
of being as being "outside" of itself, that is to say as being to sense, that
is to say as a making sense or an acting" (*PD*, 93). In this respect Nancy
is taking up and seeking to radicalize a moment already central to *Being
and Time*, that is the ectatic-temporality of Dasein thought explicitly in
terms of exteriority or "being-outside-of-itself." Dasein's "ek-sistence," for
Nancy, is also the being of Dasein as an opening of or onto sense. Thus
he reinscribes the openness and worldly heterogeneity of the categories
of *Being and Time* within the later thinking and language of *Ereignis*. To
this extent he reads the proper or "owness" in late Heidegger as always
already having passed through, and constituting itself in, the "improper,"
and the event of appropriation as appropriating nothing but the inappropriable opening, the spacing-temporalizing disclosure of the being itself as
the exteriority of sense: "The relation of existence to itself as the opening
of sense and to sense is nothing other than the relation of the 'improper'
to the 'proper'. . . . *Ereignis*: but in this it is only 'appropriating' a 'propri-

ety' where nothing is encountered other than a trembling of being" (*PD*, 102, 103). This opening, as exteriority, or the appropriation of nothing other than the inappropriable opening itself, affirms the impossibility of any subject that would maintain itself within an intimacy or immanence with itself, people, nation, polis, and so forth. At this point the extent to which Nancy's untying of the subject in his 1970s readings of Kant and Descartes is repeated and developed in his later rethinking of Heideggerian opening or *Ereignis* is evident. The centripetal movement of gathering which inflects the thinking of the event of appropriation in the *Contributions* and other Heideggerian texts written during and after the 1930s is inverted or turned inside out in Nancy's thought, transformed into a centrifugal movement of dispersal which can never be gathered back into itself or into any mode of oneness or originary unifying. To this extent Nancy remains within a discourse of ontology (albeit, as will become clear, a kind of quasi ontology). He remains within the ambit of a thinking of being, while resolutely refusing the unthought legacy of the subject, which, he believes, pervades Heidegger's thought and determines its political dimension and possibilities of appropriation within a totalitarian ideology.

When Nancy writes about being, then, about the event of being as an opening of a world and a spacing of space, a register and vocabulary emerges which is different from that of Heidegger. Against the thinking of being as gathering, sheltering, or oneness, Nancy seeks to maintain, and to hold open, a movement of opening, in which the event of being as *sense* is always a movement to, onto, or a passage and spacing of sense, which is irrecoverable and ungraspable, but which nevertheless *is* the space of the world as meaningful, intelligible, and experienceable as such. Sense, as that which the world *is*, is only insofar as it never constitutes a ground, locus, or site that has any identity or propriety, but rather exists as passage, as movement-to or as a creation or a birth. Sense never returns to itself, it opens, spaces, makes intelligible while exceeding any logic of subjectivity or any possibility of fixed and stable signification. As Nancy puts in *Une Pensée finie*:

There is sense only once this being-to itself no longer belongs to itself, no longer returns to itself. Only once it *is* this not-coming-back-to-itself: this restless refusal to come back to itself in such a way that it does not simply "remain" outside, either in the sense of a lack or in the sense of a surplus, but *is* itself the *here* of being-to-itself, the open of its openness. (*PF*, 18; *FT*, 8)

According to Nancy, then, being, world, and the spatiality of being-in-the-world have to be conceived, at their most fundamental level, as an infinitely open-ended relational spacing of sense, where being always occurs in the mode of being-to, or being-toward: "*World* means at least *being-to* or *being-toward* [*être-à*]; it means rapport, relation, address, sending, donation, presentation *to*—if only of entities or existents *to* each other" (*SM*, 18; *SW*, 8). In this context his use of the French term *être-au-monde* should be translated more properly, as has been shown above, as "being-to-the-world" or "being-toward-the-world." At the same time *sense is* the movement of being as "being-to": "Sense, for its part, is the movement of being-*toward* [*l'être-à*], or being as *coming* into presence or again as transitivity, as passage to presence—and therewith as passage *of* presence" (SM, 25; SW, 12). It is in this respect that Nancy is able to talk of the "transimmanence" of sense, since sense, as the existence of the world or opening of intelligible space, is always presupposed whenever we experience anything at all, but it exists prior to consciousness and, as it were, in between any logic of transcendence and immanence in relation to consciousness: it exists always as an arrival, passage, or movement-to upon which "presencing" occurs. This is an attempt to think an ontology, not as an event of grounding and ungrounding (Heidegger's *Grund* and *Abgrund*), but as passage or movement-to which would exceed any logic of grounding, as either ground or absence of ground or indeed as any kind of mediated movement between the two. It is also an attempt to work out an ontology which does not think being in terms of a play of identity and difference, otherness and sameness, but rather poses being as a movement of sense in its "singular plurality." Sense, here, is "singular"—that is, irreducible to any possibility of gathering, identity, or propriety—but its singularity is also constituted in its multiplicity and relationality. It is singular only insofar as it relates to or articulates a movement or passage toward other singular instances of sense. What Nancy is aiming at is nothing less than a total rethinking of Heidegger by way of Heidegger, a reworking of ontology not as a speaking or sheltering of an originary disclosure/withdrawal of being, but rather as an affirmation of its spatial-temporal opening as the singular plurality of sense. Thus Nancy announces the aim of his 1996 work *Être singulier pluriel* in the following terms: "it is necessary to refigure fundamental ontology (as well as the existential analytic, the history of being, and the thinking of *Ereignis* that goes along with it) with a thorough resolve that *starts from the singular-plural of origins*, from *being-with*" (*ESP*, 45; *BSP*, 26).

So Nancy's thinking of space, insofar as it is indebted to an existential-phenomenological account of the event of being, emerges as an amalgam of philosophical terms drawn from both *Being and Time* (sense, world, being-in-the-world) and the later *Contributions to Philosophy* (space-time, spatializing-temporalizing, event of appropriation/*Ereignis*). These terms are reinscribed into a modified philosophical idiom in an attempt to rigorously situate the thinking of being outside or beyond any possibility of propriety, where the event of appropriation is posed as a radical opening, an ungraspable being-to or being-toward of finite sense. This, it has been suggested, occurs (in part at least) as a response to Heidegger's political itinerary and within the context of Nancy's view, shared in a different way by his collaborator Lacoue-Labarthe, that the Heideggerian thinking of being fails to develop its own radical insights at crucial moments in its unfolding.

Being-to, or the being of sense as a singular plurality outside of any possibility of identity or closure, is also aligned with Nancy's rethinking of Heideggerian *Mitsein* in texts such as *La Communauté désœuvrée* (which, as indicated above, will be discussed more fully in Chapter 4). For the Heidegger of *Being and Time*, it should be recalled, Dasein occurs as being-in-the-world only insofar as it is singularized in its ownmost possibility, that is, in its projection toward the futurity of death. It is only then *with* or alongside others in a more secondary sense. Nancy's use of the term *being-with* seeks to think our worldly existence with others in a more fundamental or originary manner. Here the "being-there" of being-in-the-world can occur only on the basis of a relation with death which is (always) already shared, such that the being of the world itself is given or opened up *as* a primary being-with, which only subsequently allows for individuation or the singularizing of being-there. Thus the thinking of being-with repeats the thinking of being-to whereby the singular exists always only in a prior relation to other instances of the singular and thus always in the context of a singular plurality. It is in this sense that Nancy thinks the space of the world and the spacing of sense in terms of a shared finitude and a shared relation to death that is at once the being-to of sense and the fundamental being-with of worldly existence. Space-time as an opening or exteriority which never closes or folds onto itself is always already "with":

"With" is the sharing of time-space; it is the at-the-same-time-in-the-same-place as itself, in itself, shattered. It is the instant scaling back the principle of identity: being is at the same time in the same place only on the condition of the spacing of an indefinite plurality of singularities. Being is with being; it does not ever recover itself, but it is near to itself, beside itself, in touch with itself, its very self, in the paradox of that proximity where distancing and strangeness are revealed. (*ESP*, 55; *BSP*, 35)

The emphasis placed on "sharing" here underlines once again the status of being-with (and by implication being-to) as a spatial-temporal event, which occurs spatially insofar as the passage of sense opens up spaces and places of worldly existence, and temporally, insofar as the passage of sense produces time in its movement-to or transitivity. The opening up of spaces can occur only as temporality, and temporality can occur only as the opening up of spaces, that is, space-time:

The passage from one place to another *needs time* [*D'un lieu à l'autre, il faut le temps*]. And moving in place [*du lieu à lui-même*] as such also needs time: the time for the place to open itself as place, the time to space itself. Reciprocally, originary time, appearing as such, *needs space* [*il lui faut l'espace*], the space of its own distension, the space of the passage that divides [*partage*] it. (*ESP*, 83; *BSP*, 61)

Sharing, division, or *partage* in French, becomes a key item in Nancy's philosophical lexicon, comparable in importance to Heidegger's use of the term *sheltering* (*bergen*) but diametrically opposed to it in the emphasis it places on the originary opening of being as "being-with," such that the "with" of being is not secondary or supplementary but the very condition of the presentation or the coming to presence of a spatial world. The difference between sharing and sheltering marks, exactly, the difference between Nancy's thinking of *Ereignis* as a centrifugal dispersal or spacing of sense beyond any logic of the "proper," and Heidegger's use of the term to think being as a gathering or binding, a joining of identity through difference.

### Sense and the Body

The upshot of this is that where Heidegger, from the 1930s onward, sought to think the site of being as either the historical-destinal sending of the being of a people or nation (*Volk*), or alternatively as the work of art or poetry (Hölderlin), and in terms which resonate with a sense of near-ness or domesticity, Nancy thinks the site of the giving of being in a radi-cally different manner. The discussion of sense above underlined the extent to which this term has fundamental ontological status in Nancy, but also the extent to which the ontology of finite sense here is also a "concrete" or "materialist" ontology. Nancy exploits the many meanings of the word *sens* in French, which can refer to direction (implying the movement of "being-to"), and also, of course, can denote sense as meaning, or can refer to sense as bodily sense—touch, smell, taste, sight, hearing. The passage of sense therefore is the opening of a spatial world as meaningful or intelligible, but is also the contact or touch of something concrete or material. This reflects the manner in which Nancy comes to think the site of the passage of sense, of the giving or opening of being as in some way embodied, constituted in the materiality of corporeal existence, or as he puts it:

The ontology of being-with can only be "materialist," in the sense that "matter" does not designate a substance or a subject. . . . The ontology of being-with is an ontology of bodies, of every body, whether they be inanimate, animate, sentient, speaking, thinking, having weight, and so on. Above all else, "body" really means what is outside, insofar as it is outside, next to, against, nearby, with a(n) (other) body, from body to body, in dis-position. (*ESP*, 107–8; *BSP*, 83–84)

To this extent Nancy's use of the term *sense* cuts across the traditional phil-osophical distinction between the sensible and the intelligible in the same way that it cuts across the distinctions of transcendence and immanence, the ideal and the empirical. Cutting across or operating in excess of these distinctions, sense is "materialist" or concrete in a very specific manner (since materiality would normally imply the very distinctions which in the context of Nancy's writing it displaces). The suggestion is that our embod-ied existence implies an orientation of the body that, prior to any assump-tion of subjectivity or inscription within the symbolic dimension of lan-guage, presupposes sense and articulates the passage of sense as the spacing of space and disclosure of a shared meaningful world. Sense is therefore "material," not because it implies the notion of substance, but because it is the precondition for the bodily know-how through which, prior to conscious thought or cognition, we orient ourselves within an intelligible space, and upon which we build the symbolic dimension of signification, of signs and language.

In this respect Nancy's thinking of the body and of space has some relation to that of Maurice Merleau-Ponty, to be discussed more fully in the following chapter. It also, perhaps, recalls the emphasis Husserl places on the role of the body and of bodily orientation within space in the formation of the visual (or oculomotor) and the tactile fields, on the basis of which the constitution of space was thought in the *Thing and Space* lectures of 1907 (where the reduced phenomenon was an immanence "within the flesh"). For both Nancy and Husserl sense or meaning is a precondition for consciousness or an experience of space (and to this extent it is, for both, "unconscious"), but, whereas Husserl situates meaning within the sphere of ideality, Nancy situates it in the realm of material corporeality, on the level of touch or tact, through which we engage with, or indeed open up, a spatial world. This thinking of the corporeal is most fully elaborated in the 1992 work *Corpus.* For Nancy, here, the body is sense, it is the opening of space, the opening or sharing of spaces and of places *between* bodies: "[Bodies] are *the very discretion of the places of sense, moments of the organism, elements of matter.* A body is a site which opens, which separates, which spaces" (*C,* 18; Nancy's emphasis). Or, as he puts it later in the same text, the body is the taking place of sense: "Neither anterior nor posterior, the site of the body *is the taking place* of sense, absolutely. The absolute is the detached, the set-apart, the extended, the shared/divided [*le partagé*]" (*C,* 103; Nancy's emphasis). The body and sense, therefore, are co-originary, insofar as the body is the site of the spatializing-temporalizing opening of space, the site of the movement-to or passage of sense, without which there would be no shared being-there within a world, that is, no experience of a world as world. It is to this extent that Nancy's "ontology of sense" is also an ontology of the body and therefore materialist or concrete. It is not that, as consciousness or mind, we experience "material" things which gain their meaning through experience (empiricism) or that our minds are structured in such a way that we impose meaning on experience (idealism). Prior to any traditional distinction between mind and body, ideality and materiality, and prior to cognition per se, there is the passage of sense as a bodily event, as an opening up of meaningful spaces and a meaningful world in which such distinctions as mind/body, ideality/materiality can be made or be thinkable as such.

Nancy's account of space, then, ultimately hinges on an account of the body and of the sense of space as corporeal and material, whereby "*bodies first articulate space*" (*C*, 27; Nancy's emphasis). This is what allows him to speak of bodies as "opened space": "[Bodies] are *open* space, that is to say in a sense, space which is properly spacious rather than spatial, or what one can still call, *place*. Bodies are places of existence, and there is no existence without place" (*C*, 16). This account places Nancy's thinking firmly within the realm of worldly embodied engagements but does so in a way that seeks to emphasize the always already meaningful nature of our experience. Yet although Nancy's ontology thinks body and sense as originary, it does not allow them to be thought in terms of an origin, foundation, or ground in the traditional sense. Sense, it should be recalled, as that which is always presupposed in a meaningful world, is also ungraspable, shared, and irreducible to any closed signification or meaning. Beyond, or in excess of, any logic of grounding and ungrounding, foundationalism or antifoundationalism, sense, and the sense of the body, *is* as passage, birth, creation, the singular-plural spacing of sense which opens, discloses, and makes intelligible, but as such it can never be grasped, delimited, or mastered. It is always presupposed when we experience anything at all but it cannot be posed as a ground or foundation. Nancy is, nevertheless, willing to use words such as *foundation* (*fondement*), as in *Être singulier pluriel* when he writes, "The plurality of beings is at the foundation of being" (*ESP*, 30; *BSP*, 12). Yet what he means here is not that there are many unique beings or discrete entities which found being as substance, but rather that the presentation or coming to presence of any being is itself a (singular) plural event, a spacing or a sharing of the multiple passage of sense. Foundation here is, as it were, not a substantial ground upon which one can stand, it is movement, position or disposition, a spatial-temporal event of sense.

To this extent Nancy's bodily ontology of space obeys a strange logic whereby his philosophical writing poses sense as an ontological foundation, but rethinks the very notion of the foundational itself, not as ground (or ab-ground/abyss), but as a dispersal or sharing of sense which cannot be reduced to any signification writing can pose. It is in this sense that his writing does not ground itself upon the origin or foundation of sense, rather it *exposes* itself to, or, in another important term used by Nancy, it *touches* (*touche à*) that origin. The singular-plural passage of sense, as being or being-to, is not gatherable into words, signification, or logos, but, at its very limit, signification opens onto or touches the movement of sense. This, for Nancy, is the very task of finite thinking, a thinking that occurs within the closure or the exhaustion of metaphysics. Such a thinking involves a play with the very limit of thought and signification. This complex logic of the limit was discussed briefly at the end of the previous chapter. Its full implications will be discussed more fully in the final chapter, which is on art. It is important to note here, though, that Nancy's "materialist" ontology of sense is, more properly speaking, a "quasi ontology" (or as Derrida has put it a "quasi-transcendental ontology"), since the being of sense which he seeks to think or to make signify is irreducible to thought or signification as such.

Yet care should be taken here, for although Nancy affirms sense as an excess over signification, his quasi ontology, that is, his thinking of being as an event of finite, bodily sense, does not refuse or reject the notion of facts or the category of truth. It has been shown that his account of space builds upon and transforms the phenomenological and existential/ontological account, in order to affirm a certain kind of materialism and the concrete nature of embodied being-in-the-world. It has also been suggested that Nancy attempts to think beyond the dichotomy of foundationalism/anti-foundationalism which informed his earlier, more deconstructive readings of Kant and Descartes. Bearing this in mind, this discussion will now close with the question of truth and of factuality in Nancy's ontology of space.

### Thinking in the Singular-Plural

Given the proximity of Nancy's thought in the 1970s to Derridean deconstruction it might seem surprising that he is so willing in his later texts to work out an ontology, and to use words such as *being* or *foundation* without placing them under erasure or even within quotation marks. As will become clear in subsequent chapters, the fact that Nancy's philosophical thought remains within the perspective of being, and remains wedded to ontology (albeit a complex quasi ontology) has provoked certain reservations among some in the French literary-philosophical fraternity to which he belongs (most prominently Blanchot and Derrida). Be that as it may, it is arguable that the strength of Nancy's thought lies in its emphasis on the materiality of sense and of embodied being-in-the-world *as* finite spatial existence. Such an emphasis allows his thinking to address a worldly dimension which is both meaningful and real, in the sense that it exists as sense, prior to the dimension of the symbolic or of language. To this extent Nancy's ontology introduces a kind of realism back into a tradition of French thought that has often been associated with antirealism, with the overturning of any truth value, and with a primary focus on textuality or symbolic structures. This, of course, is no traditional kind of realism, or a return to the idea of truth as a correspondence between propositional statements and empirically observable facts (although Nancy would not deny the possibility of such a correspondence). Throughout his mature thinking, and in *Le Sens du monde* in particular, Nancy affirms the category of truth: "That one speaks of sense does not mean that one abandons or disdains the category of truth. But one does shift registers. Truth is the be-ing-*such* [*l'être-tel*], or more exactly it is the quality of the presentation of being *such* as such" (*SM*, 25; *SW*, 12). It is this "change in register" which needs to be thought here.

Truth, in Nancy, is not the truth of a proposition or axiom (Nancy, like Heidegger before him rejects the correspondence theory of truth); rather it is the being of sense, of sense as that which allows beings and entities to present themselves or to exist as such. It is in this respect that "truth can consist only, in the final analysis, . . . in the truth of sense" (*SM*, 29; *SW*, 14). The key point to retain is that the irreducible and ungraspable excess of sense does not necessarily entail a consigning of truth to the unknowable or the ineffable, nor does it imply that Nancy's ontology allows only for an epistemological relativism, a semantic free for all whereby the truth of sense can be made to signify arbitrarily in any way whatsoever. Rather the truth of an entity, fact, or event is, and therefore also proposes and indeed imposes, a sense that is singular and that must be addressed as such. But as singular, it has been suggested, sense is always also relational, it exists as a plural relationality of sense which is temporal in its unfolding.

In this respect, if the sense of an entity, fact, or event is determined as truth—that is, as the truth of the sense which that entity, fact, or event *is*—there exists a tension between the "fixing" of the determination and the necessary movement, relationality, and plurality of sense as passage or being-to; or as Nancy puts it, borrowing a famous term from Derrida:

Sense can only be determined in its truth: as the *différance of truth itself.* In this way, sense and truth belong to each other as much as they diverge from each other, and this divergence itself gives the measure of their mutual belonging. They are necessary to each other, just as they cannot fail to occult each other or to withdraw themselves from each other. (*SM,* 29; *SW,* 15)

Here truth and sense are inseparable in their belonging together. This means, however, that truth is implicated or is produced in the spatial-temporal sharing or *partage* of sense, such that the determination of truth will "distance" or occlude the movement or passage of sense, just as the tracing of movement or passage will render incomplete and partial the determination of truth (it is in this sense that they "diverge" or "withdraw" from each other). Nancy seeks to think this cobelonging and codistancing of truth and sense in terms of the "punctuality" (*ponctualité*) of truth, that is, its existence as point or puncture, and in terms of the "enchaining" (*enchaînement*) of sense:

Truth punctuates, sense enchains. Punctuation is a presentation, full or empty, full of emptiness, a point or a hole, an awl, and perhaps always the hole that is pierced by the sharp point of an accomplished present. It is always without temporal or spatial dimensions. Enchaining, on the contrary, opens up the dimensional, spaces out punctuations. (*SM,* 29; *SW,* 14)

The determination of truth, as the fixing of sense, presents itself as a piercing, a point, or a "hole" within an open-ended spatial-temporal unfolding, and thus removes the dimension of spatiality and temporality from that unfolding. This, Nancy notes, is "perhaps always" the character of an "accomplished present." That is to say, the spatial-temporal event of sense presents itself, after the event, always as a point or puncture within a wider plurality of opening or unfolding. What he is seeking to think here is the way in which, in approaching or determining the truth of a fact, entity, or event, it is necessary to be open, not just to a fixed point of sense that they may propose or impose, but also to attend to the "enchaining" of sense, the open-ended passage, relationality, or plurality of sense that allows facts, entities, and events to be in their being.

By determining truth, or fixing a point of sense, is also meant "making sense signify." Nancy's quasi ontology does not seek to think the absolute excess of sense over signification in terms which would necessitate a refusal to make sense signify, or the placing of signification per se under the sign of violence or appropriation. Rather it necessitates, or demands, an ethics and a praxis of openness vis-à-vis signification, whereby thought and language address themselves, at the limit of signification, to the singular plurality of sense; where they address themselves to the truth of entities and events, but do so in an affirmation of the tension between the fixing or "punctuality" of truth and the open-ended "enchaining" of sense, their cobelonging, but also their mutual exclusion or occlusion. In this sense, truth, for Nancy, is always determinable, but it is also always, and necessarily, inexhaustible. What his thinking resolutely refuses is what he terms in the opening pages of *Être singulier pluriel*, "the indeterminate multiplication of centripetal meanings, meanings closed in on themselves and supersaturated with significance . . . that are no longer meaningful because they have come to refer only to their own closure" (*ESP*, 12; *BSP*, xiii). His thinking articulates a refusal of closed systems of signification which would pose their truth or truths in absolute terms and thus repress the singular plurality of sense upon which any truth can be determinable as such. In turn Nancy poses his ontology of the being-to or being-with of sense as both "an *ethos* and a *praxis*" (*ESP*, 87; *BSP*, 65). As a praxis and ethos it demands that sense be made to signify, but in a way which addresses the being of sense as both singular and plural, as presentation, but also as the infinitely open-ended spatial-temporal unfolding of a shared world: "sense must be signified in all possible ways, by each and every one of us, by all 'individual' or 'collective' singulars" (*SM*, 248; *SW*, 165).

Thinking in the singular-plural, then, does not, in Nancy's terms, offer itself as a theory that presents concepts which we can subsequently abstract in order to make axiomatic judgments about being. Rather, as an ontology that is at once an ethos and a praxis it allows us to address the real existence of beings or entities in a different register, in a way that attends simultaneously to their specificity and their relationality. It demands an attention to the singular plurality of the being of entities and events as well as an openness to the inexhaustibility and open-endedness of meaning and signification. The implications of such a rethinking of ontology for diverse areas of thought and inquiry are wide-reaching. Nancy's philosophical writing, itself a singular and plural praxis of thought, constantly takes up and attends to diverse and divergent problems or proper names which make up the body western European thinking, thereby passing them through the thinking of the singular-plural. Whether it be his rereading of existential phenomenology, his "deconstruction of Christianity," his thinking of "eco-technics" or aesthetics, or his references classical thinkers (e.g., Spinoza, Hegel, Marx) or contemporary philosophers (e.g., Derrida, Deleuze, Marion, Badiou), Nancy's thought enacts itself as an ethics of, and an address to, the singular-plural of being. As such, this study suggests, his thought is irreducibly fragmentary in nature. The remaining chapters will therefore make no attempt to close or finalize an engagement with Nancy's philosophy. Rather they will focus on three motifs, body, community, and art, which themselves foreground the different ways in which Nancy thinks in the singular-plural.

# CHAPTER THREE

# Body

To write: to touch extremity. How then to touch at the body, instead of signifying it or making it signify? . . . to touch at the body, to touch the body, *touch* finally—happens all the time in writing . . . on the border, on the limit, at a point, at the extremity of writing, *that and nothing else happens.* Writing has its place on the limit. Nothing happens to writing, if something does happen to it, other than *touching.* More precisely: a touching of the body (or rather this or that singular body) *with the incorporeal* of "sense." And in consequence, a making of the incorporeal into that which touches, or a making of sense into a touch . . . writing touches bodies *according to the absolute limit* which separates the sense of one from the skin and nerves of the other.

—JEAN-LUC NANCY, *Corpus*[1]

## Introduction

The body has been a dominant preoccupation of much recent cultural theory, theory which most often has its roots in certain developments within the French philosophical scene of the 1970s.[2] Within what one might broadly call "cultural studies" the body has come to be understood primarily as a site of meaning, a site at which culture and cultural identity is expressed and articulated.[3] Such an understanding might broadly be termed "constructionist," insofar as embodiment per se is seen to be based on an experience of social construction, whereby society and social practices make the body meaningful and classify it in ways which exceed individual control or agency. In this context the body of cultural theory is determined far more as a signifying or symbolic entity than as a material or truly corporeal being. It could be argued that what is all too absent from such theoretical conceptions of the body is an engagement with its materiality and physical situatedness.[4] The body of cultural theory can all too often emerge as a rather abstract being, whereby corporeal identity, conceived primarily in terms of its constructedness in and through a social symbolic order or system of constraint, is a subject of representation rather than a messy, lived, material existence.[5]

Needless to say such discourses cannot easily enter into dialogue with scientific or medical approaches (except by treating such approaches themselves as discursive symbolic forms), where the body is largely conceived as a material thing among other things, as a mechanical and physiological or neurophysiological entity which can be scientifically determined as such through empirical investigation. The body of cultural theory, in failing to engage fully with the materiality of embodiment per se, perhaps also fails to engage with or think fully the limits of the symbolic or of signification, the point at which the socially constructed or symbolically coded corporeal identity finds itself incarnate in fleshy, perishable matter. To this extent, although such theory may engage with the concrete bodily practices which determine bodily identity and inscribe social codes in a (symbolic) unconscious, it is forms of representation which remain the object of study and not what one might call their existential-material incarnation. This point of contact between the limit of sense and signification on the one hand, and the fleshy and impenetrable materiality of the body on the other, is what Nancy's rethinking of existential phenomenology and fundamental ontology seeks to address.

The privileging of abstraction or of symbolic structures which can be discerned in cultural theoretical approaches to embodiment has its roots in a complex genealogy, and a complex and largely ignored historical relationship between phenomenology and structuralism.[6] This is a question whose scope and exact determination by far exceeds the terms of this study. However, one might note, rather schematically perhaps, that what phenomenology, in its Husserlian guise, and structuralism, in its classical or "high" forms, have in common is their "bracketing off" of the empirical referent as their object of inquiry, in favor of a description or determination of intentional structures and ideal essences (Husserl) or of overarching, signifying systems (e.g., Lévi-Strauss's structuralist anthropology). These essences, structures, or systems precede empirical reality as such and act as a kind of invariant condition of possibility or principle of production for that reality. In the account of Husserl's 1907 work *Thing and Space* given in the previous chapter it was shown that the phenomenological reduction attempted to isolate a sphere of pretheoretical experience, of immediate givenness, which would be the coming-into-appearance of phenomena and of the spatial world. It was argued that, for Husserl, consciousness and immediate perception perform the foundational disclosive function by which the world comes into appearance or is constituted, and that the question of the "things-in-themselves," of the existence of entities outside of their relation to consciousness, was not seen to be a viable object of philosophical interrogation. What phenomenology attempts to think, then, is phenomenal appearance and the logical essences upon which what appears is given identity and meaning. In the case of Husserl this leads to transcendental phenomenology, where it is always, and only, a sphere of ideality which is to be described by phenomenological analysis, a sphere of ideality which serves as the basis for all possibility of objective truth and validity in the empirical realm.

As has been argued in a recent study by the contemporary French phenomenologist Michel Henry, what phenomenology as a science of appearance appears to lack is a full account of the "stuff" of appearance itself. In his extended analysis of Husserl, Henry aims to demonstrate that, while the phenomenological reduction allows for a description of the primary flux of sensation and the temporality of intentional consciousness (retentions and protentions), and with this allows for a description of the way appearance attains a logical identity and a unifying field of signification, it tells us nothing about what he calls the "phenomenological matter" of appearance. For phenomenology appearance is disclosed, opened, or "shines," but that which shines, discloses, or manifests itself is only appearance itself; the stuff of appearance is the subject of neutrality or indifference. This is true, Henry argues, even for Heidegger's existential phenomenology, which, despite its centeredness on the concrete, situated, and historical facticity of Dasein, still remains concerned with the coming-to-appearance, disclosure, or manifestation of world-hood and not with the inner nature of phenomenality itself.[7] Henry's carefully argued contention is that this lacuna within Husserlian and Heideggerian thought leads to a series of impasses and philosophical inadequacies which render the phenomenological project incoherent and ultimately untenable. What he proposes in response to this failure is a "phenomenology of the flesh," a thinking of appearance and phenomenological essence which accounts also for its "incarnate" nature, that is, its embodiment in or fusion with material life. The phenomenology of the flesh which is developed in Henry's work ultimately also involves a careful and detailed meditation on the Christian tradition of thinking incarnation and amounts to a fusion of phenomenological and Christian thought.

Nancy's thinking of embodiment and his relation to Christianity is, as will become clear, rather different from that of Henry. Nevertheless Henry's critique of phenomenological appearance and of the Christian tradition of thinking incarnation addresses philosophical questions that are central to Nancy's understanding of the corporeal, to his thinking beyond phenomenology, and to what he has come to designate in more recent writing as his "deconstruction of Christianity." As will be shown in the account given below of his 1992 work, *Corpus*, for Nancy the Christian tradition, and conceptions of the mind/body relation which have their roots in that tradition, still dominate much of our thinking about the body and the conceptual parameters available to us to think about the presence or absence of material bodies. Nancy's "deconstruction," then, would involve a rigorous process of disassembly, whereby the various components and interlocking parts of those conceptual parameters are taken apart and reassembled in order to think the relation of mind and body, sense and matter, otherwise or differently than the tradition has allowed us to do to date. The upshot of this is twofold. Nancy's reworking of a bodily ontology leads, on the one hand, to a new conception of the body in its relation to what one might term technicity, that is, to the world of technical apparatus or of tools. Interestingly this leads to wholly new, and perhaps surprising, possibilities on the part of Nancy's postphenomenological philosophy in its approach to the world of scientific and technical discovery or invention (a world which, as the last chapter showed, has been placed in a secondary or subordinate position in the phenomenological approaches of Husserl and Heidegger). On the other hand Nancy's rethinking of the body inaugurates a thinking of the limit which has been touched upon already in previous chapters. It is a thinking of the limit of signification and of sense, and a thinking of touch, tact, or contact at the limit, which would allow signification, sense, and materiality to be thought together or alongside each other. The discourse of touch through which Nancy thinks the relation of sense and bodily matter is difficult to approach and can be easily misconstrued. Once again, what is at stake is a complex relation to, and a radical rethinking of, phenomenological thought, although in this case one of the key points of reference is, as we shall see, the philosophy of Maurice Merleau-Ponty. To date the most rigorous and extended engagement with Nancy's thinking of touch and the body has been undertaken by Derrida in *Le Toucher, Jean-Luc Nancy* (2000). This work is an important engagement with Nancy's thought as a whole, and offers an indispensable point of reference for any discussion of his thinking on the body.

The central premise of Derrida's extended essay is that the figure of touch is the philosophical cornerstone around which Nancy's thinking turns. For Derrida, touch in Nancy is a figure for that unique place or point of contact between the body or materiality and what, keeping to a more traditional vocabulary, we might choose to call soul, mind, or thought. It is also, he affirms, a philosophical figure which Nancy deploys in order to "resist, in the name of touch, all idealism and all subjectivism, whether it be transcendental or psychoanalytic" (*T*, 60). This leads Derrida to make the following startling claim about Nancy's thinking: "Touch remains for Nancy the motif of a kind of absolute realism, irredentist and postdeconstructive. . . . An absolute realism, but irreducible to all traditional forms of realism" (*T*, 60). Irredentism, a form of political ideology whose origin lies in the nationalism of the newly unified Italian state in the late nineteenth century, is a doctrine of borders or limits, a doctrine which demands the assimilation of what lies immediately beyond the frontier into the orbit of the state. There is a slight ambivalence in Derrida's comment here. On the one hand Nancy's realism is postdeconstructive; it is irreducible to any traditional realism, that is, irreducible to any traditional logic of representation or metaphysics of presence, which, of course, Derrida would reject. Yet his use of the term *irredentist* might imply a certain assimilationist tendency on Nancy's part, a desire to appropriate or master that which, at the limit, the limit of thought, of sense, and of signification, is touched in this absolute realism.

The second major premise of Derrida's argument in *Le Toucher, Jean-Luc Nancy* is that a principal strand of the European philosophical tradition is, like Nancy's philosophy, dominated by a thinking of touch or contact. This strand of the tradition within which a certain figuration or figurality of touch is at play forms what Derrida calls a "philosophical intrigue" along the limits of European thought, limits which separate German Idealism from the French tradition of rationalism, and mainland European thought from British empiricism. Integral to this philosophical intrigue is a thinking of the body, of the propriety and integrity of the individual body, a thinking which has its roots in Christian thought and in the Christian conception of incarnation where spirit is made flesh in the body of Christ. This is a heritage, we shall see, which Nancy also explicitly engages with in *Corpus*, specifically in relation to the phrase from the Eucharist, *Hoc est enim corpus meum* (This is my body). Derrida's response to Nancy, then, is to seek to further untangle this philosophical intrigue around the figure of touch, to expose its theological underpinnings, and to call into question Nancy's relation to it. Much of his discussion is devoted to this wider context and includes commentaries on figures such as Maine de Biran, Husserl, Levinas, and Merleau-Ponty. Touch, for Derrida, becomes another means to designate a tradition of thought dominated by a metaphysics of presence, one which privileges identity over alterity, homogeneity over heterogeneity, and immediacy over separation, mediation, or distance. Appealing to the Greek root *haptein* (to touch), Derrida designates this tradition as a "haptology" or "haptocentric metaphysics," in a gesture which recalls, of course, his earlier usage and understanding of terms such as *phonocentrism* or *logocentrism*.

What emerges from Derrida's lengthy and at times tortuous discussion is an attempt to discern the ways in which Nancy's thinking of touch both belongs to and diverges from the metaphysical tradition of haptology in its modern form. Broadly speaking, what he discerns in Nancy's thought is a relation of proximity with and distance from this tradition. On the one hand, Derrida is clear, the Nancean figure of touch marks a divergence or a moment of rupture: "Nancy appears to me to break with, or at least take his distance from, forms of haptocentric metaphysics. His discourse on touch is neither intuitionist, nor continuist, nor homogenist, nor indivisibilist" (*T*, 179–80). What Nancy begins to conceptualize in the philosophical figure of touch is an experience of embodiment, or of material existence, which is other than that inherited from the tradition: "another experience of the body: a different body and a different *corpus*" (*T*, 247). It is also one which, crucially, begins to push thought beyond or in excess of its Christian inheritance in order to approach a "*beyond of Christianity*" through a deconstruction of Christianity itself, or what Derrida calls a "*deconstruction of Christian 'flesh'*" (*T*, 248; Derrida's emphasis). On the other hand, Derrida maintains a degree of ambivalence or skepticism in relation to Nancy's refiguring of the figure of touch. If Nancy thinks touch against the haptological tradition which privileges presence, immediacy, continuity, and indivisibility, he does so in favor of a thinking of touch which is also a separation, a contact which occurs at distance. As will be analyzed in more detail as this discussion progresses, Nancy's thinks touch in terms of discontinuity, fragmentation, partition, and sharing. Yet for Derrida, in a classic deconstructive move, this gesture may imply a necessary belonging to, or affirmation of that which it seeks to exceed. He describes touch in Nancy as follows: "A certain way of self-touching [*se toucher*] . . . of self-touching interrupting contact, but a contact, therefore a tact which, nevertheless, we say, *succeeds in interrupting itself*" (*T*, 51). However fragmented or discontinuous the touch invoked by Nancy might be, Derrida suggests, it may imply a touch which, in interrupting itself as itself, ultimately maintains the horizon of unity and continuity which is being called into question. If this is so then the distance Nancy takes from the haptocentric tradition of thought is a distance taken in the context of a more fundamental proximity with or belonging to that tradition. By the same token, then, Nancy's "deconstruction of Christianity" would also mark a profound belonging of his thinking to Christian thought, leading Derrida to suggest that "the 'deconstruction of Christianity' announced by Nancy seems to be such a difficult and paradoxical task, very nearly impossible and forever exposed to being nothing other than a Christian hyperbole" (*T*, 249).

Derrida appears torn between a sense that Nancy's thought offers something radically new—that is, an absolute realism which breaks with a traditional logic of representation, with the horizons of metaphysics and of Christian onto-theology—and a sense that the vocabulary of touch may be fatally implicated within the forms of thought which are apparently displaced or deconstructed. His enthusiasm for Nancy's philosophical originality and boldness is matched by a certain suspicion or skepticism, and a sense of questioning or restraint. As has been indicated, much of Derrida's argument unfolds as a dialogue with other thinkers in an attempt to discern a modern haptological trajectory of thought. This trajectory is none other than that of phenomenology itself and of selected thinkers whose work has been decisive for the development and fate of phenomenological thought throughout the twentieth century, namely Husserl, Merleau-Ponty, and Levinas. It is above all in the work of Merleau-Ponty that Derrida discerns the closest proximity between Nancy and the haptological trajectory he uncovers. What follows, then, will attempt to trace Nancy's writing on the body against the background of this tension or ambivalence which unfolds across the pages of *Le Toucher, Jean-Luc Nancy*. Nancy's attempt to think another body, another *corpus*, and to move beyond the Christian inheritance, is as Derrida suggests, inseparable from his relation to phenomenological thought, a relation whose importance has begun to be discerned in the preceding chapter. In order to make sense of the manner in which *sens* in Nancy touches or comes into contact with the body, with materiality or mortal flesh, and in order to judge the validity of Derrida's skepticism and ambivalence, this discussion will now turn to Merleau-Ponty's thinking of embodiment and incarnation.

## Maurice Merleau-Ponty and the Phenomenological Body

In *Phénoménologie de la perception* (1945) Maurice Merleau-Ponty repeats the attempt, initiated by Husserl, to ground phenomenological inquiry in a sphere of primordial experience—perception—which would be situated prior to reflective thought and prior to the abstract or mathematical projections of scientific knowledge. The key difference between the two is that, for Merleau-Ponty, this primordial experience is not the reduced sphere of abstract logical essences but rather the experience of being a body, the experience of an incarnate existence which is finite and situated.[8] The exact manner in which Merleau-Ponty seeks to think this incarnation, both in *Phénoménologie de la perception* and later in *Le Visible et l'invisible*, sheds important light on Nancy's account of embodiment and his use of the figure of touch.

One of the central arguments of *Phénoménologie de la perception* is that traditional empiricist or idealist approaches are unable properly to account for the nature of embodied subjectivity, and unable to properly think what Merleau-Ponty terms, after Husserl, "the pre-predicative life of consciousness." Arguably the great and enduring strength of *Phénoménologie de la perception* is that it engages closely with the findings of experimental psychology in order to advance its arguments about the limitations of empiricist and idealist accounts of embodiment, or what Merleau-Ponty more frequently refers to as "realist" and "intellectualist" approaches. Most importantly he aims to challenge some of the deep-rooted assumptions held by classical psychology, for example, that the body is a thing or object which can be treated like other things or objects, and that experience or perception can be broken down into component elements of stimulus and response, input and output.[9] Central to this aim is the notion of bodily intentionality. In contrast to Husserl's idealist bent, the notion of bodily intentionality suggests that the event of perception through which the world is disclosed to us at the most primordial level is an event which is intimately bound up with our bodily orientation, and the directedness of this orientation within the context of a broader horizonality or environment. Yet, in placing intentionality within the sphere of bodily orientation or directedness, Merleau-Ponty is, as has been indicated, keen to avoid the assumptions that go with traditional realist accounts. He steers a path between the two alternatives by emphasizing that the body is not an object among other objects (as classical psychology would have it), nor is it a vessel through which a more abstract mind, intentionality, or transcendental ego would constitute world-hood (as idealism or Husserlian phenomenology would have it). Rather the body, and bodily intentionality, is that through which we have objects in the first instance (therefore that upon which we can subsequently treat the body as an object). What Merleau-Ponty's phenomenology is interested in describing, then, is "the primordial operation which impregnates the sensible with a sense, and which is presupposed by all logical mediation as well as by all psychological causality" (*PP*, 43; *PoP*, 34). His contention is that the psychological causality of stimulus and response, or the logical operations of reflection or cognition, both of which may play important roles in the way we make sense of our bodies and of the world, are possible only against the background of a primordial and nonobjectifiable bodily intentionality that makes bodies accessible to us in the first instance, before we can view the body as an object. The body, then, must be seen "not as an object of the world, but as a means of communicating with it, in the world no longer seen as a sum of determinate objects, but as a latent horizon of our experience, itself also ceaselessly present, before all determining thought" (*PP*, 109; *PoP*, 92). As Dermot Moran has pointed out, insofar as this sphere of bodily intentionality is irreducible to the empirical realm of physiological or psychological inquiry, and insofar as it is that which discloses the world in the first instance, it resembles a more specific characterization of what Heidegger calls Dasein.[10]

Merleau-Ponty's conception of bodily intentionality, like Husserl's more abstract conception before it, begins with the notion that all consciousness is necessarily consciousness of something. It also implies a temporal structure of protention and retention similar to that posited by Husserl. Merleau-Ponty describes this as the "intentional arc" which the body projects in its orientation to the world, a projection which understands and apprehends signification and spatial relation in a precognitive and pre-reflective manner and confers upon the phenomenal world a unity of sense. This "intentional arc" is described in the following terms:

The life of consciousness . . . is underpinned by an "intentional arc" which projects around us our past, our future, our human environment, our physical situation, our ideological situation, our moral situation, or rather ensures that we are situated within all these relations. It is this intentional arc which makes up the unity of senses, that of the senses and of intelligence, that of sensibility and motility. (*PP*, 158; *PoP*, 136)

This intentionality, as primordial transcendence toward a world, implies both spatiality and temporality; it lays down or projects spatial-temporal axes and a horizonality of sense in the context of which sensible data can be made intelligible in perception and as the disclosure of a meaningful world. Although it is not empirically measurable as a thing, Merleau-Ponty takes great pains to back up his arguments in favor of a primordial bodily intentionality by appealing to a series of studies, for example, studies of phantom limbs, visual-spatial orientation, and malfunctions in optical perception and its coordination with tactile sensation. In all cases he argues that the phenomena under study cannot properly be described within the conceptual frameworks offered by traditional mechanistic or intellectualist psychology. Indeed only when one posits something like an "intentional arc," a bodily intentionality or what Merleau-Ponty also comes to call a body image ("corps-schema"), can the worldly orientation of the body be understood and the nature of certain illnesses or malfunction be properly determined. Given the advances in cognitive science and behavioral psychology in recent decades it would be easy to imagine that Merleau-Ponty's findings might seem rather dated at the beginning of the twenty-first century. However, recent clinical research into malfunctions in spatial cognition and motor responses suggest that the central arguments of *Phénoménologie de la perception* may to some degree be supported by subsequent developments in the field of empirical knowledge.[11]

The upshot of this is a thinking of sense, not as an ideality, logical essence, or *eidos* such as it is found in Husserl, but as a meaningful directedness which is embodied or incarnate. Merleau-Ponty diverges to a large degree from Heidegger also. Despite the emphasis placed on the situated facticity of Dasein in *Being and Time*, Heidegger makes no mention of the body or of embodiment as such, and in his later writing does so only very rarely. In that sense the body, for Merleau-Ponty, is never an object, but rather always an incarnation of sense, an incarnate subjectivity or body-subject which projects a spatial world prior to any possibility of it being situated *in* a world. The body "is not where it is, it is not what it is—since we see that it secretes in itself a 'sense' which comes to it from nowhere, and projects it onto its material surroundings and communicates it to other incarnate subjects" (*PP*, 230; *PoP*, 197). To this extent the body expresses or articulates existence in its totality, it is the "pivot of the world" (*PP*, 97; *PoP*, 82), but the world here is not an objectifiable outside which accompanies the body; rather, it is something that the body itself realizes or constitutes in its secretion and projection of a horizon of sense. According to Merleau-Ponty, then, what we come to call body and mind, sign and signification, are not substantive objects or things in themselves but rather moments which we abstract and reify post-facto on the basis of a prior movement of existence which is the projection of incarnate sense and the disclosure of a world. This notion that the world cannot be seen as an outside that accompanies the body but must be viewed as that which is realized in and through the body will be central to Merleau-Ponty's understanding and use of the term *flesh* in the later *Visible et l'invisible*. What is striking here, though, is the extent to which the terminology used to describe embodied sense in *Phénoménologie de la perception* is reminiscent of a Christian vocabulary of incarnation:

The sense of a thing lives [*habite*] in that thing like the soul lives in the body: it is not behind what appears; the sense of an ashtray . . . is not a certain idea of the ashtray which coordinates its sensory aspects and which would be accessible to the understanding alone, it animates the ashtray, it is evidently incarnate within it [*il s'incarne en lui*]. (*PP*, 369; *PoP*, 319–20)

On the one hand Merleau-Ponty is attempting to develop a thinking in which terms like *mind* and *body* are an abstraction or reification of a more primordial process, on the other he continues to appeal to the language of mind and body or body and soul in order to describe phenomenologically the incarnate nature of sense. This is not necessarily to accuse him of incoherence or of self-contradiction. Rather, the reliance on a vocabulary of body, soul, and incarnation reveals the extent to which Merleau-Ponty's attempt to think beyond or outside of the oppositions that inform empiricism and idealism nevertheless situates him within a certain trajectory or tradition of thinking. While he takes pains to affirm that the union of body and soul here is in no way to be seen as the conjoining of two separate entities or opposed terms (this would be a dualism which maintained the founding distinctions of empiricism and idealism), his terminology is inherited from the Christian tradition of thought where incarnation can be seen as the moment where "the Word was made flesh."[12] At the same time the notion of embodied sense in Merleau-Ponty allows an important distinction to be made between the sphere of signification, of ideology or fiction on the one hand (all of which are secondary or derived abstractions), and of a sensible real on the other, or as he puts it: "The real distinguishes itself from our fictions because in it sense invests and deeply penetrates matter" (*PP*, 374; *PoP*, 324). It is this notion of the penetration of matter by sense which will be of key importance in discerning the manner in which Nancy thinks embodiment both similarly and differently from Merleau-Ponty, and which is developed in more radical terms in Merleau-Ponty's later unfinished work *Le Visible et l'invisible* (1964).

This work was published posthumously in its incomplete draft together with the working notes which would have allowed Merleau-Ponty to finish the volume. It follows the ambition of his earlier work insofar as it attempts to carry out "the radical examination of our belonging to the world prior to any science" (*VI*, 47; *VaI*, 27), but differs from it insofar as it aims, not simply at a phenomenological description of perception, but rather at a more ambitious and thorough reworking of an ontology, one which aims to uncover the grounds of our "first opening onto the world" (*VI*, 59; *VaI*, 37) on the basis of an interrogation and description of "the pre-reflexive zone of the opening onto being" (*VI*, 76; *VaI*, 52). *Le Visible et l'invisible* is a philosophical work of enormous scope, which like the earlier *Phénoménologie de la perception* cannot be exhaustively examined here. A large part of Merleau-Ponty's analysis is, for instance, devoted to a painstaking and highly rigorous critique of Jean-Paul Sartre's dualist ontology of the "for-itself" (*pour-soi*) and the "in-itself" (*en-soi*). Implicit in this is once again an attempt to untie the opposition which the philosophical traditions of idealist and empiricist philosophy have maintained between the sensible and the intelligible. For Merleau-Ponty, Sartre's dualism repeats this opposition and thus, like the tradition from which it inherits, misconstrues or forgets a prior experience of being in which the sensible and the intelligible are somehow interlinked or intertwined the one with the other in such a way that subsequent distinctions (such as the "in-itself" and the "for-itself") become possible as secondary or derived categories.

In a section of the working notes entitled "Chair-Esprit" (Flesh-Mind) Merleau-Ponty once again recalls the traditional distinction between mind and body but does so in order to suggest that this distinction, rather than implying a separation of the two entities designated, in fact rests on the mutual implication of the one with the other. If we say mind, we, as thinking bodies, do so only in relation to a body, and the term *mind* has no sense outside of this relation to the corporeal. In this sense Merleau-Ponty, while invoking a traditional vocabulary of spirit and flesh, is suggesting a relation between the two, or rather an originary nonseparation of the two, which is different from what the traditional opposition proposes. He is attempting to "define spirit as *the other side* of the body" by showing that "we have no idea of a mind which would not be *doubled* by a body, which would not establish itself on this *ground*" (*VI*, 307; *VaI*, 259). This thought represents a continuation of the thinking of incarnate sense developed in *Phénoménologie de la perception* but uses a slightly different vocabulary, that of chiasm or intertwining, whereby "there is a body of the mind, and a mind of the body and chiasm between them" (*VI*, 307, *VaI*, 259).

In the final section of *Le Visible et l'invisible*, entitled "L'entrelacs-Le chiasme" (Intertwining-Chiasm), Merleau-Ponty elaborates on this relation further. What is once more at stake is the way in which the body, as an incarnation and projection of sense or meaning, opens up a primordial experience of being and thus discloses a world. The key term which is used here to describe the intertwining of sense and body is not incarnation but *flesh* (however this again recalls the phrase from the Gospel of St. John, "And the Word was made flesh"). Flesh here is a term used in order to bypass all the dualist associations of mind/body, soul/body, spirit/matter, and so on, and is in the first instance characterized by Merleau-Ponty in negative terms: "Flesh is not matter, is not spirit, is not substance" (*VI*, 181; *VaI*, 139). It is not these, but rather it is the element of being, that is, it is that through which being unveils or reveals itself as embodied existence and as the existence of bodies. Thus: "Flesh must be thought, not from the starting point of substances, of body and spirit, because then it would be the union of contradictory elements, but we say, it must be thought as the element, itself concrete, of a certain manner of general being" (*VI*, 191; *VaI*, 147). In this sense flesh is not matter or the material body as such, it is that concrete embodied element in which sense is secreted, in which something like the intentional arc of *Phénoménologie de la perception* is articulated, and is therefore that in which the world of appearance comes into being. It is not the body as visible object but is rather the body of incarnate sense, the body which experiences sight and touch, pleasure and pain, or spatial and temporal orientation within a meaningful world. Thus the body, conceived solely as a visible object, is contained in or exists alongside the world of other visible bodies; it is finite, situated, and cannot be abstracted from its being alongside, or its situated perspective. At the same time there is the body that itself sees, touches, or feels and this underlies, or acts as the ground for, the body as visible object and all other visible bodies. As Merleau-Ponty puts it, "There is a reciprocal insertion and intertwining of the one in the other" (*VI*, 180; *VaI*, 138) (that is between the visible body as object, and the invisible body which gives primordial access to objects as such; hence the opposition in the title of *Le Visible et l'invisible*). The important point to retain here is that *flesh* is the term which allows an originary fusion or mutual interpenetration of the sensible and the intelligible to be thought. Flesh is the very stuff (without being a substance) of our finite embodied existence as the temporal-spatial disclosure of the world. It is the difference between inanimate matter—for example, that table, which, standing against a wall, touches the wall but knows nothing of that touch and feels nothing touching in return—and a body which projects sense, touches, is touched in return, and thus also sees, feels, and thinks. In this sense the animate as opposed to the inanimate body has a certain depth or thickness to it, the depth or thickness which is flesh, that is the dimension of sensible/intelligible experience which makes the world possible: "The thickness of the body, far from rivaling the world, is on the contrary the sole means I have of going to the heart of things, *by making myself world and by making them flesh*" (*VI*, 176; *VaI*, 135; emphasis added).

The language of intertwining or chiasmus is deployed by Merleau-Ponty to describe the way in which the body as material existence is inserted into the world of things. More precisely it describes the way in which, at a primordial level, the meaningful object seen or disclosed, and the body which sees or discloses, are fused together and do not relate to each other as an inside relates to an outside. Rather flesh, as a transcendence toward a world, is "the wrapping around of the visible upon the body which sees, of the tangible upon the body which touches" (*VI*, 189; *VaI*, 146). The language of touch in Merleau-Ponty comes to the fore in this notion of an originary interpenetration, intertwining, or wrapping around of the seen and the seer which is flesh. This intertwining or chiasmus is a primordial touch or contact of different elements which constitutes being as such, and involves a series of reciprocal touches, between that which is sensed and that which senses, between that which sees and is seen; or as it is put rather elliptically in the working notes of *Le Visible et l'invisible*: "The relation of my body as sensible to my body as sensing (this body that I touch, this body that touches) = immersion of being in touching being and of the touching being in being touched" (*VI*, 308; *VaI*, 260). At the heart of this thinking of touch lies a repetition of the notion of incarnation found in *Phénoménologie de la perception*, where sense was seen to deeply penetrate matter.

As has been pointed out, this thinking of embodiment in Merleau-Ponty can be seen as a form of naturalism since it thinks the human body as inseparable from the world and as rooted in the world of objects that flesh reveals or discloses at a primordial level. This is not to say that the existence or possibility of ideality or abstraction is denied. It is simply to think differently the condition of possibility of ideality by grounding it in the finitude of embodiment and of flesh. "Is my body a thing, or is it an idea?" asks Merleau-Ponty, "It is neither one nor the other, since it is the measurant of all things. We should recognize an ideality which is not alien to flesh, which gives it its axes, its depth, its dimensions" (*VI*, 197; *VaI*, 152). So while the notion of flesh must be situated prior to any distinction between the sensible and the intelligible, it is that which makes the intelligible and thus ideality possible, but is also that which ideality can never entirely abstract itself from or transcend. To this extent Merleau-Ponty would see all abstract projections of knowledge and theoretical thinking as always rooted in the contingency of finite embodied perspective: "Pure ideality is not itself without flesh nor is it delivered from horizonal structures" (*VI*, 198; *VaI*, 153). This is not to say that this implies an extreme, or individualistic relativism, although it may be seen as a relativism of sorts. As a kind of *naturalism*, it also implies that we *share* a world, that since we are inserted into or intertwined with the world and thus with each other, we share a horizon of being, of sense, sight, and touch, so that when one person sees another person they do so in the context of a disclosure of being, of visibility, which is a general and universal attribute of flesh (*VI*, 185; *VaI*, 142).

One might recall at this point Derrida's analysis of touch such as it is figured in the "haptological metaphysics" of the phenomenological tradition he traces in *Le Toucher, Jean-Luc Nancy*. According to Derrida this tradition privileges the notion of touch as a kind of contact which implies a relation of continuity, immediacy, and unity between that which is touched and that which touches; it implies that sensible intuition and intelligible form exist within such a relation of continuity, immediacy, and unity to constitute being as presence, within what amounts ultimately to a metaphysics of presence. The relation of reciprocity and apparent immediacy between the touching and the touched, the seeing and the seen, which the discourse of intertwining, chiasm, and wrapping around articulates would perhaps justify Derrida's assimilation of Merleau-Ponty's fleshy

ontology into this continuist and intuitionist haptological tradition. Yet, as
Derrida himself points out, there is a degree to which Merleau-Ponty's discourse of touch also implies rupture or separation, whereby flesh, although
a site of intertwining or wrapping around of elements which cannot be
thought of as distinct identities, is also a site of discontinuity:

Touch [*toucher*] and to touch oneself [*se toucher*] (self-touch = touching-touched).
These do not coincide in the body: that which touches [*le touchant*] is never exactly that which is touched [*le touché*]. That is not to say that they coincide "in
the mind" or on the level of "conscience." Something else other than the body is
necessary for the conjunction to occur: it occurs in the *untouchable*. (*VI*, 302; *VaI*,
254; cited *T*, 241)

The touch of flesh in Merleau-Ponty is, then, a touch which occurs against
the background of a discontinuity, a discontinuity which is not the separation of distinct identities or properties (mind/spirit) but rather a separation of those heterogeneous and singular elements which are nevertheless
conjoined in the contact of touch. This is a point at which Merleau-Ponty's thought is arguably at its most difficult and obscure. It is also, for Derrida, the point at which his thought is closest to the thinking which is exposed in Nancy's 1992 work *Corpus*. Derrida's ambivalence or skepticism
toward Nancy's philosophical language of touch is situated in this moment
of greatest proximity between the two thinkers, together with the sense
that Nancy in some way still belongs to the Christian tradition of thought
he seeks to interrupt or deconstruct.

Merleau-Ponty's thinking of incarnate sense in *Phénoménologie de la
perception* has been traced to a more ontological thinking of flesh, of intertwining, chiasmus, and touch in *Le Visible et l'invisible*, and finally to a
difficult and obscure notion of touch as a contact within or relation to the
untouchable. This obscure and difficult moment, so important for Derrida's ambivalent reading in *Le Toucher*, now offers a key to understanding
what is at stake in the account of embodiment given in *Corpus* and elsewhere in Nancy's thought.

## Nancy's *Corpus*: Incarnation, Touch, and the Deconstruction of Christianity

In the last chapter it was shown that Nancy's thinking of space develops as a critical rewriting of Heideggerian existential phenomenology, in which existence is seen to unfold as a passage or spatial-temporal opening of sense through which a meaningful, shared world is disclosed. It was also argued that sense in Nancy cannot be thought within the traditional philosophical categories of the sensible and the intelligible, the immanent and the transcendent, but that what nevertheless emerges from this is an ontology which is in some way materialist or bodily. The body, for Nancy, is that site or place which "is the taking place of sense" (*C*, 103), and bodies are that which "first articulate space" (*C*, 27). The body is also that limit point at which sense and matter touch or come into contact, and it is at the limit, at this point of touch or contact, that the opening of a world or the event of being (*Ereignis*) occurs. Just as it is for Merleau-Ponty, so, for Nancy, the body is the "pivot" of the world, and existence cannot be thought outside of, or in abstraction from, bodily finitude. Also when Nancy uses the term *body*, like Merleau-Ponty before him, he is not referring to the body as an object. The body here is not the body as it is constructed within discourse or within a social symbolic order, nor is it simply the material and physiological object of medical science. Like Merleau-Ponty's *flesh*, Nancy's *corpus* exists, or rather discloses existence, in a very specific kind of interrelation between discourse and matter. Bodies, he writes, "*take place neither in discourse nor in matter*. They inhabit neither 'the mind' nor 'the body.' They take place at the limit, *as the limit*: limit—external border, fracture, and intersection of the unfamiliar within the continuity of sense, within the continuity of matter. Opening, *discretion*" (*C*, 18). This thinking of the corporeal as an event at the limit of sense, as an opening or spacing of discrete places, is seen in terms of a rupturing or fracture, or what Nancy will call an "effraction," within two types of continuity, that of sense and that of matter. What makes this thought difficult is that certain key terms, *body, matter, mind,* and even *soul,* are being used in specific and rigorously defined ways which are different from, or other than, the way they might be used in more conventional or everyday contexts. What follows, then, so that the rigor and singularity of Nancy's thinking of embodiment may be understood more clearly, will attempt to trace the ways in which these terms are used outside of their normal contexts.

First, it is worth reiterating the way in which "bodily sense" in this context is being thought against all idealism and against any attempt to confer upon sense an ideal or abstract status. As was shown at the end of the last chapter, sense, for Nancy, is contingent and finite; it is neither transcendent nor immanent; it remains in excess of or irreducible to abstract systems of signification. To this extent Nancy shares the aim of Merleau-Ponty in *Phénoménologie de la perception* and *Le Visible et l'invisible*, but he is far more circumspect about the way he invokes the notion of incarnation. Rather than invoking a vocabulary of "incarnate sense," of intertwining, chiasmus, and reciprocity, to describe the way in which the world is opened up through bodily intentionality, Nancy invokes a vocabulary of rupture and discontinuity. An examination of the following lengthy quotation will give some indication of what is at stake here:

> The *body of sense* is in no way an incarnation of the ideality of "sense": it is, on the contrary, the end of this ideality, and in consequence, the end of sense, in that it ceases to return to *itself* and to relate itself to itself (to the ideality which makes "sense"), and it is suspended *on that limit which gives it its most proper "sense,"* and which exposes it as such. The body of sense *exposes* this "fundamental" suspension of sense (it exposes *existence*)—which one can also call the *effraction* which is sense in the very order of "sense," of "significations," and of "interpretations."
>
> *The body exposes the effraction of sense that existence constitutes, absolutely, and simply.* (*C*, 24; Nancy's emphasis)

Underpinning the notion of an "ideality of sense" is the notion that meaning is self-present or self-identical; that, in articulating itself as meaning, it always returns sense to itself, to that ideal concept or essence which gives or makes possible meaning in the first instance (Husserl's *eidos* for example). What Nancy appears to be moving toward in these motifs of "effraction" and "exposure" is a notion that finite bodily sense makes sense, discloses a world, and thus constitutes existence, not in a return to itself, in a gathering of its own identity and self-identity, but in a movement of dispersal, of dissemination or passage, which articulates an experience of the limit, or rather, articulates experience at the limit, or experience as limit (the limit of sense as it is exposed without return to disclose a world). "Effraction" and "exposure," then, repeat the movement that was discerned in the discussion of spacing and the event of appropriation in the last chapter, that is, the event of being as always a "being-to" of sense, which does not return to itself, but occurs as an infinitely open-ended relational spacing or sharing. It is this sense of an open-ended or centrifugal exposure of sense which determines Nancy's use of the term *suspension*, since in the absence of any return to itself in the ideality of the concept or logical essence, sense occurs always as an interruption or hiatus. Yet, crucially, this interruption or hiatus, this suspension of self-identity and self-presence, means that sense is exposed at its limit in order to open a world. To determine more clearly just what Nancy is attempting to think with this discourse of the limit (which will also be his discourse of *touch* at the limit), a further discussion of Nancy's critical response to the Christian idea of incarnation is needed.

The opening line of *Corpus* begins with the phrase from the consecration of the Eucharist, *Hoc est enim corpus meum*, "This is my body," and this provides a motif around which Nancy's thinking about embodiment will turn throughout this work (*C*, 7). We belong, Nancy reminds his reader, to a culture which pronounces this phrase ceaselessly, over and over again in millions upon millions of acts of worship, and it is a phrase which, Christian or not, we will all recognize: "It is our *Om mani padne . . .*, our *Allah ill'allah . . .*, our *Schema Israël . . .* " (*C*, 7). Yet Nancy discerns in this phrase an element which marks the difference of Christian culture from the other traditions he invokes: an obsession with naming something, of making something present, here and now, which is nevertheless a something which cannot be seen or touched here or elsewhere (God, the absolute) (*C*, 7–8). It is this making present of something necessarily absent, this incarnation of that which is without body or substance, which, according to Nancy, articulates a fundamental paradigm of Christian culture and thought in either theological or secular guise. This paradigm at once offers a degree of reassurance; it tells us that the world of appearances is fully present before us, here and now, and it thus confers upon appearance a measure of solidity in a self-present unity of the sensible and the intelligible, the corporeal and the ideal. And yet, Nancy contends, such reassurance is underpinned by a certain anguish, a fear that the world of appearance is a world of insubstantial shadows and reflections, something like Plato's Cave, where what appears is only a copy of a distant and higher truth, but a truth which perhaps has no real existence and certainly cannot be made present here and now. In this philosophico-paradigmatic reading of the Eucharist, *Hoc est enim corpus meum* is the site of a fundamental ambivalence in Christian culture, whereby the desire to see, touch, eat, and thus to participate in or in a certain sense *be* the body of Christ, is predicated on the anguish inspired by the Holy Body's invisibility, intangibility, and absence. What is taken as a rendering present in the "here" of spirit and of the absolute, in fact emerges as something like a presence which is at the same time an absence, a proximity which implies distance, a touch which implies an infinite separation. Whatever the merits of Nancy's interpretation here in terms of the wider historical and theological truth of the Eucharist and its place within the diverse traditions of Christian culture, it is arguable that the real significance of such an interpretation lies in a primarily philosophical attempt to resituate the inner logic of incarnation which lies at the heart of the biblical narrative of the New Testament. The body of Christ is spirit made flesh, sacrificed on the cross, and this incarnation and sacrifice is repeated in the act of worship that constitutes the Christian Mass. Incarnation, according to Nancy's reading, is not so much a moment of fusion, presence, or the participation of body and spirit, which is then subsequently represented and repeated in the Mass; it is a contact and a separation, a touching of the intangible. In short Nancy's reading of the phrase *Hoc est enim corpus meum* at the beginning of *Corpus* needs to be viewed in terms of his wider concern with the deconstruction of Christianity.

This is an implicit concern throughout *Corpus* but it is more explicitly engaged with as such in a later article published in *Études Philosophiques* in 1998, entitled "La Déconstruction du christianisme."[13] It has been clear from the beginning of this study that Nancy's thought gains its initial impetus and direction from the sense, shared by many in the French philosophical community in the late 1960s and the 1970s, that the tradition of European thought, characterized as an essentially metaphysical tradition, has arrived at a certain closure of the metaphysical. Clearly this relies on specific characterizations of the tradition: Nietzsche's genealogy of Christian-Platonic thought, Heidegger's conception of metaphysics as the history of onto-theology, Derrida's "logocentrism," and so on. In his 1998 article Nancy pushes this further and asks more straightforwardly whether in all this it is not simply the Christian which needs to be thought as the paradigm par excellence that has informed the history of western European philosophy over the last two millennia. Endorsing but slightly shifting the parameters suggested by Derrida in *L'Écriture et la différence*, Nancy asks "whether the 'Jewish-Greek' of which Derrida speaks at the end of 'Violence and Metaphysics' . . . is not simply the Christian."[14] In this context Nancy's working through of Christian and Christological motifs in a number of works in recent years should be seen, not necessarily as the expression of some kind of deep-seated sympathy or attachment, but rather in the context of a wider philosophical claim that the history of Christianity defines the limits and also the structure of our thinking.[15] Whether it be explicitly theological, secular, or atheistic (and even, perhaps, scientific), unless we invoke a specifically Judaic heritage (as do Levinas and Derrida for instance), these limits circumscribe the space and indeed the task of philosophical thought at the turn of the millennium.[16] As Nancy puts it, "the Christian or Christianity, is *the very thing* which is to be thought," and, in a parody of a phrase by the Italian philosopher Luigi Pareysson: "'Atheism can only be contemporary/real [*actuel*] if it contemplates the reality of its Christian provenance'."[17]

This coming to terms with, or contemplation of, the Christian inheritance of thought is not viewed by Nancy in terms of attacking or defending that inheritance, or in terms of trying to get rid of or save it. Rather he suggests that Christianity as such is, and has been, in a state of self-overcoming, a self-overcoming which belongs to its own deep structure and inner logic of development.[18] In this sense the increasing secularization or de-Christianization of culture which has occurred ostensibly since the Enlightenment, the privileging of rational and cognitive faculties, or the increasing suspicion toward, or critique of, abstract and metaphysical categories, can be seen as part of this self-overcoming of the Western tradition. Likewise the untying of teleology, eschatology, or the affirmation of an "end" of history, ideology, metaphysics, or philosophy would also, for Nancy, belong to this process of self-overcoming and cannot be thought in abstraction from Christian notions of providence and the existence of Christian eschatology seen as an essential underpinning of the culture and historical community that is the West. This is the underlying assumption of Nancy's deconstruction of Christianity, and it relies on the identification of a specific set of contingent meanings and a structure of sense which govern that tradition and determine the subsequent possibilities of sense or meaning to which that tradition then gives rise. Central to this structure, Nancy contends, is the thought of incarnation:

We know well that the heart of Christian theology is evidently constituted by Christology, that the heart of Christology is the doctrine of incarnation, and that the heart of the doctrine of incarnation is the doctrine of *homousia*, of the consubstantiality and identity or community of substance between the Father and the Son. This is what, within Christianity, is entirely new.[19]

The relationship between spirit and matter, soul and body, the intelligible and the sensible, finds in the Christological notion of incarnation an expression which is unprecedented in preceding traditions, for instance, within Hellenic philosophy or Judaic messianism. This, then, is what needs to be thought and rethought in the deconstruction of Christianity, not, as is often said, a dualistic separation of spirit and body and the privileging of one over the other in a hierarchical relation, but the manner in which this separation is in fact conceived as a fusion, a "consubstantiality" or "community of substance." One can begin to discern perhaps the extent to which Merleau-Ponty's existential phenomenology resonates with this Christological thinking despite its seemingly secular nature and its emphasis on contingency and finitude. The account Nancy gives of embodiment as the site of spacing, of worldly disclosure, and of the opening of sense is close to that given by Merleau-Ponty but divergent insofar as its latent or unthought Christological content is addressed as such in the reading given of the Eucharist at the beginning of *Corpus*.

Nancy's attempt to think and rethink the notion of fusion, consubstantiality, and identity of spirit and matter that lies at the heart of the Christian thought of incarnation perhaps finds its most accessible expression in two recent texts: "The Extension of the Soul" (2002) and *Noli me tangere* (2003).[20] The first is a reading of the way Descartes attempts to conceive the union of the body with the soul. In this text Nancy begins by citing a letter of Descartes, written in 1643, in which Descartes discusses the union of the soul and the body and invites his patron to consider that the difficulty of thinking this union lies in the fact that one must "conceive of them as a single thing, and together conceive of them as two, which is self-contradictory."[21] Nancy shows that, for Descartes, the only way to think this paradoxical union is to recognize that it is not just the body that is extended but the soul also, or as he sums up the Cartesian reasoning of the letter to his patron:

The body knows itself insofar as it is soul, or insofar as it is intimately united with it. But the soul knows itself in this way as extended, not across the body but according to the extension of the body. It is necessary to recognize an extension of the soul which is mixed with every extension of the body without sharing with it the character of impenetrability and the exclusion of extended places.[22]

Nancy offers a reading of Descartes in which body and soul are united, not as something contained within a container, and not as a pilot would be in his ship, but rather as an extension of that which would normally be thought to be without extension (soul/*res cogitans*), through which the body as the extended (body/matter) is known in its union with the unextended. Here soul emerges as a faculty of awareness or knowledge of extension and is thus extended throughout the body that knows or is aware. On the one hand the body emerges as the extension of matter, as that which is known in the extension of the soul, but which, as matter, is also in some sense *impenetrable*. On the other hand Descartes also provides the means by which Nancy can describe the body, not as object, but as that which experiences spatial relation, sensation, sight, touch, pleasure, pain, and so on. He is using the Cartesian words *body* and *soul* as another way of articulating his own thinking of "sense" and its relation to embodiment. In the body which feels, walks, sleeps, and eats, sense or soul is extended, the awareness of and meaningfulness conferred upon sensation is itself sense or soul, and it is in the extension of the sensible or animate body that the union of body and soul occurs. The two touch or are in contact with each other, or, as Nancy puts it:

The soul can be touched by the body, and the body by the soul. From the one to the other, there is touch: contact which communicates while leaving intact each of the two *res* [*res extensa* and *res cogitans*]. Touch, for Descartes, always touches the impenetrable. . . . At that point where they touch spirit and body are impenetrable each to the other and by that united. Touch brings into contact two intacts.[23]

This may well be a plausible reading of Descartes, but it is far more a pretext for Nancy to expose or elaborate his own thinking of touch and of the limit. It also highlights the difference between Nancy's thought and Merleau-Ponty's conception of incarnate sense in *Phénoménologie de la perception*. In this latter work it was shown that, for Merleau-Ponty, the incarnate sense of embodied existence "invests and deeply penetrates matter" (*PP*, 374; *PoP*, 324). Here matter is the impenetrable, that which, in its extension, is always outside or exterior to the world of phenomenal appearance. Yet through the touch or contact in which the two forms of extension, that of sense and that of matter, are exposed to each other, the world of phenomenal appearance is disclosed and the spatial-temporal event of being occurs. This touch or contact is the sensible animate body itself, it is the body which makes sense at the limit of sense, in the contact/separation of sense and the non-sense of impenetrable matter. The world, existence, what Nancy after Heidegger called "ek-sistence," is the body as extension of the soul (sense) and the touching of that sense across the extension of the untouchable (body/matter); in Nancy's own words: "The body is the extension of the soul to the extremities of the world and to the confines of the self, each intricated [*intriqué*] with the other and indistinctly distinct, extended, stretched [*étendue tendue*] to the point of rupture."[24] Where Merleau-Ponty talked in *Le Visible et l'invisible* of the intertwining and wrapping round of the seer and the seen, the touching and the touched, Nancy's intrication is a touch in distance, a contact in separation of sense and matter, which exposes the world not in the making present of a substance, or consubstantiality of spirit and body, but in a sundering/conjoining of the two. This is a reiteration of the idea that the spatial-temporal event of being, as the extension or exposure of sense to impenetrable matter, does not permit the world to be seen in terms of substances, or of the presence and self-presence of things, rather it must always be seen in terms of this separation and distancing of sense, which is also an event of touch, spacing, sharing, position, and disposition.

Nancy's reading of Descartes exposes what is at stake in his "deconstruction" of the Christian thought of incarnation, albeit not in Christological terms. In the second work referred to above, *Noli me tangere*, this Christological dimension is much more explicitly addressed as such. Published by the Christian press Bayard, *Noli me tangere* is a short meditation on the scene from the Gospel of St. John, where Christ, resurrected, appears before Mary Magdalene outside his empty tomb, and Mary, at first believing Jesus to be a gardener, then tries to touch him, to which he replies, "Don't touch me." Nancy, also an experienced and arguably highly accomplished writer on the visual and plastic arts, gives commentaries on the wealth of paintings by the European masters which have sought to interpret this scene, among others: Rembrandt, Dürer, Titian, Coreggio. In the context of this discussion though, what is interesting is the way this meditation on a biblical parable and its artistic afterlife articulates the singularity of Nancy's thinking of touch and of a deconstructed Christology. The interdiction placed on touch in the scene outside Christ's empty tomb, the *Noli me tangere* with which Christ addresses Mary Magdalene, might suggest that the sacred in Christianity, the Holy Flesh and Divine Presence, is surrounded by a taboo in relation to touch, that this is a religion of the *untouchable*, of the separation between the fallen body of Adam and the Glorious Body of Christ. Yet, Nancy contends, this is not so, for, as soon as the Body of God is given to be eaten and drunk in the Holy Communion nothing is untouchable. Indeed the Communion, as both a representation of, and a participation in, the self-sacrifice of the Holy Body, makes of Christianity a religion of touch and of contact: "Christianity will have been the invention of the religion of touch, of the sensible, of the immediate presence to the body and to the heart" (*NMT*, 27). This is a repetition of Nancy's interpretation of the Eucharist at the beginning of *Corpus*, the notion that, in its essence, Christianity is a religion of consubstantiality of body and spirit, and of the Real Presence of the Word. Yet what emerges from his meditation on the Resurrection, and on the interdiction on touch given in the *Noli me tangere*, is something rather different.

Nancy dwells a while on the uncertain status of the resurrected body of Christ. It is not, he suggests, a regenerated body, nor is it reanimated, nor is it the subject of a palingenesis, a rebirth, a revivification or reincarnation. It is a body, dead but alive, departed yet remaining, the same yet different. In this sense the resurrected body of Christ can be seen as an infinite prolongation of death within life which disrupts, displaces, or desituates the very opposition of life and death, and with that values of presence and absence, animate and inanimate, body and soul (death normally being the separation of the two). Within this moment of uncertain identity and infinite prolongation two bodies can be distinguished in their belonging together: the Glorious Body (the body of the Ascension) and the body of mortal flesh: "the one is the raising [*la levée*] of the other, the other is the death of the one" (*NMT*, 77). The body of the Resurrection becomes a figure in Nancy's reading for a moment in which the principle of identity or sameness is interrupted or subject to hiatus. This moment describes the structure of touch and separation articulated in the interdiction of *Noli me tangere*, and describes also a relation between body and spirit which is other than the relation of consubstantiality designated in the eucharistic *Hoc est enim corpus meum*. According to Nancy the resurrected body of Christ:

> refuses a contact which it could lend itself to. As resuscitated, its being and its truth are in this refusal, in this withdrawal which alone gives the measure of the touch which must be in question: not touching this body, in order to touch its eternity. Not coming into contact with its manifest presence, in order to accede to its real presence, which consists in its departure. (*NMT*, 28)

So for Nancy it is not the separation of body and spirit that may have led, within the Christian tradition, to a denigration of the former in favor of the latter, nor is it their fusion in the incarnation of spirit within the body, which, in sanctifying human flesh, may have led to a rejection of the body's baser nature. The very possibility of fallen flesh on the one hand and glorious flesh on the other is inscribed in this indeterminate status of the resurrected body, divided from itself and indistinctly prolonging its fallen mortality in its glorious eternity. It is only on the basis of this double possibility, Nancy suggests, that anything like Christian sexual morality can emerge. If we were entirely fallen bodies there would be no spirit within us to sanctify, if we were entirely spiritual there would be no mortal fleshy desires to satisfy, and only in the touch *and* separation of the two does question of sexual ambivalence or indeed repression arise. Once again Nancy's exegesis provides the means for articulating his own philosophical concerns. Here spirit and body exist within a touch which never occurs as touch but only ever as a touch in the refusal of touch. As with the use of the term *soul* in the article on Descartes, the term *spirit* is once being used as an equivalent of "sense," and the very specific usage Nancy makes of it in his thinking of spatiality and of world-hood.

One can begin to see the extent to which Nancy's "deconstruction of Christianity" is a means by which he thinks a philosophical relation between sense and body and by which his thought addresses the philosophical tradition from which it derives. His rethinking of Christian incarnation, not as consubstantiality or *houmousia*, but as a touch in separation of spirit and matter (where spirit is in fact finite sense, neither transcendent nor immanent), shows the extent to which he diverges from the latent Christological dimension of Merleau-Ponty's phenomenology. In *Le Toucher* Derrida noted that Merleau-Ponty's touch was also a touching within the untouchable and saw in this the point of closest proximity with the Nancean thinking of touch. In many ways *Noli me tangere* is a reply to Derrida's questioning of Nancy's "Christianity" in *Le Toucher*. The moment of indeterminacy figured by the resurrected body of Christ in *Noli me tangere* may appear to some much more like a Derridean moment of undecidability than a Merleau-Pontean instance of intertwining or chiasmus. Nancy, by way of his interpretation, is aiming to elaborate a more radical interruption of touch, which, he would contend, has always been at stake in his thinking of the corporeal, whatever its similarities to the thought of Merleau-Ponty: "Sense will never have been touched, there is the truth" (*NMT*, 76). To this extent Nancy is giving in this work the fullest account yet of what he understands by "deconstruction of Christianity," responding to what he calls the "rabbinical skepticism" of Derrida's commentary (*NMT*, 25–26, note 4).

These more recent texts on Descartes and on Christianity shed important light on the sometimes difficult and perhaps rather oblique formulations of the earlier *Corpus*. In particular they underscore the fact the Christian dimension of this earlier work should not be taken as a straightforward assertion of an, albeit idiosyncratic, adherence on the part of Nancy to Christianity. What one finds in *Corpus* is the mixing of a theological/Christological and philosophical registers, in which the one extends, elaborates, and/or dismantles the terms of the other. Through this Nancy exposes the singularity of his thinking of the body and at the same time acknowledges a Christian legacy which is taken apart, reassembled, and thus rethought in different terms. This can be seen in the definition given of the term *spirit*: "Spirit is the replacing, the sublimation, the subtlization of bodies in all their forms—of their extension, of their material sharing, in the distilled and revealed essence of the sense of the body: the spirit *is* the body of sense, or sense in the body" (*C*, 67). The Christian notion of spirit, as a kind of transcendence of the body, is rooted, Nancy suggests, in the body of sense, and is possible to think of as spirit only insofar as the material body of sense, neither transcendent nor immanent, a contact in separation of finite sense and impenetrable matter, is abstracted and sublimated into an idealized identity.[25] Yet however much thought abstracts, spiritualizes, or idealizes itself, it is always and only ever possible, and indeed only ever *is*, as finite embodied sense, sense which touches yet leaves intact the untouchable matter with which it is joined in the very moment of separation and distance. What Nancy is moving toward here is a thinking which, in unpicking the heart of Christianity (the Eucharist, incarnation, the consubstantiality of body and spirit), is at the same time exposing Christianity's ontological or existential ground, a ground which is not an identity or substance, and ultimately is no ground at all, but is rather a surging or opening of a world in the exposure of finite embodied sense. This is a thought in which God is neither present nor absent, where the body is not the Body of Christ, of incarnation, or the Real Presence of the Word made flesh, but is a body through which all that appears is the world itself, in its sites, spaces, and places, or in Nancy's words, "no God, not even gods, only *places*. Places: they are divine *because divested* of the Body of God. . . . Divine in the opening where all the 'divine' collapses and withdraws, leaving naked the world of bodies. Places of denuding, places of *limon terrae*" (*C*, 55). In collapsing the transcendent, the spiritual, or the ideal into the touch in separation of finite sense and impenetrable matter, Nancy is elaborating an atheism, but an atheism which "contemplates the reality of its Christian provenance." He is also elaborating a materialism, a thinking of *limon terrae*, or of the concrete, but one which, in the figure of touch, thinks outside of the material/ideal dichotomy that has informed traditional materialism. In *Corpus* this singular materialist atheism gives rise to a twofold thinking: of the body in relation to writing and the limit of sense, and the body in relation technical apparatus or what Nancy calls the "ecotechnics" of the body. Nancy's deconstruction of Christianity and of the Christian body engages in an attempt to think at the limit of the cultural tradition that, he claims, has hitherto determined our modes of thinking. Here there is no restitution, preservation, or "saving" of a Christian tradition, but, rather, the responsibility of thinking its limit at its limit: "there remains for us neither worship nor prayer, but the strict and severe, the sober yet also joyous exercise of what is called thinking."[26] This strict and severe exercise of thinking has as its outcome a specific practice of writing and an articulation of the "ecotechnics" of embodied existence.

## The Structure of Parts Outside Parts, Ecotechnics, and Writing

What seems to interest Nancy in this thinking of the body or of bodies as the opening or spacing of the world is the notion of creation or beginning. His rewriting of fundamental ontology is less interested in positing a fixed origin or a projected finality within being, but rather aims to think the event of surging into appearance or of world-disclosure as a creation in the absence of any substantive ground or specific goal: "Here is the world of worldly departure [*départ mondial*]: the spacing of *partes extra partes*, without anything overarching or supporting it, without a Subject of its destiny, taking place solely as a prodigious *press* of bodies" (*C*, 37). The notion of *partes extra partes*, of "parts outside parts," is central to this fractured thinking of body and sense, where the event of spacing occurs in a contact-separation or effraction of each term with the other, an exposure of each term to the other. *Partes extra partes* is a phrase invoked by Merleau-Ponty in *Phénoménologie de la perception*, where it is described in the following terms: "*partes extra partes*," that is, an object that "admits between its parts or between itself and other objects only exterior or mechanical relations, either in the narrow sense of a movement received and transmitted, or in the broader sense of a variable relation of function" (*PP*, 87; *PoP*, 73). The structure of "parts outside parts" describes the way in which material bodies exist in a relation of exteriority each to the other, and the way in which the components or constitutive parts of material bodies likewise exist outside of each other, never occupying the same place, and are thus able to articulate themselves as bodies and come into relation or contact with other bodies. In this sense, for Nancy, matter or materiality is always an outside or an impenetrable element, since we know that objects are touched, seen, sensed and given sense only from the outside and from this relation of exteriority, of objects touching each other in a mutual distance or separation (if we open them up, dissect, X-ray, scan, or hugely magnify them we are simply creating another exterior surface or relation of contact-separation of sense). The structure of "parts outside parts" is central to Nancy's thinking of the spacing of sense and of the effraction of sense and matter that is the "taking place" of bodies and the creation of a shared world.

Where Merleau-Ponty views this structure in terms of the "exterior mechanical" relations admitted between objects, Nancy invokes the Greek term *tekhnē* (art, craft, or technical labor). The sharing of embodied sense which gives us a world takes place in Nancy as an "originary technicity," that is, as a technical-mechanical relation (of sense) between material bodies, or *partes extra partes*, and as a means of disclosing material bodies in the contact-separation of sense and matter. The following lengthy quotation gives a clearer indication of what is at stake here:

"Creation" is the *techné* of bodies. Our world creates the great number of bodies, it is created as a world of bodies. . . . Our world is the world of the "technical," the world whose cosmos, nature, gods, whose system, complete in its intimate jointure, are exposed as "technical": the world of an *ecotechnics*. Ecotechnics functions with technical apparatus, with which it connects us in all directions. But what it *makes* is our bodies, which it puts into the world and connects to its system, our bodies, which in this way it creates as more visible, more proliferating, more polymorphous, more pressed together, more in "masses" and "zones" than they have ever been. (*C*, 78)

Nancy is not suggesting that technology or technological capacity is in any way an essential attribute of the human or something which would define the ends of the human. The "ecotechnical" creation of the world is, like the notion of "ek-sistence" discussed in the preceding chapter, something which would overturn any possibility of essence within existence. It is worth recalling at this stage the relation of Nancy's use in French of the term *sens* and Heidegger's use of the terms *Bedeutsamkeit, Sinn*, and *Bedeutung* in *Being and Time*. Heidegger's account of world-hood as a context of involvement and of meaningful assignments and references (*Bedeutsamkeit*) relied heavily upon the notion of "circumspection" (*Umsicht*), that is, the way in which objects are disclosed as meaningful because we encounter them with a view to something, a "for-the-sake-of-which," an "in-order-to" or a "with-which." This in turn gives sense to Heidegger's use of the term *Zuhandensein*, or "being-ready-to-hand," to designate the way in which we encounter things, in the first instance, not simply as present objects (*vorhanden*, or "present-at-hand"), but rather as things which serve a human purpose in some way, as instrumental or useful (thus Heidegger's famous analysis in *Being and Time* of equipment by way of a hammer as an example [*BT*, 96–98; *GA*, 2:68–69]).

The term *ecotechnics* such as it is used in *Corpus* articulates a radicalization of, and a deviation from, Heidegger's understanding of *Zuhandensein*. Where for Heidegger objects appear as ready-to-hand within a context of sense or meaning which confers upon them an instrumental or purposive quality, for Nancy, it is the body of sense itself, the body as the spacing or sharing of sense, which emerges as the site, or locus of interconnection, of tools or apparatus, and it is this interconnection which *is* the happening of the body and the spacing and sharing of sense. This does not make of the body a technical object, rather it shows an originary relation of technicity at work in the coming into appearance of bodies or in the way we disclose a world: "Attaching and connecting bodies in every way, placing them at points of intersection, of interference, and the interaction of all technical procedures, far from making of them 'technical objects' . . . ecotechnics presents them *as* bodies" (*C*, 79; emphasis added). What Nancy is trying to think here is the manner in which the relation of bodily intentionality or sense to technical apparatus profoundly shapes the way the world appears to us as meaningful. In this sense when I drive a car, speak into a mobile phone, or type into a laptop computer I am not just "using" technical apparatus; I am connected or "plugged into" them in a way which more fundamentally reveals a certain manner of being or existence and a certain experience or constitution of world-hood.[27] In trying to show that there is something technical or apparatus-related in the way in which embodied sense reveals a spatial-temporal world, Nancy is not offering an apology for, or promotion of, technology and contemporary technological and technocratic procedures. More interestingly, the affirmation of an originary technicity indicates that technology is never an end, never a subject of human progress or a finality within human history. As originary disclosure or creation of world-hood, rather, it is without end or finality: "Ecotechnics . . . substitutes projections of linear history and of final *goals* with local differences and multiple bifurcations. Ecotechnics deconstructs the system of ends, it renders them nonsystematizable and nonorganic" (*C*, 78). To this extent the thought of ecotechnics is a challenge to or contestation of any ideology which would invoke the technological progress of scientific discovery as an essential property or goal of humankind. Likewise, as a multiple sharing, connection, and interconnection of bodies and apparatus, ecotechnics does not function as a ground or foundation. Indeed it is precisely because the opening or disclosure of the world occurs as the sharing of embodied sense in and through the transversal interconnections of technical apparatus that no ground is possible; what is possible is simply the event and passage of sense as the ecotechnical creation of the world: "It is to the absence of foundation, that is to say to 'creation,' that the world of bodies owes its *technē* and its existence, or better, *its existence as technē*" (*C*, 89). Ecotechnics aims to describe a certain manner of creation, not on the basis of a foundation or origin but rather on the basis of the connection and interconnection of sense, material bodies, and apparatus, and to this extent it reiterates the thinking of foundation discussed at the end of the last chapter.

As well as offering rich potential for addressing contemporary debates around technology, particularly in the biosciences and their commercialization, Nancy's thinking of *technē* marks a decisive break from the phenomenologies of existence that have been shown to influence his philosophy of sense. The preceding discussions of Husserl, Heidegger, and Merleau-Ponty have emphasized the way in which each philosopher attempts to locate phenomenological or existential-phenomenological inquiry in a pretheoretical and prescientific dimension of experience conceived variously as the reduced sphere of logical essences, the situated facticity of Dasein, or the bodily intentionality of primary perception. In all cases scientific knowledge is placed in a secondary and derived position in relation to this more fundamental plane of phenomenological disclosure or revealing. The outcome of this approach is mixed. In Merleau-Ponty's *Phénoménologie de la perception* it gives rise to an important and still relevant critique of classical and experimental psychology and of the way in which cognitive functions are privileged at the expense of more fundamental or precognitive possibilities of bodily relation to the world. In Heidegger it gives rise to the critique of technology and technological revealing that dominates much of his thinking from the 1930s onward, leading him to invoke a more originary encounter with being (or *Beyng/Seyn*) expressed in quasi-mystical or religious language (divinity, gods, godding), and which, far more problematically, underpins his infamous comment implying that factory farming and Nazi extermination camps are indistinguishable in their inner logic.[28] Nancy's thinking of ecotechnics cuts across or exceeds the opposition posed by Husserl, Heidegger, and Merleau-Ponty between primordial phenomenological world disclosure and the sphere of scientific or technological knowledge. As technical apparatus, a family hearth, peasant's shoes, or paintbrush, a mobile phone, mass spectrometer, or electron microscope would all be connected to bodies and would all articulate a fundamental bodily intentionality or orientation of sense through which the world can be encountered as meaningful in the first instance (through which the world is "created"). In this sense the edifice of scientific knowledge, its experimental dimension, its mathematizing and objectifying revealing of the world, is no more or less dependent on an originary technicity or a relation to apparatus than is the edifice of artistic or cultural achievement in all its plurality and diversity. It is arguable that Nancy's notion of ecotechnics offers great potential for thinking across the boundaries which separate the sciences from the human sciences or arts, insofar as his reworking of fundamental ontology uncovers the shared origin of all these spheres in a bodily-technical event of sense and world.[29]

To a certain extent, when Nancy talks about an originary technicity, he is describing what much French thought since the late 1960s has called "writing." Derrida's use of the term *archi-écriture* (archi-writing), for instance, does not describe words on the page, but rather that generalized web of marks or inscriptions, which, as differing/deferring temporal-spatial traces of sense, in excess of ontological disclosure, open up or make possible time and space as we know it (this, of course, is Derrida's own rewriting of Husserl and Heidegger). Archi-writing is also governed by a logic of supplementarity whereby an originary absence of ground or transcendental signifier propels the very movement of signification and production of meaning within the temporal-spatial opening of experience. In this sense the term *writing*, such as it is used in Derrida, suggests that experience occurs not on the basis of an originary intertwining of *phusis* and *logos*, that is, the distinct identities of nature and concept, but rather on the basis of *technē*, an originary artifice or supplementarity, which would be the inscription/effacement of the signifying traces of archi-writing, and which would rupture all possibility of identity and self-presence (and, indeed, all possibility of any stable or originary opposition between nature and concept). The interest and originality of Nancy's thinking of sense, body, and ecotechnics is that it allows this thinking of "writing" as originary technicity to be thought in terms of concrete embodiment, a situated and worldly existence, where *technē* is not the iteration of signifying traces, but the touch in distance of sense and matter, of sense shared between or exposed to the *partes extra partes* of material bodies, and their interconnection or co-articulation through technical apparatus. As a quasi-transcendental condition of possibility(/impossibility) of meaningful experience, irreducible to ontological disclosure, Derrida's archi-writing and *différance* maintain, one could argue, a certain degree of Husserlian abstraction, and leave Derrida to trace the effects of contingency and finitude on discursive formations of meaning and concept, perhaps leaving him few words to address the situated and contingent existence of bodily finitude as such. Ever suspicious of words, the argument of *Le Toucher, Jean-Luc Nancy* shows Derrida's ambivalence toward Nancy's thinking of body, touch, and tact or contact, what Derrida calls Nancy's "*quasi*-hyper-transcendental-ontologization of tact" (*T*, 328). As was indicated earlier, Derrida's concern or ambivalence would be that, in talking about "touch," tact, or contact, Nancy, despite himself, risks returning thought to a continuist intuitionism and a metaphysics of presence (his "hyper-Christianity").

By contrasting Nancy's thinking of the body and of touch with Merleau-Ponty's phenomenology and with the later ontology of flesh, and by tracing the path Nancy takes through the "deconstruction" of Christianity to an elaboration of the ecotechnical creation of the world, this discussion has tried to suggest that what is at stake is a thinking, not of continuity or immediacy, but rather of separation, dislocation, or what Nancy calls "effraction." He does talk in terms of touch, contact, and materiality or the concrete. But the spatial-temporal passage, sharing, or event of bodily sense in Nancy occurs only against the backdrop of a primary fragmentation and separation of sense and matter, of parts outside parts, of a centrifugal exposure of sense without return to itself, without identity or self-presence. Unlike Derrida, Nancy is a philosopher who is happy to deploy the language of ontology or of being without invoking its erasure. Unlike Derrida, one could argue, he is happy to be a philosopher of existence, of the material and the concrete. Yet as the elaborate formulation "quasi-hyper-transcendental-ontologization" suggests, Nancy's ontology or philosophy of existence does not entail any straightforward privileging of a philosophical language which would be able to speak, represent, or appropriate the event of being. Where for Derrida the word ~~being~~ is placed under erasure, for Nancy being or existence is "exscribed." In these notions of being exscribed and of "exscription" a certain economy of writing, and of writing in relation to the body and the "archi-writing" of bodily sense, is described. If the Nancean thinking of touch and the body gives us a realism, one which is irreducible to any traditional form of realism or logic of representation, it does so only in the movement of exscription that writing enacts. It should be recalled that sense, for Nancy, is in excess of any relation of signifier to signified; it is extralinguistic yet finite and embodied, but as such exists, or makes exist, only in the separation-touch of sense and impenetrable matter (conceived of as exteriority). The body, then, is that site of touch that makes sense but that, as materiality, is at the same time outside of all sense. Likewise, sense, as bodily existence, is that in the context of which signification and language can occur, but that, as a singular bodily event, is outside or on the other side of the outer limit of language or signification. Exscription then describes the relation of exteriority, or separation which is maintained between impenetrable matter and bodily sense, and between bodily sense and linguistic signification. Nancy puts this in the following terms: "It is no doubt *because* of the body that *one writes*, but the body is absolutely not *where* one writes, and the body is not *what* one writes—but always what writing *exscribes*" (*C,* 76).

Writing here is not representation or mimesis, it does not assume the existence of a world of self-present and discrete identities or objects, which, being outside of language in their identity with themselves, can then be re-presented within the frame of linguistic signification. Writing does not copy or give an image of a ready-made world; rather, at its limit, or as passage to the limit, writing touches the real, the event of bodily sense, existence. The importance and meaning of the epigraph with which this discussion began can now be considered:

To write: to touch extremity. How then to touch at the body, instead of signifying it or making it signify? . . . to touch at the body, to touch the body, *touch* finally— happens all the time in writing . . . on the border, on the limit, at a point, at the extremity of writing, *that and nothing else happens.* Writing has its place on the limit. Nothing happens to writing, if something does happen to it, other than *touching.* More precisely: a touching of the body (or rather this or that singular body) *with the incorporeal* of "sense." And in consequence, a making of the incorporeal into that which touches, or a making of sense into a touch . . . writing touches bodies *according to the absolute limit* which separates the sense of one from the skin and nerves of the other. (*C*, 12–13; Nancy's emphasis)

Touch here needs to be understood in the terms which have been outlined throughout this discussion, that is, not as continuity and immediacy but rather as rupture, dislocation, or effraction of terms which touch only in their absolute separation. In this light, this lengthy quotation shows that Nancy's ontology, whenever it talks of sense, body, touch, being, or existence, always exscribes outside of language what it at the same time inscribes with language. Put another way, exscription is the point where writing situates itself outside of the sense it inscribes in and as writing. Nancy's "bodily ontology" then never gathers being up into the word or logos, but always points to it as the *excess* of signification, of any relation of signifier to signified. Bodily ontology is always an exscription of being. Yet, at the limit of signification there is a touch-separation of language and sense, just as there is a touch-separation of the incorporeal of sense with the corporeality of impenetrable matter. The realism here can be located in this logic of the limit, where body, sense, and signification touch at their limit in the event of existence itself as a temporal-spatial sharing of a meaningful world. Thus when I write, when I write here and now, there is a touch of fingers on a keyboard, but there also is the event of a singular existence which occurs as a touch and thus as a sharing of sense in the disposition of bodies, animate and inanimate, each outside the other, *partes extra partes*. As I write there is the literal and material touch of keys and in this also the touch of a lived existence which makes sense, itself touched in writing.

Writing in Nancy is not just what occurs in philosophy when it tries to think outside of representation, at the limit of the Christian tradition and at that limit of sense which the tradition proposes (i.e., of finite sense as limit). Touch "happens all the time in writing." What is being thought here is not representation in the classical sense (as mimesis), but may be viewed in terms of a rethinking of reference, and of the referential function of writing, conceived of as a relation to the limit of signification or as signification at its limit. Nancy's "realism" may allow us to think of the way writing "refers," not to clear and distinct signifiers or fixed moments of meaning (language as representation does this all the time), but rather to existence in its most refractory and obscure moment of becoming or creation. This, it will become clear in the final chapter, is what, for Nancy, occurs in art and in the artwork, be it narrative, poetic, or visual/plastic art. What emerges more generally from this notion of writing as the ex-scription of embodied existence is the sense that Nancy has found a philo-sophical vocabulary and discursive strategy with which he can address the world. He is not content to stay with the, albeit important, task of ques-tioning, critiquing, or deconstructing discourse or signifying structures. He addresses the world as finite and contingent, fragmentary, thoroughly resistant to any totalization within a system of goals or ideological forms. Yet he addresses the world as world, as a world of material bodies which take place in a shared becoming of sense and a shared finitude.

# CHAPTER FOUR

# Community

Prior to or in retreat from the "political" there was this, that there is the "common," the "together," and the "numerous," and that we perhaps do not at all know how to think this order of the real.

—JEAN-LUC NANCY, *La Communauté affrontée*[1]

## Introduction

What is, or should be, the relation between philosophy and politics? How ought one to address the inevitable interconnectedness of thinking and the world of political struggle and decision, where empirical realities of state power, public policy, economy, and wealth distribution are paramount? This question dominates Nancy's thought from its very beginning up to the present. An important relation of the philosophical to the political is implicit, for instance, in his early involvement with the Christian Socialist movement (and in particular with the review *Esprit* and the Confédération française démocratique du travail), but it also informs his most recent writing around questions of war, state sovereignty, technology, and globalization. Yet despite the importance of this question for Nancy, his thinking also refuses any straightforward movement between the order of philosophical reflection on the one hand and that of politics on the other. He refuses the notion that philosophy should lay theoretical grounds for a project or program which would then be conceived as the concrete effectuation, or completion of, the philosophical within the realm of the political. The expectation of such a movement from philosophical reflection to political project articulates, according to Nancy, the very essence of the metaphysical attitude within philosophy, and is deeply implicated in the recent history of European totalitarianism and the destructive, genocidal energies which that history unleashed. This is not to say, though, that thinking for Nancy is entirely divorced or removed from the political and ethical demands made upon us by the contemporary and possible future worlds.

Nancy's thought appears to be responding to two contradictory impulses. On the one hand it resonates consistently with profoundly political implications and often quite directly, and specifically, addresses the political in both its historical and contemporary dimensions. On the other hand, *as* thought it makes no attempt to found or endorse a specific politics or political program. Such an apparent conflict or contradiction can be viewed within the wider debate surrounding the political dimension of those forms of French philosophy which have been associated with the labels poststructuralism, postmodernism, or deconstruction. For instance, the "politics of deconstruction" has been a source of considerable controversy over the past three decades, specifically in relation to the Heidegger and de Man affairs of the late 1980s, but also in relation to a more general questioning of the relation of Derrida's thought to Marxism and to the politics of the left.[2] As will become clear, Nancy's thinking of the political develops specifically in response to the debates raised around the politics of deconstruction. More broadly this dimension of Nancy's thought needs to be addressed within the context of what one might term the post-Nietzschean and post-Heideggerian thinking of the political. Recently a number of Anglo-American philosophers working broadly within the "continental" tradition have made significant interventions in this area.[3] It is with this broader thinking of the political that Nancy's philosophy has been most extensively engaged to date. This has meant that the majority of responses to or commentaries on his writing have addressed his political thought, and more specifically his writing on community. As will become clear, many of these responses have also been rather critical, most often on the grounds that his thinking seemingly ignores or misjudges the empirical realm of political events and struggles. What follows here will suggest that his philosophy, while remaining inassimilable to political theory or science, offers an important rethinking of the relation between the philosophical, the political, and politics. I will also argue that, despite, or perhaps because of, the apparent withdrawal of this philosophy from the sphere of politics and its refusal to lay the ground for a political program, it does nevertheless open up new perspectives in which we might think about, and engage with, the world as a form of historical community and site of struggle and decision.

At the beginning of the essay "Guerre, Droit, Souveraineté—Techné" ("War, Law, Sovereignty—Technē"), written in 1991, in the middle of what is now known as the first Gulf War, Nancy notes how, in the face of violence, death, and suffering, the immediacy of contemporary events demand a concomitant immediacy of engagement and response: "On the one hand what counts today are the immediate factors, the dead, all kinds of suffering, the great compassion that accompanies all wars. . . . What counts on the other hand are the political determinations, gestures of approbation or criticism, motives and reasons that we can all perhaps still see as calling upon our responsibility" (*ESP*, 127).[4] And yet an immediate engagement with those political determinations which will dictate specific actions is an important (but not, for Nancy, the sole) dimension of our responsibility: "our responsibility is also, already, called upon in yet a different manner: as the responsibility of thinking" (*ESP*, 127).[5] Nancy then goes on to examine in a rigorously philosophical idiom the forms of sense which historically have been attached to the concepts of war, law, and state sovereignty, the way these forms have interacted, and the manner in which, within the context of "technological warfare," they have been transformed in the first Gulf War.[6] His opening comment reflects more broadly on the manner in which he thinks the relation between the philosophical and the political. On the one hand there is the empirical and immediate realm of politics, of events and our responsibility to decide and act in relation to them. On the other hand, and perhaps prior to this first moment, there is the responsibility of thought, which leads Nancy to consider the historical and contemporary sense of war, law, or sovereignty in a philosophical idiom, on a level which is in some way withdrawn from the field of empirical reality yet is deeply implicated in its possibility of becoming. Here the responsibility of thought realizes itself as a practice of philosophical writing. This of course does not preclude the imperatives and the real possibility of decision, position taking, and active engagement, but neither does it directly dictate the form these should take. In order to understand what may be at stake here it is necessary to trace in more detail the development of Nancy's thinking on the political, from the beginning of the 1980s in his collaborative work with Philippe Lacoue-Labarthe, to his thinking of community and what he comes to call the "compearance" (*comparution*) of shared being in the world.

## The Center for Philosophical Research on the Political

The Centre de recherches philosophiques sur le politique was opened in Paris at the École Normale Supérieure on the rue d'Ulm in November 1980 and continued its work until its closure in November 1984. During this period two published volumes of collected papers were produced, *Re-jouer le politique* (1981) and *Le Retrait du politique* (1983). The origin of the Center, set up by Nancy and Philippe Lacoue-Labarthe at Derrida's suggestion, lies in a colloquium which took place in July 1980 entitled "Les Fins de l'homme" (The ends of man).[7] This colloquium, named after an essay by Derrida (written in May 1968 and published in his 1972 collection *Marges de la philosophie*), took Derrida's work as a point of departure for a consideration of the political dimension and implications of deconstruction.[8] The various interventions and exchanges of the earlier colloquium and the broader history of the Center have been well documented.[9] What follows will retrace this history in such a way as to highlight the key issues addressed by the work of the Center and to assess some of the critical responses given to that work both during and after the four years of its life.

One of the key interventions in the "Fins de l'homme" colloquium is the political seminar given by Christopher Fynsk and Philippe Lacoue-Labarthe. In Fynsk's paper the question of the "retreat" of the philosophical in relation to the political is first explicitly addressed as such. For Fynsk this retreat is a gesture of Derrida's philosophical text itself, enacted as a kind of withdrawal from politics or political questions. Fynsk notes various moments where Derrida explicitly takes his distance from any easy assimilation of deconstruction to politics, and his refusal of any hasty attempt on the part of deconstructive thought to settle accounts or seek a "conjunction" with Marxism and Marxist thought (*RT,* 88).[10] And yet, as Fynsk also points out, citing an interview given for the journal *Digraphe,* Derrida explicitly affirms that the philosophical activity in which he is engaged is itself a form of political practice: "Philosophical activity does not *require* a political practice; it is, in every way, a political practice. Once one has struggled to get that recognized, other struggles begin that are both philosophical *and* political" (*RT,* 89).[11] This double movement in Derrida, in which philosophy is withdrawn from politics and yet remains a deeply political gesture or practice, sets the terms in which Nancy and Lacoue-Labarthe will address the relation of the philosophical to the political in their work for the Center. Fynsk's paper engages in a careful analysis of Derrida's deconstructive writing in order to highlight, within the context of its withdrawal from politics, its status as a political activity. One of the first things he draws attention to, and what most readers with a passing knowledge of deconstruction will be familiar with, is its uncoupling of philosophical activity from any logic of representation or any work of a self-grounding, representing subject. Philosophical practice, in Fynsk's words, becomes a "work of reading or writing which brings to light that point where every representing production—and that is to say, every practice which implies language—fails. Every practice, then, including its own" (*RT,* 91). This seemingly negative foregrounding of the limit-point representation and of its ultimate failure *as* representation is a moment that many would associate with the essence of deconstruction. Such an insistence on the failure of representation would also, for many, be indicative of the political vacuity or implicit quietism of deconstruction.

Yet, Fynsk argues, this moment of failure which philosophical activity affirms is an encounter with what he calls, after Granel, the "practical finitude" of all human production. By this he means the inability of human production to master the relation it maintains to its ground or foundation (this, of course, recalls Nancy's work on Kant and Descartes in the 1970s, also in part influenced by Granel).[12] By repressing or suppressing the recognition of this inability, human production in its metaphysical moment grounds itself in specific figures (e.g., God, Man, Reason) and thereby attempts to install itself as master over a specific domain of beings.[13] In this sense philosophy's affirmation of failure, the affirmation of the impossibility of mastering a ground or foundation, is less a nihilistic staring into an abyss and more an encounter with an instance of freedom and decision (that is, the recognition that our being is not predetermined by an essence or ground), a decision in which the existence of others and a shared relation to being is at stake.[14] The manner in which deconstruction foregrounds or affirms the failure of representation, its encounter with "practical finitude," means that philosophy is not and cannot be a *theoretical* practice, that is to say, one which directs itself toward the world as a work to be produced on the basis of grounded conceptual representations. Rather, in thinking existence in terms of practical finitude, as a relation to an unmasterable ground, philosophy allows for the possibility of a certain kind of decision with regard to existence or being in which something new might emerge. The effects of representation are, Fynsk admits (as does Derrida), always at work within philosophy, but at its limit and in its encounter with practical finitude philosophy "affirms itself as being both more and less than such a representing production" (*RT*, 94). Philosophy here is political because, as an attempt to interrogate or expose the limits of cultural knowledge and practices, it "would seek the conditions of an effective alteration in these practices; it would seek to open itself to what, from a past inaccessible to those practices, gives a future. It would seek to produce political possibilities for communities yet to come" (*RT*, 94). The political dimension of philosophical practice, then, is not about producing a project on the basis of theoretical reflections on, or representations of, the world; it is rather about releasing the possible unthought from that which has traditionally or already been thought, releasing future possibilities from the limit points of what we think we know about the past and the present.[15]

In his brief response to this paper Lacoue-Labarthe endorses the link Fynsk makes between the philosophical and the political and clearly affirms his own belief in the indissociability of the two. He also endorses the retreat of the philosophical with respect to politics, but takes pains to further underline the extent to which the indissociability of the philosophical and the political means that this retreat is not a simple turning away or withdrawal from politics into what might be a safe haven protected from the mess of struggle and debate. Indeed he appears to turn the meaning of the term on its head by suggesting that "retreat" "has to be *active*, offensive even" (*RT*, 97), and this is all the more the case, he adds, "given that another meaning lies beneath the term 'retreat of the political', providing a different stress is placed on the genitive" (*RT*, 97). In this second sense the "retreat of the political" would designate the manner in which, in the contemporary world, the question of the political, the question of its exact nature or essence, retires or withdraws into a kind of evidence or self-givenness, in which that which is political in politics is taken for granted or accorded a kind of obviousness which is universally accepted. The political retreats, then, insofar as it is not a question or in question, but is rather that which, in politics, goes unquestioned (e.g., the acceptance within much contemporary debate that politics is ultimately and in its last moment a function of *political economy*, and that all other considerations are necessarily subordinate to this). Within the two papers of the "Political Seminar" all the various questions which will be more systematically posed in the opening address and subsequent work of the Centre de recherches philosophiques sur le politique are present. The more systematic development or treatment of the issues raised in the "Fins de l'homme" colloquium lead Nancy and Lacoue-Labarthe to propose for the Center a twofold interrogation: first, the philosophical questioning of the political, and second, a questioning about the essential cobelonging of the philosophical with the political. This in turn leads to a clearer formalization of the distinction made by Nancy and Lacoue-Labarthe between *le politique* (the political) and *la politique* (politics), and to an account of totalitarianism which by far exceeds any traditional definition of the term understood as a particular organization of state power and social life.

The published "Opening Address" to the Center, delivered jointly by Nancy and Lacoue-Labarthe, is laced with qualifications and precisions as to the task or mode of questioning which they propose. For instance they make it clear that they have no pretension to political theory: "that is to say, to anything that could evoke a 'political science' or a 'politology'" (*RJ*, 13; *RT*, 108). They have no specialist knowledge or training in this area and claim no authority to make pronouncements within the discursive parameters such disciplines set themselves. They also underline the fact that they are working very specifically as philosophers engaged in a "properly philosophical" questioning which would have a properly philosophical value (*RJ*, 12; *RT*, 108). As philosophers, then, neither Nancy nor Lacoue-Labarthe believe that their thinking of the "political" can occur as a direct empirical approach; nor do they believe that it is any longer possible for philosophy to directly approach the political in an empirical way. This is not in the least to say that something like a political science, theory, or "politology" that is empirically grounded is dismissed, ruled out, or held to be impossible. On the contrary, the claim Nancy and Lacoue-Labarthe appear to be making (and this is a claim that many of their commentators seem to have ignored), is that any project of a theory or science of the political can only operate on the basis of fundamental concepts or forms of preunderstanding, and that these are properly philosophical in nature and need to be addressed as such, prior to their manifestation in the empirical field.[16] It is not enough, they claim, for political science to be vigilant and ever more critical about some of its founding assumptions, nor to assume that it can perform an autocritique from within the parameters of its own discourse, and through such critique transcend some of the limitations or prejudices that it may have come to recognize in itself. This, indeed, would be all too hasty and, Nancy and Lacoue-Labarthe contend, ineffectual, given the grip exerted over the human sciences by a certain kind of anthropologism which is fundamentally incapable of calling into question its prior understanding of the human and of human subjectivity (i.e., precisely that which in this context needs to be placed in question). The demand, here, is for a retrieval of a philosophical questioning of the political, which will not be too hastily subsumed into or engaged with the empirical field, since "if a new concept of the political or something which one could present as such could become clear, then any such concept would, in our opinion, necessarily derive from the philosophical field" (*RJ*, 109; *RT*, 109). Once again the key issue in all this is the question of how something new can emerge within forms of human understanding, a "something new" which would necessarily, but in no way directly, have an impact upon future possibilities of human production.

Yet this attempt by Nancy and Lacoue-Labarthe to retrieve and preserve a sphere of properly philosophical questioning in relation to the political appears to leave them exposed to criticism on two sides. On the one hand there will be those involved in philosophical or theoretical reflection who will demand that they make their thinking more directly engaged with politics and the immediacy of political struggle. On the other hand there will be those who, engaging in empirically based political science, would resent or refuse the attempt by philosophy to rework or dismantle some of its grounding assumptions. Some of these criticisms will be addressed more fully later in this discussion. Such instances of refusal would, of course, be based on fundamental differences of approach which would themselves have a philosophical dimension. As will by now be expected, Nancy and Lacoue-Labarthe's formulations occur within a preunderstanding of philosophy which is broadly, but by no means straightforwardly or exclusively, Heideggerian (it is also, as has already been shown, Derridean implying a very specific and complex "French" reading of Heidegger such as was alluded to in Chapter 1). The Heideggerian inheritance informs a series of judgments or claims with respect to the nature of the present, its relation to the Western tradition of thought and its origins in ancient Greece, judgments which, in different ways, have been shown to inflect Nancy's thinking in the previous discussions of subjectivity, space, and embodiment. In the context of the "Opening Address" the "essential cobelonging" of the philosophical and the political is emphasized, that is, the notion that the two determine each other in a fundamental manner. This is not simply a historical formation of sense inherited from Plato, rather such an essential cobelonging articulates and has articulated the historical becoming and contemporary situation of our culture, a claim elaborated in the following terms:

This reciprocal involvement of the philosophical and of the political . . . is, in reality, our situation or our state: by which we mean, in the mimetic or memorial after effect or *après-coup* of the Greek "sending" which defines the modern age, the actualisation or installation of the philosophical *as* the political, the generalisation (the globalisation) of the philosophical *as* the political—and, by the same token, the absolute reign or "total domination" of the political. (*RJ*, 14–15; *RT*, 109–10)

According to this account of the Western tradition, thought has ceaselessly striven to define and lay a ground for "the human" through various modes of figuration in order to realize these figures in cultural projects and political institutions. What Nancy and Lacoue-Labarthe are demanding is a recognition of this attempt to provide figures of the human within the tradition of Western metaphysics and a lucid account of the manner in which these figures are then proffered as a basis for political community within specific historical formations.[17] The historical epoch in which thought has attempted to "actualize" itself as the political through philosophically instantiated figures of the human is one of the defining characteristics of the "metaphysical attitude" within philosophy and defines what Nancy and Lacoue-Labarthe call, after Heidegger, the epoch of "onto-theology."[18] It is important to note that neither is claiming that philosophy or philosophical ideas have caused or entirely determined historical becoming (which might be construed to be a form of idealism). Rather they are suggesting that this becoming has occurred within a certain (metaphysical) preunderstanding of being on the basis of which appeals to philosophical or theological forms are constantly made in order to lay a ground for figures of the human and thus for human community.

In tracing a tradition in this way Nancy and Lacoue-Labarthe also proffer a specific understanding of recent history and of the present which is viewed in terms of the completion of this onto-theological tendency in Enlightenment and post-Enlightenment political ideologies. This movement by which metaphysical determinations are actualized as the political is pursued in the attempted historical realization of various progressivist discourses and culminates in the revolutionary discourse of socialism. To this extent the phenomenon of communism represents for Nancy and Lacoue-Labarthe the apotheosis and final limit of the metaphysical tradition which they are aiming to describe.[19] Revolutionary socialism emerges as the very figure of completion with regard to the metaphysical actualization of the philosophical as the political:

It seems to us as indispensable today to recognize that what completes itself (and does not cease to complete itself) is the great "enlightened," progressivist discourse of secular or profane eschatology, and that is to say the re-appropriation of man in his humanity, the discourse of the actualization of the genre of the human—in short, the discourse of revolution. (*RJ*, 16, *RT*, 111)

What Nancy and Lacoue-Labarthe appear to be suggesting is that the European Enlightenment that constructed the human in a number of specific ways (e.g., through the privileging of free will, of rational or cognitive faculties, or of the equality and rights of the individual within a universality of justice or law) is itself a secular continuation of an onto-theological tradition (that of Christian Europe rooted in its Greek beginning). Through these figures of the human, and through their various mutations or perversions, that tradition has imposed itself over the past three centuries in an attempt to actualize or "complete" itself in different political forms. These might be the various formations of liberal democracy which have emerged since the eighteenth century, fascist or National Socialist projects, and ultimately in socialist or Marxist revolutionary programs.

The broad sweep of this Heideggerian-inspired "epochal" thinking needs to be approached with all the qualifications and caveats which have been invoked in previous discussions about the dominance of a thinking of the subject (Chapter 1) or of the Christian (Chapter 3) within the Western tradition. Even if one does not entirely accept the post-Heideggerian epochal understanding of being which is invoked here, such broad judgments about the nature and unfolding of the European tradition *as a tradition* may be useful and in certain respects inevitable, insofar as they offer the means of approaching philosophically the wider field of historical becoming, on the basis of general hypotheses which can be tested against the multiplicity and detail of events (and thus can function as axiomatic judgments). At the same time such judgments may well be inevitable and always already at work in our understanding, insofar as we are always caught up in some preunderstanding of a past which we inherit in order to make sense of the present and project a future. What this epochal thinking leads to in the case of Nancy's and Lacoue-Labarthe's approach to the political is a sense that, in the wake of specific totalitarian projects (fascist / National Socialist or Marxist / socialist) and specifically in the light of the failure of these projects, the "political" has completed itself, or that it is now subject to a certain kind of closure. In this context socialism is given a privileged and dominant position since it is taken to be the "complete and completing figure of philosophy's imposition—up to and what, for us at least, could have represented the hope of a critique and a revolutionary radicalization of established Marxism" (*RJ*, 16; *RT*, 111). With the failure of socialism or any possibility of a properly revolutionary project, a failure felt acutely by the European left at the beginning of the 1980s, the political is completed in the sense that it is no longer that which is to be thought and then realized. Rather, it becomes that unquestioned evidence or obviousness (that of political economy conceived of in capitalist terms) in the face of which philosophical reflection is unable to respond or provide an alternative. This notion of *completion* repeats in a more detailed manner the second sense given to the notion of the "retreat of the political" outlined by Lacoue-Labarthe in the "Political Seminar" (see above). Indeed, for Nancy and Lacoue-Labarthe in the "Opening Address," it is this broader historical/epochal schema which gives the full sense to their use of the term *retreat*, as they make abundantly clear: "It is this double exigency—recognition of the closure of the political and political deprivation of philosophy as regards itself and its own authority—which leads us to think in terms of 're-treating the political'" (*RJ*, 18; *RT*, 112).

This theme is outlined in further detail in the paper Nancy and Lacoue-Labarthe jointly delivered to the Center on June 21, 1982, entitled "Le 'Retrait' du politique" (The "Retreat" of the Political) (*RP*, 183–200; *RT*, 122–37). In this paper an attempt is made to further clarify and elaborate the questions which underpin the activity of the Center. Nancy and Lacoue-Labarthe repeat their assertion that the political as it appears and dominates in the contemporary world is the effect of a certain retreat of the philosophical and the total dominance of the political (*RP*, 187; *RT*, 125). This leads them to give a more clearly elaborated definition of totalitarianism, both wide-reaching and highly contentious. Here they are keen to distinguish between totalitarianism such as it is defined within the discourse of political science, and a broader philosophical and nonempirical concept which would refer specifically to the notion of the "total dominance of the political." In this context "totalitarianism" for Nancy and Lacoue-Labarthe refers to the attempt to realize certain figures of the human within the totality of human social organization and relation to the exclusion of all other possibilities. Totalitarianism, in this very specific sense of the term, is a function of metaphysics and a distinctly Western historical becoming, insofar as this has been defined as the history of an attempt to actualize or realize philosophically conceived figures of the human within, or as, an existing social totality. More specifically Nancy and Lacoue-Labarthe view totalitarianism as an effect of a certain relation to transcendence such as it is played out within the metaphysical tradition. According to this account the imperial, feudal, or monarchical organization of society would, for instance, represent a relation to transcendence insofar as the emperor, lord, or king rule in the name of a principle exterior to them, the figure of the divine and participation in it through the sharing of divine authority (e.g., in the notion of the divine right of kingship).[20] This transcendent principle could affirm itself in other figures, of course, for example in an essence of the human or in an end of history which is not present, but rather project-

ed as that which is yet to come. Totalitarianism, in the specifically philosophical determination which Nancy and Lacoue-Labarthe seek to elaborate, would be predicated on a loss of the principle of transcendence and
the attempt to overcome such a loss by seeking to realize this principle in
a single figure, to realize this figure here and now within the totality of the
social body or community to the exclusion of all other possibilities. To this
extent totalitarianism is identified in Nancy's and Lacoue-Labarthe's analysis with the "closure" or the "retreat" of the political. Insofar as the political
within the totalitarian formation is no longer a transcendence or an alterity
(the divine or a "yet-to-come"), but rather is invoked as an "already here,"
an immanence governing the social whole, it cannot be questioned as such
and maintains itself in an omnipresent givenness and self-evidence. Thus,
according to this account, the "retreat" of the political *is* totalitarianism.
In this thought all the questions which the Center proposes to interrogate
come together. The retreat of the political appears "first of all as the retreat
of transcendence or alterity. Which clearly does not mean that it is for us a
matter of repeating the appeal to transcendence, whether it be God, Man
or History: these are the transcendences which have installed totalitarianism or those in which it has installed itself, converting them into the immanence of life-in-common" (*RP*, 192–93; *RT*, 129). This, for Nancy and
Lacoue-Labarthe, is a crucial and determining point. They do not seek,
in their elaboration of the historical/epochal schema of the European tradition and its relation to transcendence, to evoke a nostalgia for previous
forms of political organization. Such nostalgia is precisely that which motivates the drive toward immanence and totality proper to totalitarianism.
Rather the "retreat of the political," that is, its total dominance and withdrawal into self-evidence and obviousness, requires, not the reinstallation
of a lost transcendence, but rather a fundamental rethinking of political
transcendence per se. It requires that the political be "retreated," rethought
in its essence or essential determination.

It is here that the key task of the Center proposes itself. The "retreat
of the political" "must allow, or even impose, the tracing anew of the stakes
of the political" (*RP*, 194; *RT*, 131). This sense in which philosophy, for
Nancy and Lacoue-Labarthe, withdraws from politics, from the empirical
field of events and action, in order to "displace, re-elaborate and replay the
concept of 'political transcendence'" (*RP*, 193; *RT*, 130). It is in this sense

also that the withdrawal from politics and the concomitant "retreating of the political" is a deeply engaged gesture that does not intervene or make prescriptive/normative judgments about the present, but that demands that the present be *thought*:

> The retreat of the political corresponds to its *closure*—and by the same token to the opening of the following question: on the basis of what, against what, or along what, does this closure trace itself? It does not simply trace itself against the non-political. . . . On the contrary, the closure opens onto "something" . . . something which would be the "political"—or the essence of the political—drawn back from the total completion of the political in the techno-social. (*RP*, 196; *RT*, 132)

Or put in another way: since the political has retreated into a self-evidence or obviousness, since it now dominates our world as political economy (or what Nancy and Lacoue-Labarthe also call the "techno-social"), philosophy must withdraw from politics in order that the political might be renewed as a question, as that which, in its essence, is in question, and as that which must be retraced and thought anew. Insofar as this question is a question of essence, it is philosophical and cannot be empirical. It is in this context that the distinction between *le politique* and *la politique*, mentioned above, needs to be understood. *La politique* is the empirical field of politics, the politics "of the Chinese Emperors, the Benin Kings, of Louis XIV, or of German social democracy" (*RP*, 186; *RT*, 125). *Le politique* is a "specific dimension of alterity" (*RP*, 193; *RT*, 130), prior to politics per se but fundamental to its possible modes of articulation or becoming.

The influence of Heidegger with respect to the scope and exact framing of Nancy's and Lacoue-Labarthe's interrogation of the political would seem to be very great both in their invocation of a historical/epochal schema describing the history of metaphysics, and in their call for a reelaboration or retracing of the political in its essence. This, as will become clear, is the aspect which provokes critical responses to their specific mode of interrogation, during the fours years of the Center's activity and in more recent commentaries. The immediate question that imposes itself, at this point, relates to what might arise from this rethinking of the essence of the political. What, in the closure of the political or in the total dominance of the "techno-social," is to be retraced by thought as it withdraws and distances itself in order to engage in a more fundamental philosophical questioning? Within the text of "Retreating the Political" only a very schematic and rather undeveloped answer is given to this question, by way of listing five "basic traits." These traits that would inform the retracing of the political are:

1. "The exigency of getting away from the metaphysical *ground* of the political, from a transcendent or transcendental ground, for example in a subject" (*RP*, 196; *RT*, 132).

2. The placing "in opposition to the motifs of ground and the subject . . . the motif of finitude" (*RP*, 196; *RT*, 133).

3. A posing of "the question of relation" (*RP*, 197; *RT*, 133).

4. A posing of "the question of the mother," that is, after Freud, the question "of identification as the social constitution of identity . . . of an 'originary' or arche-originary sociality" (*RP*, 197; *RT*, 133–34).

5. The insistence that the reference to a "specificity of the political . . . is precisely not to a specificity of the *empirical* by which the political would be signaled" (*RP*, 198; *RT*, 134).

By way of a brief commentary on these five points it is interesting initially to note that the first two traits exactly repeat the concerns which underpinned Nancy's and Lacoue-Labarthe's collaboration around the question of philosophy and literature throughout the 1970s. In this sense their work on the political is very much a continuation of previous preoccupations (as is noted in the "Opening Address" [*RJ*, 20; *RT*, 114]; see also Chapter 1). Passing over the third trait for the moment it is interesting also to note that the fourth, "the question of the mother," is acknowledged to be a "risky designation" through which to address the dimension of an originary sociality. This is no doubt due to the sexual-political problems such a designation raises. What is at stake here, it appears, is a Freudian approach, in which the question of social relation is posed, at its most fundamental level, within an Oedipal or quasi-Oedipal framework of interpretation.[21] The insistence in the fifth point on the nonempirical dimension of the political is by now a familiar refrain. Significantly the third trait enumerated is described by Nancy and Lacoue-Labarthe as "*the* central question," one which "shows up almost everywhere in the Center's work, independently of the accent we ourselves had placed upon it" (*RP*, 197; *RT*, 133). The political, it seems, in its essence is a question of relation or relationality, that which is prior to politics articulates the relationality of the social body at the most fundamental level. Taken together these five points sum up Nancy's and Lacoue-Labarthe's aspirations for the kind of questions the Center posed.

The extent to which these aspirations were met during the four years of the Center's life is somewhat debatable, and a certain ambivalence with regard to this question is reflected in the letter, again coauthored by Nancy and Lacoue-Labarthe, which announces its closure on November 16, 1984.[22] They remark that, although from its outset the work of the Center sought to place the political in question (on the assumption that "nothing of the political is henceforth established" [*RT*, 144]), a certain "easily accepted consensus" emerged in place of a more essential questioning. This consensus bore directly on the question of totalitarianism and on the exact nature and legacy of Marxism and regimes of Marxist origin. With respect to Marxism, the consensus Nancy and Lacoue-Labarthe refer to has become a more widespread commonplace since the collapse of the Soviet Union, namely that "the Marxian event is henceforth null and void," that recent history has born witness to the "end of Marxism," and that any merits it may have had need to be recognized "on some sort of posthumous basis" (*RT*, 145). From this flows an acceptance that the "political" is displaced in favor of a thinking which privileges values—ethical, aesthetic, or even religious—and where the question of economy is taken to be simply a function of material reality (*RT*, 146). Implicit within this consensus is also a rejection of the definition of totalitarianism proffered by Nancy and Lacoue-Labarthe. Such a consensus with respect to the "death" of Marxism would define totalitarianism as a function of Marxist regimes, and thus define it also in strict opposition to the mode of organization proper to liberal democracy. By contrast the philosophical definition of totalitarianism outlined in the "Opening Address" and "The Retreat of the Political" is predicated on the notion of the completion or total dominance of the political, which manifests itself, albeit in very different ways, in both Marxist and liberal capitalist systems. What is clear, even from these brief allusions to the wider work of the Center in the closing letter, is that many of its contributors did not accept the broader and Heideggerian schema outlined by Nancy and Lacoue-Labarthe. This refusal to accept the terms within which the project of the Center is initially conceived is demonstrated in some of the published papers, for instance in Claude Lefort's paper on democracy or Denis Kambouchner's questioning of the distinction between *le politique* and *la politique.*[23] The closing letter seems to suggest that, for all the systematic rigor and careful qualifications of their opening formulations, many of the participants did not accept their broadly Heideggerian preunderstanding of the issue, its emphasis on epochal closure and essential questioning.

This refusal or skepticism is repeated by many of the Anglo-American commentators who have sought to give critical accounts of the work of the Center. For instance, in an article written in late 1982, Nancy Fraser argues that the distinction made by Nancy and Lacoue-Labarthe between politics and the political, and the concomitant withdrawal from one in order to effect an essential questioning of the other, "functions . . . as a means of avoiding the step into politics to which the logic of their own hopes and thought would otherwise draw them."[24] While Fraser acknowledges that they want to consider the question of essence in the hope that it will have some future impact on politics and that they are thus thinking in such a way that will allow for "an incessant sliding back and forth between two heterogeneous levels of analysis,"[25] she nevertheless sees in the distinction between *le politique* and *la politique* a refusal to engage in political debate or to be entangled in political contestation and struggle. Fraser's article is largely taken up with a fairly thorough account of the origin and work of the Center up to the time of writing. Its main argument, though, turns on this criticism of Nancy's and Lacoue-Labarthe's refusal to engage with politics, an argument which culminates at the end of her article into a call for engagement with contemporary feminist struggle. Despite the general thoroughness of her narrative account of the activity of the Center, however, it is arguable that she fails to take some of the qualifications given in the "Opening Address" seriously enough. In the text of this address, it is, for instance, made quite clear that "the ruling out or sublimating of either class struggles or political struggles has never been what is at stake for us: these are the givens of the epoch of the domination of the political and technology or of the domination of political economy. But the stake could be one of no longer subjugating these struggles, in their finality, to this domination" (*RJ,* 24; *RT,* 117). This seems to make it clear that Nancy and Lacoue-Labarthe do not seek to rule out political debate, struggle, or engagement. Rather, they are insisting that there is a philosophical questioning which can and should occur with respect to the essence of the political, and that this questioning is engaged in a specific way with a specific responsibility. This would not preclude either from dirtying their hands with struggles as citizens, professionals, or activists. As philosophers, however, they seek to rethink the determination of the political per se, such that diverse struggles, be they gender-political, class-based, economic, or otherwise, are not subjugated the total domination they have described. Fraser's demand that Nancy and Lacoue-Labarthe engage more directly in struggle and debate appears either to miss or to refuse key philosophical steps which they had made. Insofar as she misses them she does not do justice to the complexity and rigor of their argument. Insofar as she may refuse this argument she offers no alternative philosophical engagement which is clearly and systematically worked out.[26]

Nevertheless Fraser's article does testify to an uneasiness with respect to Nancy's and Lacoue-Labarthe's distinction between *le politique* and *la politique*, an uneasiness which is shared by a number of other commentators. First and foremost among these is the British philosopher Simon Critchley, who, in a Levinasian-inspired critique, makes a similar point to Fraser, although in a much more philosophically developed fashion.[27] The real problem of this distinction between politics and the political is, for Critchley, the Heideggerian "epochal" thinking that lies behind it, and the account of the closure or "total dominance" of the political to which this thinking gives rise. Critchley poses a straightforward question, namely: "is this analysis of the present political condition accurate?"[28] His contention is that Nancy and Lacoue-Labarthe, insofar as they interpret the present in terms of the completion or "total domination of the political," are essentially repeating Heidegger's understanding of the completion of metaphysics as technology or as technological revealing.[29] This repetition in turn underpins the broader philosophical definition Nancy and Lacoue-Labarthe give to the term *totalitarianism*, a definition which, for Critchley, profoundly misunderstands the nature of the democratic polity and the fundamental differences which exist between democratic and nondemocratic forms. In other words, the Heideggerian sweep of epochal thinking prevents a more nuanced understanding of the world. To a large extent Critchley joins Claude Lefort who, in the paper he delivers to the Center on January 18, 1982, suggests that democracy is different from totalitarianism, not simply on the empirical level of politics but on the level of their political essences. For Lefort totalitarianism is a distinctly modern form that emerges on the basis of a mutation or change which is in the first instance symbolic in nature. This mutation of sense lays the ground for a single party to come to power, to remove all other parties, and to claim a legitimacy allowing it to rise above existing legal constraints. It also allows the party to assimilate all aspects of communal life into its project, in what amounts ultimately to a conflation of state and civil society and an effective abandonment of the latter in favor an organicist notion of communal solidarity (*RP*, 76–77).[30] Democracy, on the other hand, is characterized by an order of sense in which a transcendent grounding of social organization has disappeared; thus it is riven with internal contradictions and traversed by disseminated sites of power, but power or authority that is nowhere specifically or exclusively located. In Lefort's words, "The locus of power becomes an empty place" (*RP*, 82).[31] While warning that this analysis risks becoming an apology for existing democratic forms which may be in need of radical reform in order to be more properly democratic, Critchley nevertheless appears to accept the distinctions Lefort makes in "The Question of Democracy."[32] According to Critchley the problem inherent in Nancy's and Lacoue-Labarthe's Heideggerian-inspired definition of totalitarianism is that, in reducing the sphere of politics to the question of the more essential determination of the political they reduce the multiplicity of the empirical field to an underlying structure which is too homogeneous and undifferentiated.

Critchley's criticism of the Heideggerianism of Nancy's and Lacoue-Labarthe's position is, in many respects, quite convincing, since it is easy to wonder whether their "philosophical" definition of totalitarianism loses more in its inability to foreground differences than it gains in its ability to highlight possible similarities or shared attributes. It is worth noting, though, that Critchley does not necessarily do justice to the rather complex nature of the "Heideggerianism" which might be at play here. For instance he asks, in explicitly Derridean terms, "whether there remains a trace of empiricity and facticity in the reduction of *la politique* to *le politique* that disrupts or deconstructs the possibility of such a reduction? Is there not an inextricable contamination of *le politique* by *la politique* and vice-versa?"[33] This is something that might easily be conceded and, as a question,

it perhaps ignores the extent to which Nancy's and Lacoue-Labarthe's understanding of Heidegger is already mediated through a Derridean reading, and a questioning of the "proper" in Heidegger, which would sus-
pend any rigid opposition between the ontic and the ontological and the
possibility of reducing the former to the latter without remainder. In this
context the distinction between *le politique* and *la politique* would correspond more to the distinction between a dissemination of sense that opens
up a meaningful world as a form of political relationality (what Derrida
would call *différance*) and a series of specific institutional and discursive
practices within that world (parties, campaign or pressure groups, nongov-
ernmental organizations, etc.). Such a distinction need not imply the reduction of one term to the other or deny their mutual interpenetration.[34]
Likewise, although the notion of the "total domination of the political"
may correspond to or repeat Heidegger's thinking of the completion of
metaphysics as technology, Nancy and Lacoue-Labarthe do not necessarily share with Heidegger an identical understanding of the technological.
In some respects what they call the "techno-social" and political economy
is more specific, and more specifically Marxian in origin than Heideggerian, and refers less to a global technological "enframing" than it does to the
dominance of economics within contemporary political formations and
neoliberal capitalist ideology. It seems that Critchley may be a little too
precipitous in drawing conclusions from Nancy's and Lacoue-Labarthe's
philosophical language and therefore ignores the degree to which something different from a strictly orthodox Heideggerian analysis emerges.

   Nevertheless the extent to which Nancy and Lacoue-Labarthe assimilate both liberal democracies and more recognizably totalitarian regimes
to a broader philosophical definition of totalitarianism remains problematic. What they are calling the dominance of the political or of political
economy in the contemporary world a political scientist might choose to
call hegemony. A hegemonic discourse or practice would not be a fundamental order of sense that discloses the world as such (it is not, therefore,
a function of *le politique*), rather it would be a discourse or practice which
has a dominant position in relation to other practices which are marginalized or suppressed in favor of the hegemon (functioning, then, within the
field of *la politique*). It is possible that the dominance of political economy
and of the techno-social within modern liberal democracies is a *hegemonic*

dominance on the level of politics rather than an *existential* dominance on the level of the political. As a hegemonic practice of politics, then, it would be open to contestation or refusal within the wider realm of politics itself (in, for example, the activities of antiglobalization or global justice movements). This would suggest that, however much democracies might tend toward the concentration of power in the hands of political, bureaucratic, and capitalist elites, and however much these elites unquestioningly accept the primacy of political economy, such democracies nevertheless maintain a field in which contestation and refusal are possible and thus remain inassimilable to the deeper political logic of totalitarianism. Despite this caveat it could still be argued that Nancy's and Lacoue-Labarthe's account usefully indicates the way in which contemporary beliefs about the primary importance of political economy are not just ideological and hegemonic forms, but form a shared substructure of the way historical and contemporary reality is perceived; that is, they are a shared order of sense that reveals or constitutes a specific understanding of world (and are thus of a more fundamental order than hegemonic political discourses at the same time that they give rise to such discourse).

Be that as it may, it is clear that the sense of ambivalence with respect to the work of the Center reflected in the "Closing Letter" testifies to certain tensions or differences in relation to the project outlined in the "Opening Address" and "The 'Retreat' of the Political." These differences are most clearly reflected in some of the published contributions to the work of the Center (Lefort, Kambouchner) and in some of the critical responses given elsewhere (Fraser, Critchley, Ingram). Yet despite the very real reservations which might persist with regard to certain aspects of Nancy's and Lacoue-Labarthe's formulations of the "retreat" of the political, the work of the Center is important in a number of ways. First and foremost among these is that it articulates a certain relation between philosophy and politics. By withdrawing from politics and refusing the notion that philosophy should have a direct theoretical impact on the formulation of a political program, Nancy and Lacoue-Labarthe mark out a space in which something like a postmetaphysical political philosophy can occur. Such a political philosophy would be distinct from the concerns and conceptual parameters of political theory or science, and free from the demand that philosophy realize or actualize itself as the political. It would seek rather to interrogate the limits of what we think the political is as such so that fundamental questions and problems might be framed in new or different ways. Closely related to this is the demand that, in the wake of the apparent "failure" of Marxist or socialist projects, we nevertheless continue to think about what is properly political in current politics, and that we do not hastily assume we know what is at stake in contemporary social and economic reality. These concerns are arguably as valid at the time of writing this study (2003–4) as they were at the time of their initial formulation in the early 1980s. A number of the "basic traits" enumerated at the end of "The 'Retreat' of the Political" are also important insofar as they set the terms for the development of Nancy's thinking throughout the 1980s and early 1990s. While the "question of the mother" (trait 4) and its psychoanalytic premise falls by the wayside, the exigency of "getting away from a metaphysical ground," the "motif of finitude," and the "question of relation" (traits 1–3, detailed above) lie at the heart of Nancy's rethinking of community in *La Communauté désœuvrée*. To this extent the real outcome and importance of the attempt to "retrace" the political lies, not in the work of the Center from 1980 to 1984, but rather in the impact it has had on subsequent developments in Nancy's thought.

## The Inoperative Community

It can no longer be a matter of figuring or modeling a communitarian essence in order to present it to ourselves and to celebrate it, but . . . it is a matter rather of thinking community, that is of thinking its insistent and possibly still *unheard* demand, beyond communitarian models or remodelings.

—JEAN-LUC NANCY, *The Inoperative Community*[35]

The opening lines of *La Communauté désœuvrée* testify to the double nature of Nancy's interrogation of the political, an interrogation which is at once philosophical and historical. As is the case in the earlier collaborative work for the Center, the question or "fate" of Marxism/communism offers a framework within which the contemporary is addressed and this in turn opens the way for a more fundamental rethinking of the nature of the political. As before, Sartre's famous comment that communism is the "unsurpassable horizon of our time" plays a key role, though again this comment is given a different emphasis or interpretation. According to Nancy, "the word 'communism' stands as an emblem of the desire to discover or rediscover a place of community at once beyond social divisions and beyond subordination to technopolitical dominion" (*CD*, 11; *IC*, 1). Here the communist imperative maintains itself in the demand for a thinking or for an experience of community which is not subjugated to the "exclusive order of privatization" (*CD*, 12; *IC*, 1). Implicit in these lines is a continuation of the claim made in the "Opening Address" and in "The 'Retreat' of the Political" that the world of liberal capitalism is one where the political per se is withdrawn into the obviousness of strictly "economic" realities and necessities, and that this atomizes the social body into the private order of the individual, itself rigorously dependent on a dominant metaphysics of the subject. Within this subjugation to an exclusive order of privatization there occurs, Nancy suggests, a "wasting away of liberty, of speech, or of simple happiness" (*CD*, 12–13; *IC*, 1). Such an order also and "more decisively" alters the form of our collective relation to finitude and to the experience of mortality. This, in turn, implies a loss of "a place to surmount the unraveling that occurs with the death of each one of us" (*CD*, 13; *IC*, 1).

The opening of *La Communauté désœuvrée* makes clear that Nancy is attempting to shift between a political critique of the contemporary (that is, a quasi-Marxian understanding of liberal capitalism as the subjugation of social life to individualism and to the order of economic exchange), and a philosophical understanding of communal identity as a collective relation to death. The rethinking of community that takes place in this work will, therefore, address the contemporary world with some degree of urgency, but will nevertheless make that address in terms of an existential or ontological questioning of a shared finitude. Of key importance in this respect is a recasting of Heidegger, and specifically of the existential structure of "being-with" (*Mitsein*), but of even greater significance perhaps is the reading Nancy gives of the Bataillian conception of community. What results from these readings is a philosophical idiom or thinking which transcribes the terms of one thinker into the terms of the other and vice-versa. This transcription of terms reflects the degree to which Nancy is suspicious of certain moments within both Bataille and Heidegger, namely a residual logic of the subject which persists in the former's use of a Hegelian language, and in the latter's invocation of the historical destiny of a people

(*Volk*). In response to Bataille and Heidegger, then, and in an attempt to think at the limits of this residual logic of the subject, Nancy develops the notion of an "unworked" or "inoperative" community.

The very term *community*, of course, might appear to be unavoidably overdetermined with identitarian or organicist connotations. Any attempt to think such a term outside of, or beyond, these connotations is likely to be highly problematic, and Nancy is acutely aware of the semantic and philosophical history which necessarily attaches itself to this concept. In particular he is interested in foregrounding what he identifies as a specifically modern paradigm of thinking about community. Within this paradigm, the "communal" is experienced in the mode of dislocation or loss. The political writing of Rousseau represents, for Nancy, an inaugural moment in this modern experience of community (*CD*, 29; *IC*, 9). The key question with regard to the political in this context is not just how the state is instituted or society is regulated. Rather, the existence of society, as a rationally or contractually organized entity, is itself experienced as a rupturing or dislocation of community, conceived in terms of a more immediate and organic self-presence of communal life to and with itself. It is Rousseau, then, who first constructs community in essentially nostalgic terms, as that which is lost in the modern experience of the social. Nancy articulates this opposition between society and community in the following terms: "Distinct from society . . . community is not only the intimate communication between its members, but also its organic communion with its own essence" (*CD*, 30; *IC*, 9). This, according to Nancy, is the essence of a modern conception of community which Rousseau bequeaths to his successors: an understanding of the communal conceived as an immediacy of self-presence and self-identity, but an immediacy which has been lost or dissolved in the modern experience of society.

Nancy begins, then, by outlining this essentially nostalgic figure of community, but does so to call it immediately into question or, more specifically, to reject it by inverting the assumptions upon which it is based. Community, he argues, is not something we have lost or something which society or the "social" has ruptured or dispersed, rather it is "*what happens to us*—question, waiting, event, imperative—*in the wake of* [*à partir de*] society" (*CD*, 34; *IC*, 11). What is being suggested here is that community is not and never has been possible on the basis of an intimate and total-ized sharing of an essence or identity, which might then be lost, ruptured, or dispersed and that we might long to regain. Rather community is possible, in the first instance and on a primordial level, only as a kind rupturing or dispersion, which is itself constitutive of the sharing or communication proper to the being-in-common of the communal. The experience of rupture or dispersal, that is, the *separation* of those entities which are "in-common" in community, would be, according to this account, precisely that which allows them to be exposed to each other, to communicate and to share an existence. In this sense the loss of intimacy, immanence, or plenitude is not something which "happens" to community in a move from archaic to modern forms of collective social organization; rather, this loss of intimacy has always already happened, and it is only on this basis that something like community can occur, or as Nancy puts it, "What this community has 'lost'—the immanence and the intimacy of a communion—is lost only in the sense that such a loss is constitutive of 'community' itself. It is not a loss: on the contrary, immanence, if it were to come about, would instantly suppress community, or communication, as such" (*CD*, 35; *IC*, 12). This is the key thought that underpins Nancy's thinking in *La Communauté désœuvrée*. What it makes clear is that his use of the term *community* is very different from, if not radically opposed to, all the conventional or traditional meanings which one may be able to ascribe to it, be they identitarian, organicist, communitarian, totalitarian, or what have you. Against all semantic expectations or received ways of understanding the term, Nancy is aiming to think about, or give a figure for, an experience of community which would exceed the principle of identity or any figure of totality. This is based on the claim, made very explicitly in the citation given above, that were any absolute identity of community to be realized, if a total immanence were to be achieved, this would mark the very suppression or obliteration of community, since, in the absence of separation, distance, or dispersal, no being-in-common, no exposure of one singular existence (you, me) to another could occur.

This summary account of the opening pages of *La Communauté désœuvrée* indicates that Nancy's unconventional use of the word *community* is predicated on an ontological or existential recasting of its traditional meaning. It does not refer to a specific social formation or mode of organization, but rather is thought in terms of the very structure of a shared existence. To this extent his transformation of the term repeats the gesture which has been shown to be at work in the preceding discussions of subjectivity, space, and body: that of reworking familiar concepts in relation to a thinking of finitude and within a displacement or questioning of their traditional metaphysical underpinnings. Heidegger's account of the being-in-the-world of Dasein is of critical importance here, just as it was for Nancy's reworking of the notions of subjectivity and space discussed in Chapters 1 and 2. In this way of thinking, subjectivity, space, and community are intimately bound up with each other, that is, each mutually implies or codetermines the other. If Heidegger gives Nancy an opening in which he can think existence in excess of any logic of subjectivity and as a plural spacing of singularities or "being-to" of sense, then he also by the same token opens up a possibility of thinking community as the fundamental "being-with" of those singularities, and not as a collection of individual subjects who bind themselves together on the basis of a shared identity.

It is in this respect that the question of death is crucial insofar as the account of being-toward-death given in *Being and Time* is precisely that which, for Nancy, places the singular existence of Dasein outside the resources or grounding of any metaphysics of the subject. In its exposure to, or projection toward, an ungraspable finitude (death), Dasein is always *hors de soi*, that is, without the intimacy or self-posing foundation proper to subjectivity. Nancy puts this in the following terms: "All of Heidegger's research into 'being-for (or toward)-death' was nothing other than an attempt to state this: *I* is not—am not—a subject" (*CD*, 40; *IC*, 14). Yet, although Heidegger gives an opening for Nancy to rework the notion of community in relation to a thinking of finitude, he does not develop such a notion within the pages of *Being and Time* itself. Indeed the, albeit brief, invocation of community in *Being and Time* as the historical being of a people or *Volk* is judged by Nancy to be a betrayal of the key insights of fundamental ontology. Dasein as "being-toward-death" may exceed any topology of substance or subjectivity but "when it came to the question of community as such, the same Heidegger also went astray with his vision of a people and a destiny conceived at least in part as a subject" (*CD*, 40; *IC*, 14). So Heidegger's existential phenomenology, insofar as it attempts to untie topologies of substance or subjectivity, opens the way for a nonidentitarian thinking of community, but itself remains fatally and unreflectively bound up with these topologies in its invocation of the historical destiny of a people (*Volk*). The problem for Nancy here is that the being-toward-death of the singular Dasein in *Being and Time* appears to have no impact on, or relation to, the collective existence of community. Insofar as Dasein is being-toward-death and being is Dasein's "ownmost possibility" (*BT*, 68; *GA*, 2:42), death is necessarily that which is each time my own death, that toward which I alone am projected. Only once Dasein is singularized in its projection toward death is it also a "being-with" others, and the relation I have to the death of others (what Heidegger refers to as the death of *das Man*) is never the same as the relation I have to my own death.[36] In *Being and Time*, then, the collective and historical being of a people is not *collectively* exposed to finitude (and therefore to a "being-outside-of-itself" or nonidentity) in the manner of a singular Dasein, or in Nancy's words, "Dasein's 'being-towards-death' was never radically implicated in its being-with—in *Mitsein*—and that it is this implication that remains to be thought" (*CD*, 41; *IC*, 14). The central aim of *La Communauté désœuvrée* is, then, to think the relation to death as "radically implicated" in the experience of community (being-with others) and to pursue the implications of this thinking of finitude in relation to a renewed conception of the political. It is in this context that the writing and intellectual itinerary of Georges Bataille comes to be of paramount importance.[37]

According to Nancy, "Bataille has gone farthest into the crucial experience of the modern destiny of community" (*CD*, 44; *IC*, 16). His contention is that Bataille's thought emerges more generally from what he calls "a political exigency and uneasiness," or from a questioning of the political as such that was "guided by the thought of community" (*CD*, 44; *IC*, 16). This crucial aspect of Bataille's intellectual career, Nancy also suggests, has so far not been properly recognized by his commentators. Twenty years after the publication of *La Communauté désœuvrée* this is no longer the case, but Nancy is certainly right to highlight the central importance of Bataille's engagement with the political.[38] This engagement is most clearly evident in the various projects and collaborations which Bataille pursued throughout the 1930s, for instance in the ethnological dimension which informed his editorship of the review *Documents* and in the more overtly political concerns which informed the work of the various reviews with which he was associated, including *Minotaure*, *La Critique Sociale*, *Contre-*

*Attaque,* and *Acéphale.* The first three of these were explicitly aligned with the revolutionary left, and many of Bataille's articles of this period show him attempting to marry his own thinking of "heterology" with a critique of capitalism and a rethinking of community based upon the idea of proletarian revolution.[39] In this context the proletarian masses are viewed (rather idiosyncratically) as a body of heterogeneous forces which are suppressed and excluded by the homogeneity of bourgeois social organization and capitalist economic exchange. Revolution is seen as that inevitable moment when these suppressed forces are violently unleashed. The review *Acéphale,* which was also a project for a secret society, appeared in four issues between 1936 and 1939 and marked a point in Bataille's thinking where he was less involved with an attempt to conjoin his interests with those of revolutionary Marxism. He aimed instead at reintroducing into modern social life an experience and a practice of the sacred in order to re-institute a form of community which would embody a certain commonality of experience characteristic of archaic societies. This ambition was also reflected in Bataille's collaboration with Michel Lieris and Roger Caillois in the work of the Collège de sociologie between 1937 and 1938.[40] This pre-war itinerary, then, sees Bataille rejecting modern social forms in favor of different conceptions of community, first in a (highly unorthodox) understanding of the proletarian masses and second, outside of any endorsement of revolutionary Marxism, in terms of an experience of the sacred and a restitution of a more "primitive" communal experience.[41]

What interests Nancy about Bataille's itinerary throughout this period is first of all the manner in which it repeats the paradigm of community he has elaborated in relation to Rousseau, that is, community conceived in essentially nostalgic terms as that which has been lost within modern society and needs to be refound or reinstituted. As will become clear, Nancy is interested in particular in the way Bataille comes to reject any nostalgic understanding of community. Just as significant, however, is the manner in which Bataille comes to understand the nature of "archaic" communities, that is, in terms of an experience of the communal based upon the principles of excess, expenditure, and above all upon a shared relation to death. This experience of excess or expenditure has, according to Bataille, manifested itself in a number of different forms in premodern societies, in what he calls practices of "unproductive expenditure," that is, "luxury, mourning, wars, cults, the construction of sumptuous monuments, games, spectacle, arts, perverse sexual activity."[42] It has manifested itself also in archaic forms of economic exchange, for instance in the ritualized act of gift giving, known as potlatch, found in various forms across the globe.[43] Perhaps the most privileged figure of unproductive expenditure for Bataille in the 1930s was that of sacrifice, and in many ways the principle or structure of sacrifice underpins all these other instances. The relation of an archaic experience of community to death finds its most explicit elaboration in this figure. For Bataille the structure of sacrifice, the ritual putting to death of another being, affirms a collective relation to death insofar as those who carry out the sacrifice (and those who partake of the ritual by bearing witness to it), also in a certain manner *participate* in the death of the one sacrificed. Bataille's interest in this idea is most clearly apparent in his project for a secret acephalic society organized as it was around the idea (although ultimately not the reality) of human sacrifice.[44]

At the heart of this conception of sacrifice lies an understanding of death which is both different and similar to that of Heidegger. Where in *Being and Time* the death of others is the death of *das Man* and is never the same as *my* death (my ownmost possibility which each time is always and only my own), for Bataille it is conversely and exclusively in the death of others that our mortality is revealed. It is in seeing others die, and in our participation in that same potentiality for (or being-toward) death, that we encounter our own finitude. Death, then, in Bataille's terms is not something which can be thought in isolation from community; indeed it is on the basis of the fact that our mortality or finitude is always already shared that something like community can exist in the first instance. This is why sacrifice becomes such a privileged figure, since it represents a ritual in which the very structure of community, that is to say, a shared or collective relation to death, is experienced or affirmed. This is also why, for Bataille, those premodern societies organized on the basis of sacrificial practices or a sacrificial experience of the sacred are also given a privileged position in his various projects of the late 1930s. Importantly, sacrifice conceived as irrecoverable loss, wastage, or expenditure signifies that death is not a horizon that can be mastered. It is not something that can be directly encountered or grasped by consciousness and thus in any way triumphed over or overcome. In the Hegelian/Kojèvian terms used by Bataille death cannot be "put to work," that is to say, incorporated into the dialectical activity of negation and determination which makes up the life of the subject.[45] Since death, as the annihilation of subjectivity, is only ever encountered indirectly in the death of others, it is not something that is assimilable to the principle of identity, or, in Nancy's words, to the "resources of a metaphysics of the subject" (*CD*, 41; *IC*, 14). In this sense it is arguable that Bataille in fact repeats Heidegger's understanding of existence, as a being-toward a horizon of death which cannot be grasped or mastered as such, but he situates this (non)relation or exposure to death on the level of the collective, of community, and not on the level of the singular Dasein.

Bataille's central importance in *La Communauté désœuvrée* lies in the way he thinks this fundamental relation between community and death. The political dimension and impetus of Bataille's thinking such as it developed throughout 1930s gives Nancy a framework within which he can rethink community outside of any figure of identity or totality. An exposure to a potentiality for death, inassimilable to the logic of a subject, is that which is shared in community and not a principle of identity or communal essence. Nancy expresses this in the following terms:

Community . . . is calibrated on the death of those whom we call, perhaps wrongly, its "members" (inasmuch as it is not a question of an organism). But it does not make a work of this calibration. The death upon which community is calibrated does not *operate* the dead being's passage into some communal intimacy, nor does community, for its part, *operate* the transfiguration of its dead into some substance or subject—be these homeland, native soil or blood, nation, a delivered or fulfilled humanity, absolute phalanstery, family, or mystical body. Community is calibrated on death as that of which it is precisely impossible to *make a work*. (*CD*, 41; *IC*, 15)

What Bataille bequeaths to Nancy, then, is a thinking of community as "the presentation to its members of their mortal truth . . . the presentation of the finitude and irredeemable excess that make up finite being" (*CD*, 43; *IC*, 15). It is from this Hegelian language of "putting to work" that the notion of an "unworked" or "inoperative" (*désœuvrée*) community is derived and from which *La Communauté désœuvrée*, of course, takes its title.[46] Yet although Nancy takes on this understanding of community and death from Bataille, he also, as has been indicated, rejects all nostalgic conceptions which assume that an intimacy or communion has been lost and needs to be regained. He therefore rejects Bataille's privileging of the archaic, or the primitive, and indeed argues that Bataille himself came to realize "the ridiculous nature of all nostalgia" (*CD*, 47; *IC*, 17). This changed attitude to a nostalgic conception of community has its origin, Nancy argues, in the experience of failure which resulted from Bataille's political engagements of the 1930s. This failure was in the first instance that of the communist project, that is, its betrayal by the Soviet state. In the second instance Bataille experienced this failure in the relation to the history of European fascism and specifically in relation to fate of the Nazi state. The catastrophe, horror, and sheer absurdity to which Nazism gave rise, led Bataille, in the wake of the Second World War, to be far more skeptical about the possibility, or indeed the desirability, of any attempt to realize a nostalgic conception of community. Against the backdrop of wider political events, Nancy argues, Bataille "went through the experience of realizing that the nostalgia for a communal being was at the same time the desire for a work of death" (*CD*, 46–47; *IC*, 17). In this context the Nazi project of grounding community in an intimacy or communion of a historical people appears as an inversion or as a perversion of Bataille's conception of a sacrificial community. Instead of an experience of shared finitude and collective exposure to a horizon of death which cannot be mastered or put to work in the production of a communal subject, the Nazi project enacted the very opposite process, that is, a putting to work of death, in the act of genocide on the one hand and sacrifice of German blood on the other, in order to found a community and realize it as the immanence of a shared essence or identity (native soil, blood). In Bataille's terms, and as is indicated in Nancy's comment cited above, such a project would necessarily fail since death is precisely that which cannot ultimately be subsumed into a work of subjectivity: "it does not *operate* the transfiguration of its dead into some substance or subject." The attempt to restore a sacred community within the modern world is not played out in the historical arena according to a logic of sacrifice such as it informs the secret society of *Acéphale*, but rather occurred as a necessarily failed attempt, catastrophic, genocidal, and ultimately suicidal, to put death to work. It is the experience of this that led Bataille beyond any nostalgic conception and to a "withdrawal from communitarian enterprises" (*CD*, 47; *IC*, 17).

It is certainly clear that Bataille's work on and around the review

*Acéphale* and his activity in the Collège de sociologie mark the endpoint of his attempts to engage in projects which would seek some form of revolutionary change within the modern world.[47] In terms of Bataille's postwar itinerary what interests Nancy is the way Bataille comes to think the figure of community in relation to eroticism, as the "community of lovers." Nancy's reading of Bataille effectively, and rather schematically, splits the latter's career into two halves: the prewar period marked by revolutionary projects and a nostalgia for archaic social forms and the period after 1939, marked by a thinking of community in which "communion" occurs not in ritual practices of the sacred but comes to be more and more located in the realm of erotic experience. Yet, if Nancy finds in Bataille's thought a model for thinking community both in relation to death and outside a logic of subjectivity, he also identifies key aspects in which a legacy or a work of the subject persists. As has been indicated, the risk in the logic of sacrifice is that the subject or subjects who expose themselves to a shared yet ungraspable horizon of death in the sacrificial act do not in fact enact community as an unworking of identity, but rather seek (impossibly) to appropriate death and put it to work in order to realize its transfiguration into a substance or subject. Nancy notes that in the postwar period Bataille acknowledged that for the logic of sacrifice to be properly sacrificial, not only would the victim have to die but the sacrificer would also then have to commit suicide (CD, 47; IC, 17).[48] Only in this way would there be any real sacrifice (loss without gain), and only then would death be the unworking of a subject, rather than a subject putting death to work (which Bataille now sees as an inevitable outcome of any sacrificial *project*). According to Nancy it is this admission which lies at the heart of Bataille's shift in the postwar period, away from the notion of sacrificial community toward the notion of a community of lovers.

Yet he goes on to argue that this shift to an extent exacerbates, or at least certainly does not overcome, the problem in Bataille's thinking of a residual and unthought legacy of the subject. Bataille, of course, rejects any metaphysical understanding of subjectivity as an autonomous, self-posing, or self-grounding identity. This, as has been indicated, is why Nancy is so drawn to the thinking of community as a shared relation to death which unworks any communal assumption of identity or subjectivity. For both it is impossible to properly think community on the basis of a community of subjects, since this isolates each singular existence in its own autonomous sphere, and thereby suppresses the communal relation (shared finitude). Or as Nancy puts it, "For Bataille, as for us all, a thinking of the subject thwarts a thinking of community" (*CD*, 60; *IC*, 23). Yet the manner in which Bataille comes to think the limits of the subject, its irrecoverable excess and exposure to a shared finitude upon which community can occur, is framed within a (Hegelian/Kojèvian) language of the subject-object relation. It is this that Nancy questions in his reading of the "community of lovers." This invocation of a Hegelian/Kojèvian language signifies that in the very moment Bataille seeks to think beyond any logic of subjectivity, he also remains to a degree implicated within the orbit of that logic. Nancy puts this in the following terms: "Properly speaking, Bataille had no *concept* of the subject. But, at least up to a certain point, he allowed the communication exceeding the subject to relate back to a subject, or to institute *itself* as subject" (*CD*, 63; *IC*, 24). The term *communication* here refers to the manner in which Bataille comes to understand the excess of the subject over itself. This excess is, precisely, that which allows community to occur (since it means we are not isolated from each other as discrete identities), and is marked or affirmed in the sphere of eroticism (just as it was previously marked in the notion of a sacrificial community). Within this sphere of communication any self-enclosure of the subject, or any immanence of the subject to itself, is impossible and the separation of subject and object is dissolved. In *L'Expérience intérieure* Bataille gives an explicit account of the manner in which he understands communication as the dissolution of the subject or as the fusion of subject and object.[49] Nancy foregrounds the extent to which, in his view at least, Bataille's formulations in this text remain tied, not just to a Hegelian understanding, but to the broader context of European philosophy from which the Hegelian system emerged. If the communication of erotic experience is a place or site, then "the equivalence between this place and a 'fusion of the subject and the object' . . . leads Bataille back to the core of a constant thematic in speculative idealism" (*CD*, 61; *IC*, 23). In this context Nancy questions whether, in Bataille's Hegelian language of subject and object, the existence of others is ever really posed as *other*, since the other person is not in fact conceived in terms of a radical alterity: "This other is no longer an other, but an object of a subject's representation" (*CD*, 62; *IC*, 24). As long as this is the case the subject remains intact and subsumes all excess to itself rather than being undone in the exposure to an excess it cannot master or appropriate.

This is a crucial point since the stakes, for Nancy, always turn around the possibility of rethinking community, according to a thinking of finitude (a relation to death) that exceeds the resources of a metaphysics of the subject. What his readings of Bataille and Heidegger in *La Communauté désœuvrée* show is that both these thinkers offer an opening to thought in which such a fundamental reworking of the concept of community might occur, but that both, in different ways and at different moments, fall back into an unreflective and unthought logic of subjectivity. On the one hand, Bataille is able to think community as a shared relation to death, but he is compromised by his thinking of each singular existence in terms of a subject-object relation. On the other hand, Heidegger thinks singular existence as a relation to death which unties subjectivity, but "goes awry" when he thinks community as the assumption of the historical destiny of a people (and thus conceives of them, in identitarian terms, as a subject). Put very schematically then, Nancy's readings in *La Communauté désœuvrée* expose the latent thinking of subjectivity in both Heidegger and Bataille but seek to think community anew by combining the way Heidegger conceives singular existence (Dasein) with the way Bataille thinks communal existence (shared finitude). The philosophical idiom which results from this will be Heideggerian, but without the concomitant invocation of community as historical people, and Bataillian, but without the invocation of singular existence as a relation of subject to object.

Nancy's community is "unworked," then, insofar as it is a multiplicity of singular existences who are "in common" only on the basis of a shared mortality which cannot be subsumed into any communal project or collective identity. This relation to death is not the communication, communion, or fusion of a subject and object. It is the exposure of each singular existence, its being-outside-of-itself, to a death which is revealed in and through the death of others. Community reveals, or rather *is*, our exposure to the unmasterable limit of death, and thus our being together outside of all identity, or work of subjectivity. This is expressed in the following terms:

Sharing comes down to this: what community reveals to me, in presenting to me my birth and my death, is my existence outside of myself. . . . *Community does not*

*sublate the finitude it exposes. Community itself, in sum, is nothing but this exposition.*
It is the community of finite beings, and as such it is itself a *finite* community. In
other words, not a limited community as opposed to an infinite or absolute community, but a community *of* finitude, because finitude "is" communitarian, and
because finitude alone is communitarian. (*CD*, 68; *IC*, 26; Nancy's emphasis)

What is perhaps most striking about this passage is the repetition of the
language of being. The verb *to be* is used six times in the third-person singular and this, of course, is a reiteration of Nancy's insistence that community be thought as an ontological dimension. Community here is not a
project to be realized, it does not occur as a series of social practices, and it
is not a value or an ideal—rather, it *is* only as shared finite existence. This
understanding responds in a very precise manner to four of the five "basic
traits" which were listed in "The 'Retreat' of the Political" (see p. 166). The
figure of community which emerges in *La Communauté désœuvrée* refuses
the dominant contemporary understanding of the political as the "techno-
economical organization or 'making' operational of our world" (*CD*, 59;
*IC*, 23), based on an essentialized understanding of the human as *homo
ecomomicus*. As has been indicated earlier in this discussion, this dominant
understanding is, according to Nancy, nothing other than a prolongation
or historical transformation of bygone communitarian projects, which in
each case invoke specific figures of human essence or origin in order to lay
a metaphysical ground for the political and for a project of political community (e.g., God, Man, Proletariat, People). The figure of an unworked
or inoperative community recasts the political outside any possibility of
grounding or any assumption of collective identity, and outside any possibility of project or historical process.

On the basis of this account of *La Communauté désœuvrée* a number of questions might be posed. Indeed a number of questions have been
posed about this work by a variety of commentators writing from very different perspectives. These range from specific but important questions,
such as whether Nancy's critical reading of Bataille is entirely accurate or
fair, or whether, despite his reworking of Bataille, he does not still remain
too involved with a Heideggerianism in relation to which philosophical,
ethical, and political objections might persist. More broadly the question
of the manner in which one can move from an ontological recasting of
community to the empirical realm of politics and political judgment has

again arisen. Such responses to this thinking of an unworked community have come from within the literary-philosophical circles to which Nancy himself belongs (e.g., writing by Maurice Blanchot and Jacques Derrida) but also have emerged within Anglo-Saxon academic debates (among philosophers, political theorists, and literary critics). One of the earliest and most important of these interventions is Blanchot's *La Communauté inavouable* (1983). This work is important insofar has it has had an impact on the wider reception of Nancy's work within the English-speaking academic world, and also because it highlights various divergences and differences within the specific French literary philosophical community to which he belongs.

*La Communauté inavouable* is a response to an early version of Nancy's work on community published in 1983 in the fourth issue of the review *Aléa* (see note 37 above). It is also, as Blanchot himself points out, a reprise of a reflection with regard to "the communist demand" which has informed his writing throughout much of his career. This reflection responds to the demand made on thought by the communist ideal, calling into question "the possibility or impossibility of community in a time which seems to have lost all community" (*CI*, 9; *UC*, 1). From the outset, then, Blanchot indicates, albeit indirectly, that Nancy's concerns such as they emerge within the context of his work for the Center have also for some time already been his own. They were also, Blanchot reiterates, those of Bataille, and by signaling the presence a certain uninterrupted questioning of community within his own writing, Blanchot is also, perhaps, indicating the extent to which he shared a certain itinerary with his friend. What follows in the pages of *La Communauté inavouable*, then, is a reading of Bataille, and specifically of the Bataillian understanding of community, which takes some degree of distance from Nancy's account while emphasizing many of their shared concerns. This gives rise to a rather different approach to the way in which the existence of community might be thought, or more specifically it raises a number of implicit objections to Nancy's formulations.

As Leslie Hill has pointed out in the account he gives of *La Communauté inavouable*, much of its opening section, "La Communauté négative," is devoted to restating and reaffirming Nancy's understanding of community. Blanchot, for instance, repeats Nancy's understanding of hitherto existing communism as resting on a totalizing conception of immanence, and of totalitarianism and individualism as intimately linked in their shared affirmation of closure (of the social whole or atomized individual).⁵⁰ He also repeats Nancy's rejection of any project of community founded on the nostalgia for a fusional communion or for a sharing of communitarian essence (*CI*, 11; *UC*, 2). Most importantly, Blanchot reaffirms the understanding of community as a shared relation to finitude (*CI*, 24; *UC*, 11). Yet, as Hill also shows, while Blanchot endorses these positions up to a point, he nevertheless introduces another vocabulary into his discussion, and this shift in philosophical lexicon articulates a rather different understanding of community.⁵¹ In the account of *La Communauté désœuvrée* given above it was argued that great importance was placed on the language used to describe the question of relation upon which community or being-in-common can be thought. The Hegelian language of subject and object was rejected in favor of a reworked and reinscribed Heideggerian language of the being-with of Dasein (*Mitsein*). The language used in *La Communauté inavouable* to address the question of relation is neither Hegelian nor Heideggerian, but Levinasian, as the following citation reveals:

If the relation of man to man ceases to be the relation of the Same [*du Même*] with the Same but introduces the Other [*l'Autre*] as irreducible and, in its equality, always in a relation of asymmetry to he who contemplates it, it is an entirely different kind of relation which imposes itself or imposes a different form of society which could hardly be called a "community." Or one could accept to call it thus while asking oneself what is at stake in the thought of community and if it, whether it has existed or not, does not always in the end affirm the *absence* of community. (*CI*, 12; *UC*, 3)

Any reader familiar with Levinas's thought will know that the relation of self and other occurs, not in the mode of being-with, but rather as a relation to a transcendence or alterity which escapes all ontological disclosure or recuperation within the horizon of being. Prior to any horizonality or preunderstanding of being this relation to alterity constitutes the self, and thus imposes an indebtedness to, and therefore responsibility toward, the other (which in its transcendence is capitalized as Other); hence the Levinasian insistence on the primacy of ethics over ontology. Significantly, at the very moment Blanchot introduces this Levinasian terminology he also questions whether the term *community* could apply to any conception of the communal which takes the asymmetrical relation of self and other as its starting point. In the context of this Levinasian thinking of relation Blanchot appears reluctant to the use the term *community* in anything that might resemble positive terms. If others are always experienced as a radical alterity or as a transcendence inassimilable to any horizon of being as such, can community be thought in terms of "being-with"? Must it not always be a community thought, not in terms of its coming to presence but rather in terms of its absence? Such, as the above citation shows, is Blanchot's question, and it leads him to dispute the account Nancy gives of Bataille in *La Communauté désœuvrée*.

A key argument of *La Communauté inavouable* is that Bataille, after the failure of his quasi-Marxist engagement, comes to experience community, not as a project (acephalic/sacrificial), but rather as an absence, or more specifically as a community of absence. This emphasis on community as inassimilable to any project or to any logic of being represents an implicit refusal of Nancy's suggestion in *La Comunauté désœuvrée* that the secret society of *Acéphale* can be thought as in any way related to the Nazi project of "putting death to work" in order to affirm an immanentized communal essence. The motif of an absent community also refuses Nancy's contention that the project of *Acéphale* was experienced as a failure. Blanchot expresses this in the following terms:

The absence of community is not the failure of community: it belongs to community as its extreme moment or as the test which exposes its necessary disappearance. *Acéphale* was the common experience of that which cannot be placed in common, nor properly maintained, nor reserved for an ulterior abandon. . . . The community of *Acéphale* could not exist as such, but only as imminence and as withdrawal. (CI, 31; UC, 15)

The failure of *Acéphale* would, in these terms, always be its success since, as an absence of community or as a community of absence, it was never a question of a communal project as such: it was never a work which could be unworked, nor that which could be inverted or perverted into the National Socialist nostalgia for a community of blood and soil. Blanchot seems to be implicitly calling into question the whole language of working and unworking which informs the argument of *La Communauté désœuvrée* and asking whether the motif of unworking does not perhaps always im-

ply a prior work or operativity. If this is so Nancy's invocation of "unworking" might in fact be always taking as its starting point the notion of community as work or project and would thus ultimately remain rigorously
held within the thinking of work or project it seeks to displace. Hence the
significance of Blanchot's use of the term "unavowable" (*inavouable*). Unavowable here emphasizes the importance of the fact that *Acéphale*, as a society, was *secret*. It did not declare itself, it did not present itself as project
or program, but rather withdrew and only to this extent did it represent
the "experience of that which cannot be placed in common, nor properly
maintained." As that which was secret and unavowable, *Acéphale* was also
withdrawn from any project or horizon of being; it was that which "could
not exist as such."

Underpinning Blanchot's repetition of Nancy in *La Communauté inavouable* is a divergence and, indeed, a reproach. The reproach is implicit
in the way he differentiates Bataille's understanding of community from
any nostalgic *project*, and thus refuses any comparison, however indirect,
of that understanding with the National Socialist experiment. It is divergent insofar as it refuses to think community within a logic of working or
unworking, and within any horizon of being or of being-with. The source
of both the reproach and the divergence, then, appears to be the degree to
which Nancy remains tied to a thinking of being and to the language of
ontology. This is clear from Blanchot's, explicitly Levinasian, affirmation
of ethics:

Ethics is only possible if ontology—which always reduces the Other to the Same—
gives way, and can affirm an anterior relation in which the self is not content simply to recognize the Other, to recognize itself in the Other, but is placed in question by it to the point where the self can only respond through a responsibility
which cannot be limited and which exceeds it without being exhausted. (*CI*, 73;
*UC*, 43)

Underpinning the argument of *La Communauté inavouable* is an affirmation of the primacy of ethics over ontology, since the latter is irredeem-
ably implicated in the violent gesture of a philosophical tradition which
reduces the Other to a logic of the same.[52] On this basis Nancy's attempt
to think community (however inoperative or unworked) in terms of a being-in-common, or being-with which occurs on the basis of a shared relation to finitude, can only miss, or pass over the real relation which struc-

tures our encounter with others, that is, the ethical relation, the relation to transcendence or alterity prior to any horizon of being. By the same token Nancy fails to detect the degree to which Bataille's account of community already escapes the horizon of ontology, since it is only ever a community of absence.

This critical reading given in *La Communauté inavouable* is to a certain extent quite persuasive. Blanchot, for instance, gives a more detailed and nuanced account of the Bataillian understanding of existence as always already incomplete, contested, and exposed to its own impossibility. According to this account the excess of our shared finite existence is inassimilable to ontological disclosure or to any working or unworking of subjectivity (and hence also to any dialectic) (CI, 16; UC, 5). This in turn leads Blanchot to dispute the account Nancy gives of communication, the fusion of subject and object, and of the "community of lovers." Although a Hegelian language of subject and object may be invoked in key works such as *L'Expérience intérieure*, what is ultimately at stake in eroticism is not the ecstatic self-forgetting of erotic union, but rather the "putting into play" (*mise en jeu*) of an existence, which, as *always already* insufficient, contested, and exposed to impossibility, is affirmed prior to any logic of recognition or dialectical work (*CI*, 18–19, 21; *UC*, 6, 8). It is arguable, therefore, that Blanchot elaborates Bataille's thinking with greater precision than does the account given in *La Communauté désœuvrée*. At the same time the reservation he expresses vis-à-vis Nancy's use of the language of ontology may also seem persuasive and has certainly gained a degree of wider critical currency through the influential work of Simon Critchley. It is worth noting, however, that Nancy would probably be skeptical of any invocation of Levinas in the context of a rethinking of community or of the ethical relation. As the discussion of the preceding chapters have argued, Nancy's philosophy, his thinking of the "being-to" of sense and its effraction or exscription in relation to bodily existence, articulates an ontology which does not necessarily "reduce the Other to the Same." For Nancy ontology or, more properly speaking, a quasi ontology of excess in which being is always exscribed, does not *reaffirm* the violence of the philosophical tradition insofar as it situates its thinking of being outside of itself (that is, it always exscribes the thought of being it inscribes and to this extent is closer to a thinking of exteriority or alterity [and therefore to the positions of both Blanchot and Levinas] than Blanchot admits). This is, though, the key difference between Nancy's thought on the one hand and that of Blanchot/Levinas on the other: the latter pair distance themselves from a primary emphasis on the language of being, while the former seeks to rework it and think it anew. Indeed, he would claim that the Levinasian insistence on the priority of ethics over ontology rests on a significant misreading or misrepresentation of Heidegger's thought and a failure to engage philosophically with the fact that, in the last instance, all thought necessarily begins and ends in a reference to that which *is*. It is not within the scope of this discussion to give a full account of the critical distance Nancy takes from Levinasian ethics. It is important rather to underline the extent to which Blanchot's reading of *La Communauté désœuvrée* and his refusal of the language of "being-with" rests on this broader divergence with respect to Heidegger and to the Heideggerian legacy within French thought. A similar though not identical divergence informed Derrida's ambivalent response in *Le Toucher Jean-Luc Nancy* (such as it was discussed in the preceding chapter) and is evident also in works such as *Politiques de l'amitié* and *Spectres de Marx.*[53]

Blanchot's response to Nancy is therefore important on a number of fronts. It highlights the extent to which the concerns of *La Communauté désœuvrée* are central to those of a broader literary-philosophical community in France in the postwar years.[54] It also highlights the degree to which Nancy's reworking of the interlinked questions of relation, community, and the political within an explicitly ontological perspective or language sets him apart from the thought of figures with whom he can, to greater or lesser degrees, be most closely associated: for example Blanchot himself, Bataille, and in a slightly more ambiguous way, Derrida. Maintaining this ontological perspective allows Nancy to think community as something that always necessarily *is* by virtue of our shared finitude, and not as something which may be lost or gained, regretted in nostalgia for a past or projected in a program for the future. As such community, in Nancy, can only be affirmed or denied. The choice or instance of decision which presents itself in this context relates to whether the shared finitude of existence is recognized and affirmed as such (together with the unworking of collective identity this implies) or whether this finitude is negated in the continued appeal to metaphysical figures of essence or ground, and to an identitarian understanding of political community. It is within this perspective, or possibility, of affirmation and negation that the vexed question of the relation between the political and politics in Nancy needs to be addressed.

### Literary Communism

As was indicated earlier in this discussion many of the critical responses to Nancy's collaborative work on and around the political have called into question the usefulness of his thought for addressing in a more direct fashion the empirical realm of politics and of political action or struggle. This was evident both in Nancy Fraser's contemporaneous response to the work of the Centre de recherches philosophiques sur le politique and Simon Critchley's work around ethics and politics in the early 1990s. In both cases the very act of distinguishing between the political and politics was seen to be overly reductive and, indeed, entirely counterproductive in relation to immediate possibilities of political or ethical engagement. The thinking of community which emerges in *La Communauté désœuvrée* might well appear to confirm the general thrust of these criticisms. If, as Nancy says, "community is given to us with being and as being, well before all our projects, aims and enterprises" (*CD*, 87; *IC*, 59), then it is difficult to see how this might be relevant to any engagement with the empirical realm as such, since, as an ontological given, our shared finitude would seem to be posited prior to any order of political decision or commitment, action or inaction. However, it is worth underlining once more that, from the very outset, the whole logic of "retreat" or of "re-treating" the political that informed the work of the Center was predicated on a refusal of any direct move between the order of philosophical questioning and engagement with political projects, programs, or parties. To this extent the thinking of *La Communauté désœuvrée* remains rigorously within the parameters which Nancy and Lacoue-Labarthe set for themselves at the outset of their collaborative work on the question of the political. Yet, from the very outset, both held to the assumption that the attempt to retrace or replay the political was not entirely disengaged from commitment per se, and indeed that such a retracing was in itself an important form of engaged activity. At some point, then, there has to be a point of connection between the act of "retracing" the political and the sphere of politics, or rather a way of thinking their mutual implication such that the former will have an impact, albeit indirectly, on the way we think about or engage with the latter.

Fraser and Critchley are not alone in suggesting that Nancy does not entirely succeed in addressing this point of connection or mutual implication.[55] One of the most interesting interventions in this context has come from a political scientist. In an article published in the journal *Constellations* Andrew Norris highlights the strengths and what he sees as the important shortcomings of Nancy's conception of community.[56] From the perspective of political philosophy or theory the notion of an "inoperative community" is important, Norris suggests, insofar as it constitutes "one of our most comprehensive arguments against [the] understanding of politics as a form or expression of identity."[57] The contention here is that Nancy's work fundamentally challenges received notions of political community and thus provides a conceptual framework within which political concepts of all kinds can be rethought and their history reevaluated. An ontological recasting of our "being-in-common" would, by this account, change the way we think about the empirical field and how we might address it, while stopping short of the traditional (metaphysical) philosophical gesture of laying a ground for an overarching project or program. Norris's article, then, marks an important gesture of recognition by a political scientist of the way in which Nancy's thought can have an impact beyond the area of strictly philosophical endeavor. Philosophy here may not lay a ground for political thought or courses of action, but it can offer new perspectives which would alter the manner in which political events, both historical and contemporary, are understood. To this gesture of recognition, however, Norris adds an important reservation. What the thinking of community as shared finitude lacks, he suggests, is an effective and properly rigorous theory of political judgment. While Nancy's thinking gives us the conceptual tools to articulate critical suspicion of all politics and ideology based on assumptions of identity, it fails to develop criteria for judgment, or offer any standard which would allow us to differentiate between alternatives. Norris argues that the ethics or politics of this thinking amounts to whether or not we recognize and affirm "being-in-common" as our fundamental state. It does not, he suggests, go far in telling us *how* we might affirm being-in-common or what a good or bad, or wise or foolish, affirmation might look like. Hence Nancy's thinking turns on whether we have an authentic or inauthentic relation to our shared finitude: "For Nancy . . . to be inauthentic is to deny our being-in-common. Instead of a lifeless conformity, this denial produces xenophobia and violent conflict, the oppression and rejection of the 'other,' be she Muslim, Croatian, Mexican or Black. To be authentic is to 'consciously' undergo the experience of our sharing—and this entails a resistance to such violence."[58] To a large degree this is a fair account of Nancy's position, consistent with the accounts he gives of totalitarianism (in particular of Nazism). Norris is also right to suggest that a key aspect of this thinking relates to a gesture of affirmation or denial in relation to the ontological structure of shared finitude. Yet his call for a proper theory of judgment and for some kind of legislative framework that would give criteria for decision and action is fraught with difficulty. Such a theory would, albeit in a limited or residual manner, reintroduce the principle of identity or of foundation within thought. As will be clear by now, Nancy would question or refuse such a notion in the name of a fully rigorous thinking of finitude. For Nancy questions of decision and judgment are important but they can only be viewed in the context of the way his reworking of ontology implies, or is inseparable from, an ethos or ethics, that is, a mode of comportment which is consistent with the structure of being he describes. Insofar as Norris values the thinking of community which emerges in *La Communauté désœuvrée* but calls also for a more legislative theory of judgment, he is attempting to combine modes of thought which may ultimately be rigorously incompatible.[59] It may be wrong, then, to suggest that a theory of judgment is necessary in order to connect Nancy's thought of the political with the empirical realm of politics. Indeed Norris's article largely ignores the fact that the issue of praxis is in fact a central concern in *La Communauté désœuvrée*. The manner in which the structure of shared finitude may be affirmed is addressed very explicitly in the two sections entitled "Interrupted Myth" and "Literary Communism" (albeit in a rather different fashion than Norris envisages). What the thinking of finite community leads to is not a theory of judgment, but rather, and rather curiously, to a thinking of literature and a specific notion of writing.

It was clear from the analysis offered by Nancy and Lacoue-Labarthe in the "Opening Address" to the Center that their understanding of the European metaphysical tradition affirmed a cobelonging of the philosophical with the political. Implicit in this cobelonging was the sense that metaphysical understanding has historically sought to complete itself within or *as* the political, that is, to realize itself fully within the field of relations which constitute human community. This further implies a necessary cobelonging or mutual interpenetration of the political and the sphere of politics. Central to this account was the notion that the completion or realization of metaphysical understanding occurred in and through an appeal to specific figures of the human which would then function as the foundation or source of legitimation for specific political forms or programs. The key issue within this context would be the question of how, and by what means, the foundational figures which structure the political are communicated to, or instantiated within, the sphere of politics. In *La Communauté désœuvrée* Nancy addresses this issue within the context of a specific understanding of myth and mythic narratives. "Myth," here, does not refer simply to fabulous tales transmitted by tradition or to what we usually understand by "mythology" (in, for instance, its Greek, Roman or Nordic forms). Myth, in this context, is that to which a political community appeals in order to found its existence as such and to perpetuate that existence as the intimate sharing of an identity or essence. The passage from the political to the sphere of politics occurs, then, in myth, insofar as it is in myth that the existence of lived community is founded and perpetuated. According to Nancy, "Myth is above all a full and original speech, which both reveals and forms the intimate being of a community" (*CD*, 122; *IC*, 48). Myth, then, would be a language or discourse which allows the world of shared finitude to be known and understood in specific ways which would in turn dictate the manner in which we live and interact together within political and communal structures or institutions. In this sense myth has a foundational, structuring power in relation to communal life; it is "the name of a *structuring logos* . . . , the name of the cosmos structured as logos" (*CD*, 125; *IC*, 49). Such a conception is entirely consistent with Nancy's broader understanding of being as that spatial-temporal dissemination of sense which opens a world and constitutes shared existence as such. Myth, in this context, would refer to the manner in which sense, as the shared stuff of finite existence, is organized into a signifying discourse or narrative, a series of figures or fictions upon which specific communal formations and practices can be based. To this extent it represents both a formal articulation of the order of sense that is constitutive of existence, and that which gives ground and meaning to specific communal institutions or practices. As a foundational fiction or narrative it traverses or communicates between the order of the political and the order of politics: "Myth communicates the common, the common-being of what it reveals or of what it recites. Consequently at the same time as each one of its revelations it also reveals community to itself and founds it" (*CD*, 128; *IC*, 50–51). In this sense, Nancy suggests, it is impossible to think the existence of community outside the appeal to myth, or rather it is necessary to think the mutual implication or inevitable coexistence of the one with the other: where there is community there is myth and vice-versa.

It is arguable, then, that this understanding of myth offers a way of thinking a movement or passage between the fundamental order of the political on the one hand and the sphere of politics on the other. This is not to say that the mess of political events is entirely reducible to the mythic narratives which give them life, but they could not exist in the way they do without an appeal to, or a grounding in, such narratives. This does not necessarily imply that the founding fictions of myth function as causes of events such that any one event can only be understood in terms of its mythic foundation. Rather it implies that a fundamental articulation of sense (existence) and the formalizing of that sense into the signifying discourses of myth (the communication of an "in-common") gives an overall context of sense and meaning which would underpin historical causality (and agency) per se. In this sense the processes of cause and effect which might interest the historian would themselves occur on the basis of a mythic understanding and within the context of an appeal to the fictions of mythic narrative. Yet insofar as this account does not seek to explain processes of cause and effect at the empirical level, it may appear to lack an explanation of the way in which historical communities change over time or how one mythic narrative gives way to or is superseded by another. Indeed the model of historical community which emerges here might appear to be rather static, and necessarily so since the more usual sense of myth implies a temporality which is outside of historical time. Insofar as mythological forms are usually taken to embody or symbolize natural forces, timeless essences or eternal aspects of the human condition, they traditionally are situated in a sphere that would be prior to the time of historical progression.

It is important to note, however, that the discussion of myth in *La Communauté désœuvrée* invokes two different understandings of the term *community*, the traditional notion of community as a sharing of identity or essence (requiring a foundational myth), and the sense given to the term by Nancy, a shared finitude which cannot be subsumed into any work of identity or project (and which is therefore always without foundation). If community requires or necessarily appeals to myth as a founding fiction it does so in order to articulate itself in the first sense, that is, as a sharing of identity or essence. Yet, Nancy maintains, community exists always and already in the second sense, that is, as the nonidentity of shared finitude. Thinking these two moments together allows Nancy to address the way in which the latter necessarily disrupts or, as he puts it, "interrupts" the former. If the shared world of sense is that which can be formalized or organized within the signifying systems of mythic narrative, it is also, as the discussion of previous chapters has shown, that which, in excess of signification, cannot ever be entirely reduced to or mastered by those systems. So just as the appeal to myth will found community as a shared identity, so the existence of community as an unworked and unworkable finitude will always interrupt any full assumption of identity or any total realization of myth within finite historical existence. Indeed the insufficiency of myths and founding narratives to properly account for existence in all its refractory, ungraspable, singular plurality is what reveals the finitude of human community. Nancy, aligning his own thinking with that of Blanchot, puts it like this: "It is the interruption of myth which reveals to us the disjunctive or hidden nature of community. In myth, community was proclaimed: in interrupted myth, community affirms itself as what Blanchot has called 'the unavowable community' . . . the unavowable community, the withdrawal of communion or communitarian ecstasy are revealed in the interruption of myth" (*CD*, 147; *IC*, 58). This play between the founding of community as identity on the basis of myth, and the interruption of myth by the existence of community as shared finitude, would account for the process of historical change in an interesting way. It suggests that the mythic narratives which function as a foundation for identitarian community are always themselves necessarily without foundation, that is to say, always exposed to existence as an unworked or "unavowable" community.[60] The interruption of myth in this context would be its exposure to the plurality of finite sense for which it cannot account, and thus its exposure to new forms of sense or meaning. These might then be organized into new mythic narratives which would displace the old; hence the difference between one historical epoch and another would turn around the shifts which occur in relation to the mythic narratives that found an affirmation of community. In this context historical change cannot be conceived in terms of a dialectical or teleological process, but rather in terms of a constant birth or becoming of singular-plural sense that interrupts established foundational narratives and opens the way for future narratives to emerge.

Nancy's account of myth implies, therefore, the constant interruption of myth and ceaseless instability within the experience of community. The affirmation of community as shared identity is constantly interrupted by its existence as shared finitude. This would imply that the relation between the political and politics is always multiple and unstable and that one term is never entirely reducible to the other.[61] Just as the political gives figures for community in foundational, mythic narratives and thus gives meaning and structure to the specific practices and institutions of politics, so specific practices and institutions exist only within and *as* the singular-plural becoming of sense, itself irreducible to the totalizing aspirations of foundational, mythic narratives. What emerges here is a complex conceptual framework which allows the dominant structures of meaning that inform historical epochs to be addressed as such, but which at the same time allows the contingent and plural mess of historical becoming to be taken into account without entirely reducing it to the logic of dominant structures. It also gives a framework for understanding how dominant mythic narratives will always and necessarily be contested in favor of other divergent or emergent narratives, or new and different forms of sense. In this sense the political force of Nancy's thought lies less in the way it might prescribe specific modes of contestation and more in the way it allows us to understand the inevitability of contestation per se. In this thinking of unworked community there is no experience of mythic foundation without experience itself, as shared finitude, countering or interrupting myth. For Nancy, the key issue of praxis within this context relates to the means by which the interruption of myth and with this the experience of finite be-

ing-in-common can be affirmed. In *La Communauté désœuvrée* this experience of interruption finds its most important affirmation in the practice of
writing called "literature."

That such an extended meditation on the political, politics, and
community should have its outcome in a theory of literature may seem
strange, but it is entirely consistent with Nancy's overall attempt to think
rigorously according to a certain understanding of finitude. Literature in
this context has a privileged position insofar as the practice of writing affirms a sharing of sense which is irreducible to any fixed identity or meaning. To this extent the being or existence of literature *is* that of existence
or being per se. That is, in communicating sense outside of any figure of
identity, literature communicates shared existence as such, or in Nancy's
rather refractory formulation:

> Being-in-common *is* literary, that is, if one can say that it has its very being in 'lit-
> erature' . . . it will be necessary to designate by 'literature' that being itself, in it-
> self, that is to say that singular ontological quality which gives *in* common . . . but
> which means that that being is only shared *in common*, or rather that its quality of
> being, its nature and its structure are sharing. (*CD*, 161; *IC*, 64)

If being-in-common is the sharing of finite sense then literature is the very
sharing of sense which reveals to us our being-in-common. Nancy is as-
cribing to a certain practice of writing a power of ontological disclosure
which is reminiscent of the later Heidegger's thinking of art and poetry
(*Dichtung*), an association that will be discussed in the final chapter. In this
context literature is also, and necessarily, the interruption of myth. Insofar
as it communicates or shares the finite sense literature affirms community
as a singular plurality of beings and not as shared essence or identity. Literature is "the common exposure of singular beings, their compearance"
(*CD*, 165; *IC*, 66). On the basis of this ontological understanding of literature the most important way to affirm the shared finitude of human
community and a certain retraced conception of the political is to write
and think in a manner that Nancy calls "literary communism." By this
he means a practice of thought and of writing, of thought in and as writing, which articulates our shared being beyond any figure of identity, and
which affirms the singular plurality of sense as the very stuff of our finite
becoming.

Once again one might respond that this is an insufficient basis for a call to arms, or for any specific political engagement or project. Yet Nancy's response once again would be that all these can only occur within a certain preunderstanding of sense, and that it is the responsibility of thinking to address sense as a singular-plural becoming, to affirm it as such. A practice of writing can never be divorced from what Nancy would call an ethos, or "habitus," that is, a specific manner of being-in-the-world, and a specific way of comporting oneself toward the world and toward the existence of others. The notion of literary communism repeats the thinking that was discussed at the end of Chapter 2, namely that ontology and ethics are co-originary. A certain understanding of being implies a certain mode of comportment and vice-versa. What the notion of literary communism which is developed in *La Communauté désœuvrée* suggests is that only on the basis of a certain practice of sense, a practice which finds its most privileged expression in literature, can the order of the political and of finite community be addressed *as* finite. To this extent Nancy maintains his refusal to lay a ground for specific political engagements. The thinking of *La Communauté désœuvrée* does not give criteria for decision or judgment, it does not prescribe or endorse this or that course of action. Yet it does open the way for a thinking in which the ontological, the ethical, and the political can be thought in terms of a necessary interrelation or mutual implication. In the thought of (interrupted) myth which emerges in *La Communauté désœuvrée*, a way is also opened to think anew the nature of historical change, and with this the nature and future possibilities of political contestation. The thinking of finitude clearly has its limits, and these, Nancy would argue, are the ungraspable limits of finitude itself, which exposes itself as "inoperative" community in excess of all ground or identity. It involves a sober renunciation of foundationalist attitudes, and of political projects grounded in figures of essence or of the absolute. Yet for all its sobriety it maintains interruption as a ceaseless and inevitable condition of all political becoming, and thereby maintains the future as that in which something new and different can and will always emerge. It might then seem strange that Nancy's thinking of the political and of community should have its outcome in a theory of literature, but literature is where the sharing of human voices and community occurs; it is where the new and the different can be affirmed.

# CHAPTER FIVE

# Art

Art today has the task of responding to, and taking responsibility for,
this world.

—JEAN-LUC NANCY, *The Muses*[1]

## Introduction

To talk about "realism" in relation to Nancy's philosophy, and in particular in relation to his thinking about art, may seem a little strange or un-
expected given the predominantly antirealist and antimimetic tendencies
of the philosophical and theoretical contexts with which it might be most
obviously associated, for example French poststructuralism or more specifically Derridean deconstruction. Yet, as this study aims to show, while
Nancy's thought is deeply rooted within these contexts and consistently
aims to displace, or think outside of, topologies of subject or substance,
it nevertheless develops into what one might call a postphenomenological philosophy of existence. Here, questions of world-hood, situated contingency, and a certain understanding of materiality are central concerns.
Within this broader context Nancy's thinking on art can be qualified, albeit tentatively, with the term *realism*. Tentatively because his realism bears
little resemblance to what might traditionally be thought under this term.
For instance he rejects any notion of art as imitation or mimesis, and rejects also any logic of representation whereby art could be thought, like a

mirror, to reflect or give an image of some determinate and determinable preexisting reality. Yet art, in Nancy's thought, exists in, or as, a relation to the world, a relation to shared finite existence, and more specifically to that movement of sense which is, or opens up, world-hood itself in all its singular plurality. In this context it becomes clear that Nancy does not take the existence or the definition of art for granted; he does not presuppose what art or the division of the different arts might be and then go on to think how each art form functions. Rather, the whole concept of art is rethought in terms of his wider philosophical thinking of existence and his rereading and reworking of existential phenomenology.

Indeed the question of art, of its philosophical determination, and of the relation between art and philosophy, is perhaps one of the dominant concerns in Nancy's writing throughout his career, and it emerges within a number of different contexts. In the 1970s it is a question which is posed in the context of the specific interrogation concerning the relation of literature to philosophy and the post-Kantian theories of art developed by the Jena Romantics (see Chapter 1). Yet, across his career, Nancy's writing on art also emerges within the context of collaborations with individual artists or of occasional pieces devoted to such artists (e.g., prefaces to exhibition catalogues, short pieces on writers, or in one instance a collaborative work with the Iranian filmmaker Abbas Kiarostami).[2] Also, his interest in the visual arts has been developed most recently in two small but important books devoted to philosophical-critical readings of Christian painting, *Visitation (de la peinture chrétienne)* and *Noli me tangere*. Perhaps most importantly though, his thinking about art emerges in a number of detailed readings of, or responses to, writing on art by Hegel and Heidegger. These more classical philosophical meditations are dispersed throughout some of Nancy's mature works (e.g., *Le Poids d'une pensée* [1991] and *Le Sens du monde* [1993]), but are also the central preoccupation of a number of full-length works (e.g., *Les Muses* [1994], *Le Regard du portrait* [2000], and *Au fond des images* [2003]). The dispersed and heterogeneous nature of this writing on art once again testifies to Nancy's general manner of thinking, which eschews systematizing gestures in favor a more fragmentary approach, an approach which responds to, and develops from, readings of specific texts and which is itself literary or literary-philosophical in nature. In order to gain some sense of a guiding thread within this diverse body of writing, what follows will focus on Nancy's responses to Hegel's thinking on aesthetics and Heidegger's meditation on the essence and origin of the artwork.

The third chapter concluded that Nancy's "bodily ontology," his thinking of sense, of touch, of originary technicity, and of bodies as *partes extra partes*, were all implicated in an economy of excess irreducible to the restricted economy of signification and symbolization, or any possibility of ontological disclosure. It is in this context that writing is always governed by a logic of "exscription," whereby it necessarily exscribes the sense of that which it inscribes as signification. This logic of exscription, as was suggested at the end of the first chapter, articulates or traces a passage to the limit of thought or signification. At the same time, it was argued, such a logic affirms the undecidable relation of literary to philosophical language and with this the syncopation or interruption of any attempt to lay metaphysical foundations for thought. In light of Nancy's early work around the relation of literature to philosophy and his sustained affirmation of a persistence of the literary within the philosophical, it is not surprising that the logic of exscription which governs the writing of "bodily ontology" is also that which governs his thinking about art. The "realism" of this thinking, the "postdeconstructive absolute realism" about which Derrida wrote in *Le Toucher*, can be ascribed to art also, insofar as both obey the logic of exscription, of touch, or of what Nancy also comes to call "exposure." In this sense his thinking on art is inseparable from the manner in which he conceives of thinking per se, and thus inseparable from his thinking of sense, body, materiality, world-hood, and so on. Art, here, is "realist" insofar as it touches or "exposes" the passage of sense, and insofar as sense *is* or exposes finite, concrete, worldly existence. One of Nancy's most helpful and explicit comments on the logic of exscription can be found in the short essay entitled "Le Poids d'une pensée" (The Weight of a Thought):

Sense requires a thickness, a density, a mass and therefore an opacity, an obscurity by which it gives purchase, it lets itself be touched *as sense* precisely there where it absents itself as discourse. This *there* is a material point, a point which weighs: the flesh of lips, the point of a pen or a style, all writing insofar as it traces the edge and the beyond of language. It is the point at which all writing *is exscribed*, places itself outside of the sense it inscribes, in the things of which this sense is supposed to form the inscription. And this *exscription* is the final truth of inscription. (*PdP*, 8; *GT*, 79)

As was the case in Nancy's much earlier use of the motif of the "speaking mouth" (*la bouche*) in *Ego Sum* (discussed in Chapter 1), at stake here is the way in which any signifying discourse, be it speech or writing (in the more restricted and usual sense of inscribing words on the page), is in contact with, touches, but is also separate from, a material instance and a technical apparatus (lips, pen, keyboard) that is an event of finite sense or embodied existence, an existence which is, or which makes, sense. There is no homogeneity or continuity between signifying discourse and that finite instance of sense and body which is, or opens, a world. Yet neither are they entirely absent from each other; they exist in contact/separation, in a "tact" which leaves "intact." Because sense in Nancy is always embodied, that is, is always in a relation of touch/separation to a material, concrete existence (or ek-sistence), any act of speaking or writing (and indeed drawing, painting, composing, and so on) can (and must) have a relation, itself one of touch/ separation, to that embodied existence which is or makes sense. This is a relation which is explicitly marked or affirmed, articulated or traced, both in philosophical writing as Nancy practices it, and in literary writing and other forms of artistic production. Art, as with a certain philosophical thinking at the limit, has, is, or opens onto, a certain relation to sense.

Despite the seeming complexity or possible obscurity of Nancy's formulations around the motifs of sense, touch, and exscription, his thinking here is attempting to address something straightforward and relatively commonplace or accessible, namely that works of art, be they paintings, literary fictions, films, sculptures, musical compositions, or whatever, in their sensible materiality present to us a world or an experience that makes sense in ways not reducible to any fixed signification or order of the signified. Nancy, if you like, is sensitive to the sensible qualities of art, be it the materiality of canvas and color, the visual quality of the written or filmed image, the sensuous or sonorous qualities of sculpture or music. Yet this sensible or sensuous quality is also bound up with, or opens onto, a singular site or instance of something both sensible and intelligible, that is to say, sense. In this way Nancy is seeking to interrogate, without relying on notions of art as representation or mimesis, the manner in which artworks have the capacity to affect us, to touch or stimulate our senses, and to make sense in ways which other signifying discourses or practices do not. Nancy's contention is that art touches existence, touches sense, and in

a certain sense "makes sense," in ways which are not reducible to signification or to any logic of representation. In this context art, for Nancy, is signifying discourse which exceeds or interrupts signifying discourse—it articulates a relation to sense in excess of signification. This relation to sense
is conceived as that thickness, density, or mass, that singular site or passage, of material, bodily existence. Art, here, is therefore always implicated
in an exposure of sensible/intelligible physicality or materiality as much as
in an experience of more abstract meaning or signification proper. It is in
this context that Hegel plays such an important role in Nancy's thinking
about art.

### Untying Hegel: Art, Sense, Technicity

Nancy and Hegel have much in common when it comes to their
various formulations on the nature of art. Both refuse the notion that art
functions as an imitation of a pregiven phenomenal reality; both are interested in the material, sensuous, or sensible aspects of the artwork and the
relation of these to meaning or sense. These shared concerns provide an
opening for Nancy to develop his thinking about art on the basis of close
readings of Hegel's writing on aesthetics. What follows, then, will focus
principally on Nancy's reading of Hegel in two specific essays: the first,
"Le Portrait de l'art en jeune femme" (The Portrait of Art as a Young Girl),
appeared in the short volume published in French as *Le Poids d'une pensée* (1991), the other, "Pourquoi y a-t-il plusieurs arts et non pas un seul?"
(Why Are There Many Arts and Not Only One?) was published in the volume *Les Muses* (1994).[3]

Hegel's lectures on aesthetics were given throughout the 1820s, and
edited from notes and transcripts into three (substantial) volumes in 1835,
and, with revisions, in 1842. As readers familiar with Hegel will know,
these volumes offer a vast overview of the history of art, taking in non-
European forms and tracing the history of European art from classical
Greece through to Hegel's own time. At the same time this history is very
systematically organized and interpreted through the lens of Hegel's own
philosophical thinking of logic and the history of human spirit or idea.[4] It
should go without saying, then, that what follows will make no attempt to
give any full overview or broad philosophical account of Hegel's lectures of

aesthetics. Rather it will focus more specifically on the points which Nancy himself addresses, and on the manner in which he reads Hegel, largely for his own purposes, in order to follow a certain path of thinking about art. In this context Nancy's reading of Hegel emerges more as a productive rewriting of Hegel, a reading of Hegel passed, as it were, through the crucible of the thought of being (or sense) in the singular-plural.

Two central aspects of Hegel's thinking about art are crucial for Nancy. First, Hegel conceives of art as the unity of an ideal content and a sensuous form, that is, the presentation of universal spirit in an individualized and sensuously particularized configuration. Second, art, for Hegel, has a history. It develops through periods or phases, and in each period spirit is configured differently in the artwork and various forms of art predominate. Closely related to the second point and of great interest to Nancy is Hegel's understanding of art in relation to the five senses—sight, hearing, touch, taste, and smell—and his privileging of the first two senses over the latter three.

These two central aspects of Hegel's thinking on aesthetics have a common root and justification in his dialectical method and his understanding of the history of spirit as a dialectical movement. Dialectic in this Hegelian context refers to the process by which human understanding takes certain concepts or categories as distinct from each other, discovers through reflection that contradictions emerge in them, and subsequently produces a higher category which embraces the earlier categories and resolves their inherent contradictions. Thus art, as the unity of an ideal content and a sensuous form, is a dialectical resolution or conciliation of opposites: the Idea (God, universal morality, the sublime) on the one hand, and sensible, presentable form on the other. At the same time, and in a rather more complex manner, the history of art is dialectical insofar as it participates in the history of absolute spirit itself. Put rather schematically one could say that, for Hegel, the history of spirit is the progression of that pure activity of the human mind which overreaches itself and idealizes what is other than spirit (nature, the environment) through its rational and practical activities. In this sense Hegel's system is an attempt to think the manner in which the human mind progressively frees itself from, and in so doing masters, its contingent material environment (the result being absolute spirit or knowledge). The mind does this in distinct phases, in which the relation between mind and the objective world is configured differently, with each phase moving on from and canceling the contradictions inherent in the previous phases.

The history of art for Hegel plays a fundamental role in this progression. In the lectures on aesthetics, he divides this history into three distinct periods: symbolic art, classical art, and romantic art. In each period humans consider spirit and its relation to the natural world differently and this produces a different relation of ideality and sensuous form in the works of art which that period produces. In the (preclassical) "symbolic" period, spirit is conceived in a diffuse, undeveloped, and overly abstract manner and thus cannot find an adequate sensuous form through which it can be presented. This for Hegel, is the art of the East and of ancient Egypt, in which architecture is the dominant form, for example temples and pyramids, constructions which may attain a certain perfection or symmetry of sensuous form but which do not correspond in any adequate way to spirit (since it is conceived in such underdeveloped abstract terms). In the period of classical art spirit is manifest in the figures of the Greek gods. Here the possibility of a perfect unity between ideal content and sensuous form is opened up, since the Greek gods themselves are spirit married with human form, the ideal and the natural embodied in a perfect union. For Hegel, Greek art, in the dominant art form of sculpture, is the most perfect form of art possible in that it represents par excellence the conciliation of the ideal and the sensuous which is the proper vocation of art per se. The period of romantic art, according to this schema, is inaugurated by the Christian era, in which spirit, or God, has a concrete or incarnate form in the figure of Christ *and* a progressively more abstract spiritual depth in the respective figures of the Father and the Holy Ghost. Romantic art, then, seeks to embody a higher and more developed form of spirit than is found in its symbolic and classical precursors, yet at the same time loses the perfect correspondence between ideal content and sensuous form which was proper to classical art. The subject matter of romantic art is what Hegel terms a "free-concrete spirituality," presented in the artwork not as a correspondence to sensuous form but as an excess, as a "spirituality toward the spiritually inward" (*LA*, 80; *As*, 87). Like symbolic art, then, romantic art carries with it an inadequacy of presentation, but the spiritual dimension is far more developed. The privileged art form of the romantic period, according to Hegel, is poetry. Hegel refers to poetry as "the universal art of the spirit which has become free in itself and which is not tied down for its realization to external sensuous material" (*LA*, 89; *As*, 94). This is a key moment for Hegel since romantic art, and that means first and foremost poetry as the universal art of the spirit, signals the end or final phase of art itself; the end, at least, of art insofar as it plays a key role in the history of spirit. Insofar as romantic art configures ideal content and sensuous form in a relation of inadequacy the one to the other, and has as its content an absolute inwardness, or free-concrete spirituality, it paves the way for the resolution of this contradiction in the discourse of philosophy. Art, for Hegel, has an inherent limitation or restriction (that of sensuous form); as spirit develops to its highest level art is necessarily superseded by pure rational thought, that is, philosophy itself, meaning, of course, Hegel's own speculative idealism and his own dialectical method.

The implicit occidentalism and teleology of Hegel's system should be clear from this summary account, as should his privileging of certain art forms over others (e.g., sculpture over architecture). What interests Nancy in relation to the two aspects of Hegel's thinking on aesthetics outlined above is their dialectical nature, that is, the way in which art is presented as the reconciliation of opposites on the one hand and as a historical development on the other, a development in which dominant forms successively give way to each other in order, finally, to be superseded *as art* by the pure, rational, and universal activity of speculative philosophy. In "Le Portrait de l'art en jeune femme" this dialectical, historical progression from art to philosophy is Nancy's central concern. The opening pages of his essay give an exposé of Hegel's aesthetic thinking and pay particular attention to the notion of art as the conciliation of opposites, and as that which, from one historical phase to another, is superseded by or sublated into (*relevé* in French, *aufgehoben* in German) "higher" forms. In so doing, Nancy suggests (in what resembles a classic deconstructive move) that the dialectical movement which is seen to be at work in art and the sublation of art by philosophy is far more problematic than Hegel will allow. Nancy follows Hegel's reasoning closely: if the task of art is to reconcile the idea (or spirit) with a sensible presentation or manifestation (form), then artistic beauty itself, such as it is manifest in the artwork, is not an abstraction of the understanding, but a concrete presentation of the absolute (*PdP*, 37;

my trans. in this section). Thus it follows that if artistic beauty is of the order of the concrete concept, it is also of the order of speculative knowledge (what Hegel would call absolute knowledge or philosophy). With what may appear to be a slight forcing of Hegel's text, Nancy suggests that it is entirely possible on this basis to turn such reasoning around and hold that speculative knowledge is, effectively and necessarily, of the same order of presentation as art (*PdP*, 37). Nancy here is calling into question the manner in which Hegel treats "pure speculative reason" as a sublation of the inadequacy of presentation in poetry or romantic art, and with this calling into question the manner in which Hegel differentiates between art and philosophy more generally.[5] However much Nancy might be forcing Hegel's text, a legitimate question perhaps is being raised here, namely why the relation of spirit, idea, or universal reason should be any different in the form of poetic language than it is in the form of philosophical language (since both are, after all, language, and in both cases what is at stake is the concrete presentation of a concept or of the absolute). Nancy is suggesting that the contradiction or inadequation which emerges in the language of poetry, the "universal art of the spirit," is *not* sublimated or canceled in the language of philosophy, but rather persists:

It is possible that there is a contradiction between the dialectical resolution (or sublation) in speculation, or in (philosophical) "pure thought," and the necessity of (artistic) manifestation. It is possible that this necessity is *itself* speculative. And that, in consequence, the contradiction which is in question is a contradiction which blocks, in sum, dialectical movement, and which *maintains* art exactly at that point where it should disappear—or better: *exactly at that point where it disappears.* (*PdP*, 38)

Where Hegel would see a necessary progression from romantic art to speculative philosophy, Nancy locates an interruption or blockage in the dialectic. As has been indicated above, this reading to a large extent repeats the problematic of presentation (*Darstellung*) that formed the substance of Nancy's reading of Kant's first *Critique* in *Logodaedalus*. Philosophy finds itself unable, on its own terms, to differentiate itself from the language of literature and to inaugurate itself as pure reason. The argument of "Le Portrait de l'art en jeune femme" follows Hegel insofar as it appears to affirm the romantic conception of art as an inadequacy of presentation, but sharply differs from the account given in the lectures on aesthetics insofar as it locates an unresolvable, unsublatable contradiction within, and thus a failure of, the passage from art to pure speculative thought. This means that, for Nancy at least, both art *and* philosophy are inadequate forms for the content they propose. They enact, or are, the presentation of something which exceeds any possibility of presentation, an excess which is irreducible to dialectical resolution or sublation, and thus irreducible to the work of reason or absolute knowledge. This outcome in irresolvable contradiction or aporia is as necessary and unavoidable for Nancy as the outcome of resolution and conciliation is inevitable for Hegel. "It is as if," Nancy writes, "in art an immemorial past does not cease to be born anew. . . . This immemorial past, whose 'passage' repeats itself, could this be the repeated moment of a *coming to presence*? Of an *arrival that Hegel's knowledge cannot and does not want to know—and yet cannot avoid*?" (*PdP*, 38–39). What is interesting here is that, although Nancy has located and affirmed what he sees to be an impasse in Hegel's thought (one which renders undecidable the difference between art and speculative thought itself), his emphasis is on art as a birth or a coming-to-presence. To this extent his reading of Hegel is not content to rest with the simple affirmation of an impasse or with the untying of dialectical progression, but is more insistently focused on the consequences of this for the nature or structure of artistic (and philosophical) presentation or exposition. It is in this context that Nancy highlights, as he did in *Logodaedalus* in relation to Kant's thought, an ontological dimension within Hegel's thinking of spirit and dialectical resolution.

By this view the Hegelian dialectic is not just a matter of understanding, reason, or logical process, but is tied up far more fundamentally with the manner in which human reality is made manifest, disclosed, or constituted as an objective world. Such an emphasis might lead one to believe that Nancy is once again taking an explicitly Heideggerian turn. Yet it would be fair to say that, just as the ontological reading of Kant's first *Critique* can find ample justification in the pages of the "Transcendental Aesthetic," a similar reading of Hegel's lectures on aesthetics (and no doubt of his system generally) is borne out by the text itself. For instance it is made clear from an early stage in the introduction to these lectures that truth, such as Hegel conceives it, is necessarily tied up with manifestation, presentation, or the appearance of truth: "Truth would not be truth if it did not show itself and appear, if it were not truth *for* someone and *for* itself, as well as for the spirit in general too" (*LA*, 8; *As*, 19). By the same token, art as the presentation of an ideal content in sensuous form is necessarily also the presentation of truth: "Art liberates the true content of phenomena from the pure appearance and deception of this bad, transitory world, and gives them a higher actuality, born of the spirit" (*LA*, 9; *As*, 20). In this sense Hegel's general account of history as the history of the dialectical unfolding of the spirit and the progression toward absolute knowledge, is at the same time a history of the different modes of appearance or manifestation of the world, of different worldviews and modes of understanding worldly reality. In this history art plays a key role in the disclosure of the truth (of the world) such as it is understood in any one period. So, what is important for Nancy in relation to his understanding of art is not just the suspension of the dialectical operation of the artwork, or of the progression from art to philosophy, but also the manner in which this dialectical operation is fundamentally tied up with the question of the presentation or manifestation of truth or world-hood. This is expressed in the following terms:

( . . . Sublation [*la relève*] is always revealing [*révélante*]; the dialectic is in its essence [*en son cœur*] revelation, that is to say the appearance of that which makes itself of itself appear, and which only makes that appear, which it makes appear. Hegel knows this very well, as could easily be shown. This should lead us to think that if art is held suspended in this "in-between" of the revealing dialectic, it is because it will never itself be revealing, nor revealed. Its manifestation or its presentation is not revelation).

All that interests us is located in this interval, this interstice—all is suspended in this syncopation. (*PdP*, 47–48)

The suspension of the Hegelian dialectic such as Nancy thinks it not only leaves art held "in between" the status of poetry and speculative thought; it also interrupts its function as the revelation of truth. Thus art is left suspended or syncopated (Nancy recalls this term from his reading of Kant in *Logodaedalus*) and in this state of suspension presents, not the progressive revelation truth or spirit, but simply the very act of presentation. In Nancy's reading of Hegel, art, in the interruption or suspension of its dialectic, becomes the pure presentation or manifestation of nothing other than pure presentation or manifestation itself. The untying of the dialectic here is not the ruination of art, nor its salvation in the face of the all-embracing grasp of the Hegelian system. Rather art, and this is the very crux of Nancy's argument, as presentation of that which exceeds presentation, becomes "the presentation of presentation." Through this seemingly difficult and rather elliptical formulation Nancy is trying to think art, that is, the sensuous and sensible form of the artwork itself, as a kind of proffering or gift: "The singular transmission of art, neither lost nor saved, would be the offering [*offrande*] of an offering, and perhaps the offering of offering itself, absolutely. Or indeed, the presentation of presentation itself. Art is presented, by itself in sum for itself, or for the presentation that it forms" (*PdP*, 56). This, then, is the offering or proffering of nothing other than the act of offering itself, the tracing of a figure or form, which figures nothing other than itself and its own act of figuration. It should be clear that, despite Nancy's close attention to the detail of Hegel's text, a very different conception of art and of artwork emerges within the pages of "Le Portrait de l'art en jeune femme." Given the discussions of subjectivity and sense in the preceding chapters of this study it should not be surprising that Nancy is unwilling to follow or endorse the teleology of speculative reason such as it unfolds within the Hegelian system. Nor, given his earlier reading of Kant in *Logodaedalus*, should it be surprising that Nancy locates within this system an instance of interruption or hiatus which suspends or syncopates the dialectical progress of the entire edifice of speculative thought itself. Yet, as was indicated earlier, what interests Nancy most, perhaps, is less his rather unorthodox reading of Hegel than the way in which this reading produces a philosophical language and idiom through which a different thinking about art can emerge. Hegel's thought allows Nancy to formulate in rigorously philosophical terms the question of "presentation" in art and to suggest that what art presents is nothing other than presentation itself. This is a difficult thinking, for, according to Nancy, this "presentation" is "neither an impresentable, nor a present, neither a transcendence, nor an immanence, but the arrival [*la venue*] or the happening [*l'advenue*] of presentation" (*PdP*, 60). In order to clarify this difficulty, the ontological dimension of Nancy's interrogation needs to be explicated further. It is clear that Nancy's thinking about sense and ek-sistence is rather different from the manner in which Hegel conceives of spirit, idea, and concept. In thinking art as the "presentation of presentation" it is the thought of sense which is at stake, or in the words which Nancy himself uses to conclude "Le Portrait de l'art en jeune femme": "In the birth of art, it is a question existence (of being) such as it must from now on be thought" (*PdP*, 61). This task of thinking is taken up and pursued in the reading of Hegel given in the opening essay of *Les Muses,* "Pourquoi y a-t-il plusieurs arts et non pas un seul?"

As the title of this essay suggests, a general question about art is being posed here and the argument is less oriented toward the close reading of a specific text. Yet, despite important references to other thinkers (for example, Plato, Kant, Heidegger, Adorno), Hegel's aesthetics once again plays a key role in the way Nancy frames or poses his question. The question itself appears, at first sight, to be directed toward an issue of division or categorization and suggests a theoretical interrogation of the different art forms: painting, sculpture, writing, music, and so on. Yet, for Nancy, the existence of a plurality of arts is inseparable from the question of the essence of art itself. Originally, the opening of this essay indicates, there were Muses and not just *a* Muse, a detail, it is suggested, that points to an originary plurality within the essence of art itself. Nancy's essay, therefore, aims neither to interrogate the empirical plurality of artistic production nor to pose the question of the essence of art in terms of a single governing principle. Rather, it aims to think the essence of art in terms of its plural origin or to think the plural *as* its origin. This in turn entails a twofold interrogation of the technical and sensory dimension of art, or rather the manner in which art itself is divided in its origin through its necessary dependence on this technical and sensory dimension. Using the French term *la technique* (meaning technique but also technology) Nancy draws attention to the manner in which, within contemporary thinking, art and technology (*technique*) tend to be thought of as entirely distinct, rather than mutually interdependent categories, and suggests, intriguingly, that this tendency has led to a thinking about art devoid of properly artistic invention and a proliferation of technology devoid of proper thinking about technology (*LM*, 18; *TM*, 5). The dependence of art on a sensory dimension is much more readily admissible, indeed undeniable, and much more ingrained in traditional thinking about aesthetics. Importantly, Nancy draws attention to the way in which, for Hegel, the sensory dimension of art and the division of the five senses governs the division of the different arts. "Art too,"

Hegel writes, "is there for apprehension by the senses, so that, in consequence, the specific characterization of the senses and of their corresponding material to them . . . must provide the grounds for the division of the individual arts" (cited in *LM*, 24–25; *TM*, 9–10). In the Hegelian system the question of the plural origin of art is inseparable from its material form. By addressing this materiality in terms of both the sensory *and* the technical dimension of art Nancy once again follows Hegel but also diverges from him.

The divergence between the two lies in the way Nancy thinks about the technical aspect of artistic production, but also in the different account he gives of sensible form and its relation to the senses. If Hegel views the division of the arts on the basis of the division of the senses, then, Nancy suggests, the difference between different art forms (painting, sculpture, music, and the rest) must be rooted in the difference between the senses. Yet how are we to think the identity of the different senses and thus their difference from each other? And if the division of the five senses provides the basis for the division of the arts why are there not five arts, one for each sense? Why, also, if Hegel really thinks sight and sound to be essential to aesthetic experience do the other three senses play any role at all in the division of the arts?[6] Touch, for instance, as Nancy points out, offers no basis for a type or category of art and yet has long been taken as the essence of the senses in general (*LM*, 26–27, *TM*, 11). Indeed Nancy questions whether the faculty of sense is not so heterogeneous as to be impossible to fix into five categories. Such heterogeneity, he suggests, is emphasized by thinking about sense or sensation in both classical philosophy (Aristotle) and modern physiology, as well as in a certain tradition of modern French thought (*LM*, 27–28; *TM*, 11–12).[7] All this leads Nancy to suggest, contra Hegel, that the division and integration of the senses is no basis upon which to think the division of the different arts. It also leads him to suggest that the plural origin of art is therefore not the five senses, but rather the plurality and heterogeneity of sense itself. This plurality or heterogeneity cannot be categorized or enumerated; rather, it emerges as a plurality of singular instances of sense irreducible to any governing principle or unity. Nancy, then, returns the thinking of the senses in art to a thinking of the singular-plural, or as he puts it, "The *singular-plural* is the law and the problem of 'art' as it is of 'sense,' or of the sense of the senses, of the meaningful [*sen-*

*sé*] sense of their sensible difference" (*LM*, 30; *TM*, 13–14). The plural origin of art, then, emerges in Nancy's account as the singular plurality of the senses, and this in turn is inseparable from a thinking of touch.

As was shown in the third chapter, touch, in Nancy, exceeds what is normally understood by this term. Touch, here, is not simply one of the five senses, but that which in the irreducible singular plurality of the senses is itself sensible, that which is sensuous in the senses. Nancy puts this in the following terms:

Touch is nothing other than the touch of sense altogether and of all the senses. It is their sensuality as such, . . . touch presents the proper moment of sensible exteriority, it presents it *as such and as sensible.* . . . Touch is the interval and the heterogeneity of touch. Touch is proximate distance. It makes one sense [*fait sentir*] that makes one sense (what it *is* to sense): the proximity of the distant, the approximation of the intimate. (*LM*, 35; *TM*, 17)

Touch here is not, for Nancy at least, a governing principle which would resolve the singular-plural of sense into a unity or homogeneity. It functions rather as a mode of relation by which the singular-plural of sense is articulated as singular plurality. This, once again, is a logic of contact in distance which singularizes the singular insofar as it makes of sense a relation to something other than itself (to another instance of sense) but maintains the singular as an irreducibly fragmentary plurality insofar as such a relation occurs only on the basis of an originary separation or rupture. In this sense touch, for Nancy, is neither a transcendent principle governing the senses, nor an immanence which underpins their ultimate unity or homogeneity, but rather, according to the logic of contact in separation, it is both a transcendence and an immanence, a "transimmanence" of the senses or of sense. This is perhaps Nancy at his most difficult and most refractory. Yet once again it is worth noting that what is being thought here is a rather basic or fundamental experience, with which we are all familiar, namely that we all have bodies and that we all experience a meaningful world through our bodily senses or sensations. These sensations are irreducibly plural yet nevertheless are articulated with each other, or as Nancy would say, they "touch each other." Thus, for Nancy, touch is not just one of five senses but is rather "the general extension and particular extraposition of sensing [*sentir*]. Touch *forms one body* with sensing [*fait corps avec le sentir*], or it makes of sensing a body [*il fait des sentirs un corps*], it is simply the *corpus* of the senses" (*LM*, 35–36; *TM*, 17, Nancy's emphasis).

The plural origin of art, therefore, is not as Hegel would have it, the five senses, themselves rationally deducible and subsumable into an ultimate unity of sense, but rather the senses in their irreducible singular plurality. In this way Nancy's account of art is intimately bound up with the motifs of sense, touch, and body such as they were discussed in the preceding chapters. His untying of Hegel's dialectical thinking about art has a twofold outcome. In the first instance art emerges as the presentation of its own figure or form, or in Nancy's words as the "presentation of presentation." In the second instance the sensuous form of artistic presentation is articulated in terms of the singular plurality of the senses, a plurality which in turn is articulated or rather maintained in the "proximate distance" of touch. The "realism" of art in this context can be located in the way in which these two moments or points of issue can be thought together such that art, that is, the sensuous and sensible form of artistic presentation, has a privileged relation to the presentation or manifestation of worldly existence. Where Hegel locates the revelatory power of truth proper to the artwork in the unity of ideal content and sensuous form, Nancy locates its "presentative" power in the sensuous form or figuration it proffers or offers, and the manner in which such sensuous form or figuration touches (in contact/separation) "sense," that is the sense of the world, sense that is or makes a world. This "presentative" power of art is described in the following terms:

What does art do if not, in sum, touch upon [*toucher à*] and touch by the principal [*principielle*] heterogeneity of "sensing" [*sentir*]? . . . it touches on the immanence and the transcendence of touch, or put another way: it touches on the transimmanence of being-in-the-world. Art does not engage with [*n'a pas affaire au*] the "world" understood as a simple exteriority, as a milieu or as nature. It engages being-in-the-world in its very springing forth [*dans son surgissement même*]. (*LM*, 36; *TM*, 18)

Thus when Nancy says that art is the "presentation of presentation," when he thinks of it as the birth or creation of a figure or a form, such a presentation is analogous to, or in a way a repetition of, the presentation or manifestation which is the coming-into-being of world, that is, the disclosure (or *surgissement*) of being-in-the-world itself. Art here does not re-present a world that would be exterior to it, rather it presents or makes manifest a sensuous figure or form which makes sense, or is a "touch at" sense, just as the being-in-the-world which we encounter through our bodies makes sense. Or again, as Nancy puts it in his own terms: "Art isolates or forces the moment of the *world* as such, the being-world of the world, not as a milieu in which a subject moves, but as exteriority and exposition of a being-in-the-world, exteriority and exposition grasped formally, isolated and presented as such. Therefore the world is dislocated into plural worlds, or more exactly, into an irreducible plurality *of* the unity 'world'" (*LM*, 37; *TM*, 18). Nancy's thinking about art here is inseparable from the manner in which he thinks world disclosure, or being-in-the-world, as a spacing of space, an originary unfolding of spatiality, in a temporal-spatial passage of sense (such as it was discussed in Chapter 2). It is not that art presents a world as a totality or as a fixed signification. Rather it manifests or presents a figure or form, which, as a "touching" of sense, opens up a world, not as totality, but as fragment. If world-hood is, according to Nancy, in irreducible singular-plural opening of sense (both sensible and intelligible), the work of art, as a sensuous configuration, figuration, or presentation, is itself an opening of a world: "Each work is in its own way a synæsthesia. And the opening of a world. But is so only insofar as 'the world' itself, in its being world . . . is a plurality of worlds" (*LM*, 58–59; *TM*, 31). For Nancy, an artwork, that is, a painting, a sculpture, a musical composition, or a poem, functions to present a fragment of world; the sensory aspect or configuration of all these art forms has as its origin an originary plurality of the senses and of sensible figuration (of the figuration of sense *as* world).

It might be useful to recall at this point that "sense" in Nancy, as transimmanence, is that which is or which opens worldly existence per se—it is always an excess. As the discussion of previous chapters has shown, sense here is in excess of any relation of signifier to signified and is that which "exceeds the phenomenon in the phenomenon itself" (*SM*, 35; *SW*, 17). Sense is that which there always already is whenever there is any embodied experience or awareness of being in a world that is or makes sense. Nancy's thought persistently attempts to think the limits of, or think at the limit of, the phenomenological account of world-disclosure. Sense cannot be subjected to the rigor of the phenomenological reduction such as it is conceived by Husserl (see Chapter 2). Although Nancy does talk about the world in terms of its surging forth (*surgissement*) or its coming to presence (*venue à la présence*), his writing also consistently shifts away from the phenomenological language of appearance, donation, shining, brilliance, and so on, into a different register (position, disposition, touch, contact, etc.). In "Pourquoi y a-t-il plusieurs arts et non pas un seul?" it is suggested, once again, that the language deployed by phenomenology to account for the nature of world-disclosure is insufficient: "In truth it is not a question of donation, nor of intention, nor even of a signifying. The coming [*venue*] of the world is not even a coming. The world is simply *patent* [patent]" (*LM*, 60; *TM*, 33). Nancy is trying to find a postphenomenological language or idiom to express the way in which, through our bodily senses, the world is always already there for us as that which makes sense prior to theoretical understanding or more abstract forms of cognition. This is why he talks of the world in terms of its "patency" (or in French its *patence*), that is, its simple, straightforward, but always already intelligible, *thereness*. In this context Nancy views the sensible configuration of the artwork not as a representation of or imitation of phenomena (not as mimesis) but as a sensible/intelligible figuration which, like the world, is an "evidence": "The objects of art do not depend on a phenomenology . . . because they are prior to the phenomenon itself. They are of the patency of the world [*Elles sont de la patence du monde*]" (*LM*, 61; *TM*, 33). In this respect "sense," that is, the sense that is or makes a world, is that which in the artwork, as in the phenomenon, exceeds the artwork itself. Both art and world are evidence or presentation as the touch/separation, the contact-in-distance, of sense. "Sense," Nancy writes:

is not "given," it is only patent *and* suspended in its very patency, patent-non-apparent. . . .

Art exposes this. That is not to say that art represents originary patency [*patence originaire*] . . . but that there is art, and that there are many arts, this is what is exposed as evidence. Or again: this is what is patent about patency. In another lexicon one could say: it is the presentation of presentation. (*LM*, 61–62; *TM*, 34)

Clearly this is not an easy formulation. Yet what Nancy appears to be drawing attention to is the way in which the figurative form of the artwork figures only itself, only the act of figuration, and in so doing presents itself as a singular existence, having no meaning or signification other than the presentation of its own figure or form. In this it is, or *exposes*, the existence or manifestation of the world as evidence, its being as sensible/intelligible *thereness*, prior to any system of signification or relation of signifier to signified. The work of art, as evidence, thus has a privileged relation to the existence or evidence of the world itself, or in Nancy's more elliptical formulation, the work of art is *of* the evidence of the world. In this sense the meaning of the work of art is both inseparable from its sensible form or presentation and necessarily in excess of any fixed signification. Its meaning is the touch of sense, the transimmanence of sense and world, or, as Nancy puts it: "The transimmanence, or the patency, of the world takes place as art, as the works of art" (*LM*, 63; *TM*, 35).

In "Pourquoi y a-t-il plusieurs arts et non pas un seul?" the plurality of different art forms is seen as an inevitable manifestation of the plural or singular-plural origin of art itself. A view of art emerges here which to a certain extent repeats Hegel's account but at the same time significantly diverges from it. On the one hand, art is a sensible form which maintains a privileged relation to the truth of the world or world disclosure; on the other, the thinking of sensible form and the truth of the world or world disclosure have been reworked in the perspective of the singular plurality of sense, touch, exposure, and evidence (or what is termed elsewhere the "ek-sistence" of being-in-the-world). This untying of Hegel's account of art and of the revelatory power of the artwork might seem to bring Nancy's position very close to Heidegger's such as it emerges in the essay "Der Ursprung des Kunstwerkes" (The Origin of the Work of Art). For Heidegger the origin of the work of art lies in the essence of art itself, which he conceives of as the "setting forth" or "putting to work" of truth, where truth, as elsewhere in his thought, is aletheia, or the unconcealing of a world. In "The Origin of the Work of Art" he puts this in the following terms: "The artwork opens up in its own way the Being of beings. This opening, i.e., this revealing, i.e., the truth of beings, happens in the work. In the artwork the truth of beings has set itself to work. Art is truth setting itself to work" (*BW*, 165; *GA*, 5:25). Thus Heidegger in his famous analysis of the "peasant shoes" in a painting by van Gogh sees in the figurative dimension of art, not the imitation or representation of an object, but the disclosure or manifestation of the truth of a world. This is born out by his poeticized evocation of the rural earthbound way of life of which, he imagines, the shoes form an integral part: "In the stiffly rugged heaviness of the shoes there is the tenacity of her [the peasant woman's] slow trudge through the far spreading and ever uniform furrows of the of the field swept by raw wind" (*BW*, 159; *GA*, 5:19). As was indicated in the earlier discussion of space and spatiality (Chapter 2), Nancy is sharply critical of the Heideggerian privileging of rural, bucolic, and domestic motifs, together with the pious and reactive tone which accompanies the deployment of such motifs. At the same time it is to a large degree undeniable that Nancy's account of art as the touching of sense and as the "opening up" of a world is very close to Heidegger's formulations in "The Origin of the Work of Art." Yet, as always in Nancy, such an apparent similarity belies deeper differences in tone and emphasis; in certain respects his thinking about art sharply diverges from that of Heidegger. Once again the nature of this divergence hinges on the manner in which Nancy conceives of sense, and, in particular, of the manner in which he relates sense to an originary technicity.

As was indicated earlier in this discussion, the essay "Pourquoi y a-t-il plusieurs arts et non pas un seul?" places a key emphasis on the technical dimension of the artwork. This, for Nancy, is inseparable from its sensible dimension.[8] Indeed it is the technical dimension of art, the paintbrush, pigment, and canvas, the sculptor's tools and materials, and even words themselves, for the writer and poet, which makes of art a sensible form that engages the intelligible materiality of sense such as Nancy conceives it (*LM*, 52; *TM*, 27). As was indicated in the previous chapter, this thinking of an originary technicity is entirely opposed to Heidegger's account of technology as the "enframing" (*das Gestell*) proper to modernity that sends the question of being into oblivion. In relation to art, Nancy's thinking of technicity displaces the Heideggerian account of the "origin" of the artwork and also the understanding of the work *as* work, that is, the "putting to work" of the truth of being. For Heidegger technological enframing and the poetic saying of the artwork are entirely opposed to each other. The one is an obliteration of the truth of being, the other a preserving of its originary unconcealment, gathering, and sheltering. If, according to Nancy, "the sensible and technical plurality of the arts engages intelligible sense" and thus make of artworks that which "opens a world," then at the same time this sensible and technical plurality disperses the notion of origin or originary gathering and unties any possibility of "putting truth to work." In this way Nancy's account of art sets itself squarely against the piety and pathos of poetic saying in Heidegger, and the manner in which such saying is viewed as speaking an originary, pretechnical giving of being:

> The technicity of art dislodges art from its "poetic" assurance, if by that is understood the production of a revelation, or art conceived as a *phusis* unveiled in its truth. Technicity [*la technique*] unveils here nothing but itself, but as itself, this will already have been understood, it is not simply in the first instance processes, instruments, calculations—all of which nevertheless are also its bare truth. Technicity *itself*, is also the "unworking" of the work, that which puts it outside of itself, to touch the infinite. Technical unworking does not cease *forcing* the fine arts, dislodging them ceaselessly from aestheticizing repose. (*LM*, 66; *TM*, 37)

Truth, here, is not put to work, set forth, gathered, or preserved; rather, as sense, as that sense which the sensible and technical plurality of the arts engage, truth is put outside of the artwork itself. To this extent, Nancy's account of the originary technicity of art is aimed at untying Heidegger in the same way that his account of the singular plurality of the senses unties Hegel. The synthesizing or gathering movement one finds in both, whether it be the dialectical sublation of the ideal content and sensible form, or the putting to work of an originary truth of being, is, as it were, turned inside out in Nancy's account and becomes a dispersal, an exposure to an irreducible exteriority or being of sense "outside of itself."[9] It is in this context that art as technical-sensible figure or form is the presentation of presentation, but also at the same time the contact-in-separation, touch, and exscription of sense.

This, then, is Nancy's realism, deeply rooted in the accounts of art given by speculative idealism and existential phenomenology, but placing the sense of art in excess of dialectical conciliation or resolution, in excess of an originary setting forth of the truth of being. The sense of art is also placed, according to the logic of touch, exposure, or exscription, in excess of the figural presentation of the artwork itself. The preceding discussion has highlighted the way in which the realism of Nancy's thinking about art turns on the manner in which the sensible form of the artwork exists in a relation of exteriority (touch-separation) to sense. This sense is always in excess of the artwork and yet is that onto which the artwork nevertheless opens or to which it is exposed insofar as it is the "presentation of presentation." In order to clarify this logic of exposure or exscription further, this discussion will draw to a close by examining how Nancy thinks about figuration or presentation in art in terms of the image and what he calls, in a more recent work, the "distinct trait" (*trait distinctif*) of the image.

Image—Touching the Real

Much of Nancy's most recent work has placed a more clearly em-
phatic emphasis on the motifs of separation, discontinuity, and distance.
This, for instance, was shown to be the case in his short meditation on
the resurrected body of Christ, *Noli me tangere* (2003), discussed in Chapter 3, and no doubt reflects a desire to follow through the radical implications of the "deconstruction of Christianity" and perhaps more specifically
to respond to Derrida's ambivalent analysis of the lexicon of touch in *Le
Toucher*. Another rather more substantial work published in 2003, *Au fond
des images* (In the Depths of Images), develops this emphasis on separation
and discontinuity in relation to the notion of the "distinct" and to the role
of the image within the artwork.

If, for Nancy, art *is* only as technical-sensible figure or form and as
the "presentation of presentation," then it *is* so only insofar as it figures,
presents, or traces an image. In the opening essay of *Au fond des images*,
entitled "L'Image—le distinct" (The Image—the Distinct), Nancy discusses the central role of the image in art, drawing on a number of examples
and different genres: an extract from Edith Wharton's *Summer*, Hans von
Aachen's painting *Young Couple*, and a "musical image" from Verdi's *La tra-
viata*. Citing and analyzing Wharton's prose description of an open door,
the emergence of a young girl and an expanse of city and sky, Nancy takes
pains once again to resist any strictly mimetic interpretation, according to
which the reader, assimilating a string of images, would visualize a scene
which could then be said to represent a recognizable preexisting external
reality. "It is less a question," he suggests, "of an image which we cannot
fail to imagine (one which each reader forms or forges in their own way
and according to their own models) than it is a question of an image function [*fonction d'image*], light and precise relation of shadow, framing and
detachment, opening [*sortie*] and touch of an intensity" (*AI*, 17). What interests Nancy is the manner in which the image traces or figures a form
which has no preexisting model or "reality" (for the image to work as it
does it is not necessary that Wharton actually witness and reproduce the
open door, emergent girl, city, and so on, or that they ever really existed).
What is of interest here is what Nancy terms the line of the image (*le trait
de l'image*). The French word *trait*, translated here as "line," serves the
double function of suggesting a tracing or figuration (such as one might

associate with the term "line-drawing"), but also a separation or differentiation: a line is that which separates or divides two volumes or planes of
space. In terms reminiscent of the discussion above of presentation and
sense, Nancy suggests that with the appearance of the young girl through
the open door a world also appears. Yet he also suggests that this world,
like the girl, stops at the threshold, stops, and stops us the readers at the
threshold of the novel, at the line or figure traced by its writing, such that
we enter a world but are held before or at a distance from it. In the image
the reader does not simply visualize an environment but rather is exposed
to "an indefinite totality of sense" or world. This is an exposure in which
the tracing or figuration of form in the line of the image also marks the infinite separation and distance of that which is traced. The reader is held on
the threshold of the line which divides/shares (*partage*) inside and outside,
light and shade, life and art (*AI*, 18). If, Nancy adds, it is possible that the
same line (*trait*) can both separate and communicate, "it is because the line
of the image (its tracing, its form) is itself . . . its intimate force: because the
image does not 'represent' this intimate force, but it is that force, it acti-
vates it, it draws and withdraws it [*elle la tire et elle la retire*], it extracts just
as it withholds it, and it is with that force that it touches us" (*AI*, 18). In
"L'Image—le distinct," then, Nancy returns his analysis once more to the
motif of touch: the image touches us but not in a way which suggests emo-
tion or sentiment or which implies a continuity or homogeneity of that
which touches and that which is touched. What touches here, in the very
instant of a proximity-in-distance, is the force of sense, the tracing of a line
which both presents and withdraws, brings into contact and separates. The
language of touch is doubled with a language of force, intensity, or affect.[10]
That which is drawn in the image is also withdrawn, but in this double
movement of presentation and withdrawal an intensity makes itself felt, it
touches in the very movement of its being held at a distance.

   This is a language of contact-in-separation, which, as was shown in
Chapter 3, is the constant refrain of Nancy's thinking of touch, sense, and
body. Yet, as has been indicated, the discussion of the image here places a
sharper and more central emphasis on the articulation of separation and
distance, or what Nancy terms "the distinct." "L'Image—le distinct" begins with a discussion of the sacred and its relation to the images of art and
religion. While art may always have been associated with religion, Nancy

suggests, it does not have its origin in religion per se but in the sacred (itself closely bound to but not coextensive with the religious). The sacred is that which is set apart (from the everyday or the profane), separated or withdrawn—that which, in a sense cannot be touched. In order to differentiate this sense of the sacred from its entanglement in religious practices, and in order to underline the radicality of the separation and distance designated here, Nancy invokes this term *distinct*. In the first instance this separation might be seen, rather straightforwardly, as the separation of the image from any empirically existing object or thing. In this sense the image is distinct from things per se, or as Nancy puts it, "The image is a thing which is not a thing: it distinguishes itself essentially from the thing [*essentiellement elle s'en distingue*]" (*AI*, 13). This initial emphasis on distinction as a separation from the world of things once again underlines the way in which Nancy seeks to untie the functioning of the image from any logic of representation. "The distinct," he writes, "holds itself apart from the world of things as a world of available objects [*en tant que monde de la disponibilité*]" (*AI*, 13).

At a more fundamental level, however, this distinction from the world of things implies a much more radical dimension of separation or distance. There is a sense in which the image, as distinct from the being-there of things, has a unique ontological status, a "being-image," as it were, which is in and of itself a relation of separation. The line of the image (*le trait de l'image*), it might be recalled here, "is itself . . . its intimate force" (AI, 18), it draws but also withdraws, and is thus the presentation *and* withdrawal of that force of the image which touches. The "distinctive line" (*le trait distinctif*), Nancy notes, "separates that which is no longer of the order of touch" (*AI*, 12). In these seemingly paradoxical, difficult, and altogether rather obscure formulations around the motif of distinction and separation Nancy appears to be intensifying his language of touch through an ever more intensified language of the untouchable. If the image touches us if its line or *trait* is the drawing of an "intimate force," this is so only on the basis of withdrawal, of the tracing into visibility of that which is invisible, the bringing into contact of that which is distant, separate, always intact. This, then, is the importance of the thinking of the distinct such as it emerges in this essay: "The image must touch at [*toucher à*] the invisible presence of the distinct, at the distinctiveness of its presence. The distinct is invisible . . . because it does not belong to the domain of objects, of their perception and their outline, but to that of forces, of their affections and their transmissions. The image is the evidence of the invisible" (*AI*, 30). The distinct emerges here as another means of designating the infinite excess of finite sense, that which "exceeds the phenomenon in the phenomenon itself" (*SM*, 35; *SW*, 17). Yet the motif of the distinct more radically underlines the order of sense *as* excess, as the untouchable of that which is touched in the line of the image. The image exposes an "indefinite totality of sense" or world, it presents or traces a figure, but does so only insofar as it traces a relation of unbridgeable distance or separation from the instance of sense which it exposes. The image, such as it is thought here, closely resembles the account given by Maurice Blanchot in his 1955 text *L'Espace littéraire*. According to Blanchot the image obeys a logic of "contact in distance," it is "a way of seeing which is a kind of touch," or again: "What is given to us by a contact in distance [*un contact à distance*] is the image."[11] Interestingly Blanchot, like Nancy, shifts away from the language of "seeing" or "vision" in relation to his account of the image (these terms may be too laden with both phenomenological and religious connotations) and adopts the term *fascination*. This potentially has a parallel with Nancy's adoption of the term *distinct* in order to disengage his thinking of the image from the religious context and heritage connoted by the term *sacred* (see above). For both Blanchot and Nancy, then, the image is a relation of touch-in-distance with that which is withdrawn from phenomenal disclosure. The difference between the two lies in the way each characterizes that which withdraws, and this is brought out further in the way Blanchot talks about "fascination": "Whoever is fascinated does not see, properly speaking, what he sees. Rather, it touches him in an immediate proximity; it seizes and draws him close, even though it leaves him absolutely at a distance. Fascination is fundamentally linked to neutral, impersonal presence, to the indeterminate They, the immense faceless Someone."[12] Where, for Nancy, the "distinct" is an indeterminate totality of sense or world, for Blanchot the image opens onto or touches what he comes to call the neuter, or the "other night," or, following Levinas, the *il y a*. This echoes, quite precisely, the difference which emerged between the two thinkers in the discussion of community in the preceding chapter. Where Blanchot is attempting to think of a radical alterity prior to any phenomenal disclosure or giving of being or world, an alterity which is anonymous, indeterminate, and impersonal, Nancy thinks this alterity as distinct sense, distinct from or in excess of the world of phenomena, but that which nevertheless *is*. The difference between the two still needs to be marked, but in *Au fond des images* Nancy's thinking of the image, indeed his thinking in general, is closer to that of Blanchot than it has ever been. This, it could be argued, is because of the more radical emphasis that has been placed on the moment of separation or rupture articulated by the use of the term *distinct*. It may well be that in his more recent works (for example *Noli me tangere, Au fond des images*, and *La Création du monde*), Nancy has shifted emphasis away slightly from a language of finitude and being-with, which so heavily dominated *La Communauté inavouable*, to a language which much more clearly foregrounds separation, distance, and the infinite excess of finite sense over any instance of phenomenal disclosure or presentation. If this is so it is surely a response to his longstanding dialogue with Blanchot and to Derrida's important intervention in *Le Toucher*.

Yet despite these shifts in emphasis and a certain renegotiation of philosophical lexicon, Nancy maintains the demand that thought always address and place itself in relation to the world and the question of worldhood. This remains true for Nancy's treatment of the image in *Au fond des images*. As was indicated earlier the artistic image is on the one hand set radically apart from the course of worldly presentation, since, as presentation of presentation, it presents or exposes an "indefinite totality of sense" or of world, in the absence of, or in a radical separation from, finite being-in-the world itself. Yet it does this only in order to expose the *sense* of a world in a purer and unmediated form. Nancy expresses this in the following terms: "The image suspends the course of the world and of sense . . . but affirms all the more a *sense* . . . *directly with* what it makes felt (itself)" (*AI*, 27). The image, then, is the presentation (and withdrawal) of a distinct sense, which *as distinct* is separate or infinitely distant from worldly manifestation, that is, withdrawn from finite being-in-the world. It is in this sense also that the artistic image can be seen as "pure" presentation of presentation. Yet this is not to say that the image is abstract or idealized, detached from the world in the sense of being immaterial or an "ideal form." The image, Nancy takes pains to point out, is always material, it is "the matter of the distinct, its mass and its thickness, its weight . . . " (*AI*, 29). All this is consistent with the thinking of sense, addressed earlier in the discussion of body and embodiment (Chapter 3), as a relation to a material or concrete instance. It also recalls the reading of Hegel's aesthetics discussed above, according to which art in general emerged as the sensible-technical presentation of a figure or form. To this extent it is clear that Nancy's discussion of the image and of the distinct in the opening essay of *Au fond des images* is very much a continuation of his previous meditations on art.

Yet what is perhaps most interesting about the thinking of art here is the way in which the image occurs as the "touch" of an indefinite totality of sense, which, as always in Nancy, is necessarily in excess of any determinate relation of signifier to signified. In this way the sense of the image is the presentation/withdrawal of a world in the absence of being-in-the-world and thus also of an instance of truth. At the same, time as an excess over any relation of signifier to signified, the artistic image resists any imposition of fixed meaning or signification. It touches us; in its sensible form or line (*trait*) it has an affective force or intensity which makes sense but does not articulate any determinate meaning. Nancy puts this in the following terms: "At a stroke, which is its stroke [*D'un seul coup, qui est son coup*] the image delivers [*livre*] a totality of sense or a truth. . . . Each image is a singular variation on the totality of distinct sense: of sense which does not enchain the order of significations" (*AI*, 30). In this way Nancy thinks the image, and with that artistic presentation in general, as an exposure of the truth of a world which is not tied to, or recuperable within, any logic of signification. Artistic truth in this context can be made to signify, that is, its sense can be appropriated by a signifying discourse (for example a work of critical interpretation or evaluation) but it also always necessarily exceeds such discourses. This, of course, would explain why works of art offer themselves up to multiple or potentially infinite interpretations, since their sense is always an irrecuperable excess, and why at the same time they cannot be made to signify in an arbitrary or random manner, since they exist as the presentation/withdrawal of an indeterminate totality of sense, which imposes itself as touch, force, or intensity. The artistic image is, according to this account, necessarily tied up with an experience of ambivalence or equivocation: it both infinitely exceeds the order of signification and, as a touch of sense or exposure of truth, always necessarily touches that order in its very withdrawal:

The image touches at [*touche à*] that ambivalence by which sense (or truth) cease-lessly distinguishes itself from the interrelated network [*réseau lié*] of significa-tions, which at the same time it never ceases to touch: each formed phrase, each accomplished stage, each perspective, each thought puts into play an absolute sense (or truth itself) which does not cease also to distance itself and absent itself from all signification. But more than this: each constituted signification . . . also forms by itself a distinctive mark of the threshold beyond which sense (truth) ab-sents itself. (*AI*, 31–32)

This is none other than a repetition in different terms of the logic of ex-scription around which Nancy's thinking ceaselessly turns. Between signi-fication and sense there is always a line of separation (*trait distinctif*), which means that sense is always distinct, apart, withdrawn, in the very moment of its presentation in the figure or form of the image. This means that in the artistic image, however it may be interpreted or made to signify, sense withdraws always at the vanishing point or limit of any possible significa-tion. At this moment of vanishing or exhaustion of signification the image, as residual line or tracing of a form, affirms the force or intensity of sense, of a truth which absents itself in this tracing of pure form or presentation (of presentation).

It is clear that Nancy is less interested in posing art as that which can be given fixed meaning or invested with a sacred or transcendental pur-pose. It has no redemptive function and does not represent or signify a pre-given and determinable "reality." Rather, as the pure presentation of pre-sentation, the tracing of a figure or form beyond whose line sense absents itself, art, for Nancy, is an exposure of truth, a touching of the "real" of a world, beyond or in excess of any mediation through signifying systems or discourses. Art exposes or touches a fragment of world. This thinking of art is realist, then, but only insofar as art touches, only insofar as it is an "eternally intact touch of being" (*SM*, 196), in which a fragment of world is exposed.

It is arguable that the interest and strength of Nancy's account of art lies in the way he returns art to an unmediated relation with the sense of the/a world in the very moment that it is held at a distance from the repre-sentation or manifestation of beings in the world. Artistic form is thought in terms of a complex logic of presentation that exceeds any possibility of mediation through discourse or a signifying system. The implications of this are twofold: on the one hand when we talk about a work of art—be it a painting, sculpture, symphony, poem, or novel—we are likely to focus less exclusively on its status as discourse, that is, as a symbolic order or certain set of signifying structures which we can determine and interpret in the context of wider concerns (cultural knowledge, specific theoretical frames, questions of value). On the other hand the sensible-technical and formal aspects of the artwork are likely to be the focus of an intense interest. The interest here is directed not simply toward the way in which formal innovations disrupt expectations of meaning and interrupt signifying systems.[13] Rather it is in the figuration or the "line" of sensible-technical form that the work of art really has its truth-value, its affective and properly "artistic" impact. It is *in* the presentation of pure form, and *at* the vanishing point where signification is suspended, that art exposes the sense of the world, touches existence. In this sense when we talk or think about art and artistic images we are likely to talk less about symbolic structures or economies of signification and more about the point at which these give way to a pure presentation of presentation, an exposure to, and thus an engagement with the indefinite totality of sense which makes up a world. As Nancy wrote in *Le Sens du monde*: "sense must be signified in all possible ways, by each and every one of us, by all 'individual' or 'collective' singulars" (*SM*, 248; *SW*, 165). Talking less about symbolic structures or economies of signification articulated within an artistic image or production does not mean that we would simply behold the line of the image, the tracing of its figure or form. It does not mean that we bear witness to the suspension of signification and the excess of sense in order then simply to affirm suspension and excess as such. Rather, by attending to the vanishing point of signification in the artistic image, to that line of separation beyond which sense absents itself, we may begin to signify, to find some kind of symbolic expression, for that which has no symbolic expression but is nevertheless the very stuff, being, and sense of worldly existence. In this sense art, for Nancy, not only disrupts, interrupts, or suspends already existing discourses and representations, it exposes the real of the world which those representations leave behind, elide, or omit. Art can never be mere decoration or recreation, it is always a creation, a creation of the sense of the world. Art, as art, proposes or exposes sense, truth, world. This is the guiding thread and ultimate point of issue of Nancy's meditations on art: "Art today has the task of responding to, or taking responsibility for, this world" (*LM*, 151; *TM*, 93).

# Conclusion: On the Creation of the World

*To create the world* means: immediately and without delay to reopen every possible struggle for a world, that is to say for that which must form the opposite of a global injustice taking place against the background of a general equivalence. But also to pursue this struggle precisely in the name of this, that this *world* comes from nothing, that it is without precondition and without model, without given principle or end, and that it is exactly *that* which forms the justice and the sense of a world.

—JEAN-LUC NANCY, *La Création du monde*[1]

By means of five motifs or specific instances—subjectivity, space, body, community, and art—this study has sought to interrogate the general trajectory and movement of Nancy's thought. This general trajectory does not necessarily form an easily reducible unity which can be presented as a philosophical system. Nancy's thinking always emerges in a contingent practice of writing which traces diverse paths and traverses a multiplicity of specific philosophical contexts, primarily and most obviously those of speculative idealism and existential phenomenology. The paths taken across these other bodies of thought ceaselessly follow a line up to the limit of thought itself in order to trace that limit and to expose thought to its own excess. Each of these paths and instances of exposure are necessarily contingent upon the philosophical context or signifying system that thought engages, but also, and necessarily, they expose a singular instance which exceeds the determinations of that context or system. In this sense

Nancy's thinking maintains itself as fragmentary, as a practice of thought which unfolds as a plurality of singular gestures or exposures to/at the limit of thought.

Despite Nancy's fragmented and nonsystematizing approach to the writing of philosophy, the preceding chapters have sought to highlight certain continuities of concern or approach and to foreground the philosophical rigor and precision which his writing articulates. Each motif, subjectivity, space, body, and so on has offered a way into Nancy's corpus, enabling a tracing of its development from the late 1960s on. At the same time the preceding chapters have sought to show the manner in which each of these motifs articulate a relation or point of contact with the others: the thought of subjectivity exceeding any topology of substance or ground necessarily opens onto the thought of the spatializing-temporalizing of space and of the body as the site of that spatial-temporal opening. Likewise the thought of space and body necessarily implies a specific ontological understanding of community, which in turn opens onto a specific thinking of art and literature and their relation to the real of a shared world of sense. The articulation of these motifs, the one with the other, does not necessarily imply their possible or inevitable subsumption into an overarching unity, totality, or system. Rather one could say, following Nancy's own formulation, that these instances touch each other in their unfolding as singular gestures of thought, but that as singular discursive articulations of, or exposures to, that which exceeds speculative rationality, they resist resolution into the logic of any transcendent signifier or to any underlying immanence or unity. Or, put another way, Nancy's philosophical writing is itself governed by the logic of spacing and transimmanence, of touch-in-separation and exposure to the singular-plural of sense. This, indeed, is the point at which this study began.

Within this complex yet perfectly rigorous logic of philosophical writing and within the overall trajectory of thought which this study has sought to trace there is a specific instant or instance which is of decisive importance for Nancy, the instant of what he comes to call *creation*. Even in the early writings of the 1970s, writings oriented toward the question of the overcoming of metaphysics and toward antifoundationalist readings of Kant and Descartes, Nancy was not content simply to affirm the abyss of foundation and the negation of substance or ground. Rather the inability of thought to ground itself in pure reason (Kant) or in the autonomous self-positing of a subject (Descartes) exposed, on the one hand, the syncopation (or nonidentity) of philosophical production, and on the other, a site (in excess of symbolic determination) of spacing, sense, and embodiment (*ego* and the "speaking mouth"). As Nancy develops his critique of existential phenomenology in the 1980s, 1990s, and the first years of the new millennium, the direction of his thought is less immediately oriented toward antifoundationalist readings and increasingly focuses on this site of excess as a site of creation or birth: of the being of world-hood, or of the arrival and spacing of the world in the singular-plural passage of sense. The absence of ground within being (its ek-sistence beyond any topology of substance) is seen in terms of an arrival or coming which is or makes a world. As was suggested in Chapter 2, Nancy's thinking of the sense of the world as a singular-plural passage, arrival, or birth takes his thought beyond specific concerns of foundationalism or antifoundationalism. It is this which arguably opens the way for a thinking of creation.

In a recently published essay, entitled "De la création" (On Creation), collected in the volume *La Création du monde* (2002), Nancy takes pains to differentiate his own understanding of "creation" from any theological or monotheistic understanding of the term. Creation here does not mean the production of something from nothing, whereby "nothing," as the material cause of "something," necessarily supposes a prodigious efficient cause and the prior existence of a creating subject who would be the agent of this efficient causality, an agent who would create with a view to a certain end or purpose (*CM*, 86–87). This theological conception of creation, particularly in its more vulgar orthodox forms, is, Nancy suggests, "the most disastrous of concepts" (*CM*, 87). Disastrous, it should by now be clear, because such a conception poses the ground of being in monological terms, subsumes the singular-plural arrival of being to that ground, and is thus a form of ontological denial and with that the condition of possibility for violence (of all kinds). Against this theological understanding of creation Nancy opposes a conception which more radically conceives the absence of origin or nonexistence of the nothing. While the theological conception must maintain the being of an originary agency or subjectivity prior to creation (the creator God), Nancy suggests, invoking Nietzsche, that the absence of origin within being and the thinking of creation need to be thought in more absolute terms: "There is nothing withdrawn in the very depths of the origin, *nothing but the nothing of origin* . . . no longer is there the thing in itself nor the phenomenon, but there is the transitivity of being-nothing. Is that not, in the end, what Nietzsche was the first understand?" (*CM*, 90–91).[2] This is the thought that has ceaselessly motivated Nancy's use of the term *opening* in his account of the being of the world and of being-in-the-world, a term which he draws from existential phenomenology (Heidegger, Merleau-Ponty) but whose sense he reworks in the context of his thinking beyond phenomenology: a thinking of limits, of the disposition and touch-in-separation of bodies or *partes extra partes*: "Opening is neither foundation nor origin. Nor is opening a sort of receptacle or prior extension for the things of the world. The opening of the world is that which is opened along [*le long de*] these things and between them, that which separates them in their abundant singularities and which relates the ones to the others in their coexistence" (*CM*, 93–94). In this context Nancy's thinking of creation emerges as different from the theological (and specifically Christian) understanding of the term but also as an intensification or radicalization of that understanding. As such the thought of creation, as Nancy himself emphasizes, forms a "nodal point in a 'deconstruction of Christianity,' insofar as such a deconstruction proceeds from monotheism itself" (*CM*, 93). It emerges also as a post-Nietzschean affirmation of active production as opposed to any reactive nostalgia for a lost ground or godhead, or a negative thinking of the absence of foundation as that which needs to be mourned or lamented.[3] In this respect the use of the term *creation* in this recent text is provisional and strategic. It is a term bequeathed to Nancy by the tradition which, in an intensification of its meaning, allows him to interrogate the spatial-temporal arrival of the world in terms of a more radical "nothing of origin," and in terms of a production of the new or the unknown.

Importantly, this emphasis on the creation or on the opening of the world itself opens onto a thinking of engaged being-in-the-world, of decision and of judgment. This study has highlighted the extent to which, for Nancy, ontology and ethics are co-originary. It may also be recalled from the discussion of community in Chapter 4 that some commentators have called into question the manner in which Nancy's ontological and ethical concerns can be related to the those of politics, and to the question of political engagement and judgment.[4] In *La Création du monde* and specifi-cally in the essay "De la création," Nancy addresses the issue of engaged praxis, decision, and judgment in relation to Kant and Lyotard. Decision, such as it is conceived here is not the decision taken in favor of one or an-other possible course of action or alternatives; it is not the kind of decision which can be prescribed or verified according to specific criteria or estab-lished norms. Rather, it is a decision for "that which is in no way given in advance, but which is an eruption of the new, unforeseeable because with-out figure [*visage*]" (*CM*, 67).[5] As such the question of decision is insepa-rable from that of judgment and from the way in which, through an act of judgment, we might differentiate between a good and a bad decision and a desirable or undesirable outcome. In this context Nancy (along with Lyotard and Derrida) is seeking an understanding of the concept of judg-ment which does not rely on the prior existence of a universal norm or prescription, what Lyotard, after Kant, calls "reflective judgment."[6] Not-ing that, for Lyotard at least, the problem of "reflective judgment" or ab-sence of the universal has become the general formula of "postmodernity," Nancy adds: "if the universal is not given, this does mean that it should be mimed or dreamed of . . . but that it is to be made [*à faire*]" (*CM*, 69).

This is important insofar as it indicates that, in untying the inter-related questions of decision and judgment from established criteria or universal norms, Nancy does not aim to endorse any form of arbitrariness or relativism, nor to promote decisions made for or in the name of this or that particular *against* the notion of the universal. Rather he is aiming to think the event of judgment, the judgment of ends or of desired out-comes, as that which engages the instance of void (the "nothing of origin") from whence a world emerges or arrives. Judgment here engages the cre-ation of the world and of a sense of the world in the absence of any prior model or already established end. In this sense the absence of criteria or norms upon which judgment *as* judgment occurs is not simple arbitrari-ness or relativism, but rather the "nothing" from which the world emerg-es as the singular-plural arrival of sense. Thus what is engaged is not this or that particular determination but rather the shared world of finitude as such, the event of this sharing and the spacing of all those singular-plural instances of sense which are, or make, the world. It is in this sense that the "universal" for Nancy is not presupposed but "made," since a judgment is itself made on the basis of, and as a necessary engagement with, nontotal-izable totality of singular plurality as such. This absence or void is that be-fore which judgment is placed. It is the absence of any originary intuition which might guide judgment according to a rule or law, or what Nancy also calls an "inconstructible."[7] Judgment here:

finds itself placed before—or provoked by—an inconstructible, which responds to an absence of intuition. . . . The inconstructible of an absence of intuition . . . defines the necessity not to construct in the void . . . but to let void surge forth, or to make with this void that which is in question, namely *the end*, an end which henceforth forms the stakes and the business of that which is more a praxis than a strictly intellectual form of judgment.

To put it succinctly: this is not an act of construction but of creation. (*CM*, 70–71)

As an act of creation or praxis judgment is in effect conflated with deci-sion, since both are removed from strictly theoretical concerns and orient-ed directly with the creation of the world. The void of judgment, like that of decision, is always also the void from which the world springs—the goal or end of both is always the "creation of the world." This needs to be un-derstood not as the creation of this or that particular world but rather as the creation of the world of shared finitude as such, the creation of sense as singular plurality and in the name of singular plurality. In this sense Nancy's understanding of judgment implies or rather necessitates a cer-tain responsibility toward the singular-plural. It necessitates the ethics of openness discussed toward the end of Chapter 2 and with this a reworked understanding of the concept of justice, the need in the act of judgment to "do justice to the multiplicity and the coexistence of singulars, to multiply therefore and to infinitely singularize ends" (*CM*, 72). To a large extent this formulation recalls Derrida's thinking of justice such as it emerges in *Force de loi*.[8] Yet where Derrida appeals to justice as an experience of impresent-able and absolute alterity, and as that which is always "to come [*à venir*],"[9] Nancy more immediately and directly turns his understanding of the term toward worldly engagement and the production or creation of the world as such. The engagement of philosophy here is "the judgment of ends . . . of a destination or sense of the world" (*CM*, 68). In this context the universal which is "to be made" in an act of judgment such as Nancy understands it is a "multiple universal" that imposes itself as a binding *to* and *by* the singular plurality of shared finitude, and therefore necessarily obeys "the schema of a differential" or a "general absolute incommensurability" rather than a general equivalence or logic of identity (*CM*, 75).

This conclusion began with a citation from the opening essay of *La Création du monde*, "Urbi et orbi" (To the City and to the World), where Nancy, in the name of creation, appears to affirm the need to "immediately and without delay . . . reopen every possible struggle for a world" (*CM*, 63). The invocation of "every possible struggle" might at first suggest that Nancy's thinking gives us no means to differentiate between the relative value of different struggles or to proscribe or counter those who struggle by means of violence and terror for this or that particular view of the world (for instance those who struggle in the name of racial or religious purity, or in the name of ideologies which justify economic and military oppression). Yet the qualification he immediately adds to the invocation of "every possible struggle for a world"—"that is to say for that which must form the opposite of a global injustice taking place against the background of a general equivalence" (*CM*, 63)—necessarily implies that the struggle invoked can never be one for this or that particular world; it must always be for a world of shared finitude and for the sharing of that finitude. The struggle, every possible struggle, which Nancy invokes will always be a struggle bound by a certain responsibility toward the making of a "universal multiple," toward the creation of a world of sense which would affirm the singular plurality of existence as such. Across the accounts of subject, space, body, community, and art, it is arguably the creation of the world, groundless, multiple, and fragmentary, which makes an insistent and persistent demand on Nancy's thinking. Nancy's thinking makes this demand on us as well; it is a demand that calls for our decision and judgment. The demand here is that we engage with the world, or that we be engaged by it, in the absence of any appeal to a human essence, to pregiven realities, or to prospective teleologies. Nor should there be any appeal to the specificity or possible preeminence of particular identities or communities. The demand here is for the creation of a world as the exposure of singularities each to the other and as a sharing of finitude. In the end it is perhaps a rather simple injunction: "That it is for us to decide *ourselves*" (CM, 101).

# Notes

INTRODUCTION

1. Maurice Blanchot, *L'Entretien infini*, 526; *The Infinite Conversation*, 359.

2. Nancy himself takes up this phrase in order to refer to the fragmentary aesthetic of the Jena Romantics in his collaborative work with Philippe Lacoue-Labarthe, *L'Absolu littéraire*, 57–80; *The Literary Absolute*, 39–58.

3. Blanchot, *L'Entretien infini*, 201–55; *The Infinite Conversation*, 136–70. For Blanchot's commentary on the Nietzschean thought of the eternal return, see ibid., 391–418; 264–81.

4. In relation to Nietzsche's possible synthesizing or popularizing moments Blanchot suggests that it is "as if he had suffered from this fragmentary demand"; ibid., 206; 139.

5. Ibid., 234; 156.

6. Ibid., 211; 141.

7. See Jean-Luc Nancy, "Un Certain Silence"; "Marx et la philosophie"; "André Breton"; "Catéchisme et persévérence"; and "Nietzsche: Mais où sont les yeux pour le voir."

8. See Nancy, *Corpus*; and "La Déconstruction du christianisme." For some of Nancy's recent writing on Christian painting see *Noli me tangere* and *Visitation (de la peinture chrétienne)*. Nancy's "deconstruction of Christianity" and its relation to his thinking of embodiment will be discussed in Chapter 3, "Body."

9. Most prominently this criticism has been raised by Simon Critchley in *The Ethics of Deconstruction*, 200–219.

10. A single and obvious exception to this is Derrida's seminal work *Le Toucher, Jean-Luc Nancy*. There has been no full-length introductory study of Nancy's philosophy to date. A vast number of critical and philosophical engagements with his work do exist, mostly in the form of journal articles (see "Other Works Cited" in the Bibliography), or by way of works partially devoted to his thought, such as Simon Critchley's cited above. Works in this category include also Critchley's later work *Ethics—Politics—Subjectivity*, 239–53; see also Gayle L. Ormiston and Alan D. Schrift, eds., *Transforming the Hermeneutic Context*; Miami Theory Collective, ed., *Community at Loose Ends*; and Todd May, *Reconsidering Difference*. Important

assessments of various aspects of Nancy's thinking have been given in introductions to translations of his work, most notably by Simon Sparks, in Jean-Luc Nancy and Philippe Lacoue-Labarthe, *Retreating the Political*, xiv–xxviii, and by Christopher Fynsk, in *The Inoperative Community*, vii–xxxv; see also Philip Barnard and Cheryl Lester's introduction to Jean-Luc Nancy and Philippe Lacoue-Labarthe, *The Literary Absolute*, vii–xxii; and also Jeffrey Librett's preface to *The Sense of the World*, vii–xxvi. A number of important volumes of collected essays devoted to Nancy also exist, for example, Peggy Kamuf, ed., *On the Work of Jean-Luc Nancy*; and Darren Sheppard, Simon Sparks, and Colin Thomas, eds., *On Jean-Luc Nancy*. See also *At the Heart: Of Jean-Luc Nancy*. At the time of writing two volumes have appeared or will soon appear which testify to a growing interest in Nancy's work: the collectively edited *Le Sens dans tous les sens*; and B. C. Hutchens, *Jean-Luc Nancy and the Future of Philosophy*.

11. Martin Heidegger, "Das Ende der Philosophie und die Aufgabe des Denkens," in *Zur Sache des Denkens*, and *The End of Philosophy and the Task of Thinking*.

12. Although he does not refer to them directly, Nancy's target is likely to include French *nouveaux philosophes* such as André Glucksmann and Bernard Henri-Lévi. The rejection by the *nouveaux philosophes* of the Marxist heritage and their return to a neo-Kantian perspective marked a decisive shift away from the radicalism which informed the dynamic of French philosophy in the late 1960s and early 1970s, a radicalism personified most clearly in the work of figures such as Jacques Derrida, Gilles Deleuze, Michel Foucault, and Jean-François Lyotard. See in particular André Glucksmann, *Les Maîtres penseurs*, and Bernard Henri-Lévy, *La Barbarie à visage humain*. For an excellent polemical account of this philosophical retrenchment see Domique Lecourt, *Les Piètres penseurs*. From the 1980s onward Nancy is also concerned with the manner in which the event of Marxist thought is more generally forgotten or suppressed in favor of the triumphalist assertions of neoliberal capitalism and economics in the wake of the failure of the European left and, subsequently, the collapse of the Soviet Union; see Chapter 3, "Community," in particular "The Center for Philosophical Research on the Political."

13. As will become clear in Chapters 2 and 3, "sense" in Nancy is not posed as either a transcendent condition of possibility of experience or as an empirical determination. It is neither entirely material nor ideal, rather "the element of sense is a reality indiscernibly and simultaneously empirical and transcendental, material and ideative, physical and spiritual" (*OP*, 90–91; *GT*, 59).

CHAPTER 1: SUBJECTIVITY

1. Jean-Luc Nancy, "Monogrammes," *Digraphe* 20 (1979): 134.

2. Jacques Derrida, *L'Écriture et la différence*, 409–28; "Structure, Sign, and Play in the Discourse of the Human Sciences," in *Writing and Difference*, 279–93.

Hereafter *ED* and *WD* respectively.

3. Mostly notably in the essay on Jean Rousset, "Force and Signification" (*ED*, 9–49; *WD*, 3–30); on Michel Foucault, "Cogito and the History of Madness" (*ED*, 51–97; *WD*, 31–63); and on Husserl, "'Genesis and Structure' and Phenomenology" (*ED*, 229–51; *WD*, 154–68).

4. This, of course, is a central concern of Derrida's other seminal text, *De la grammatologie*. See, in particular, *De la grammatologie*, 11–41; "Exergue" and "The End of the Book and the Beginning of Writing," trans. Gayatri Spivak, in *Of Grammatology*, 3–26. Hereafter *DG* and *OG* respectively.

5. See, in particular, "The Written Being the Being Written" (*DG*, 31–41; *OG*, 18–26).

6. *Poétique*, no. 1 (1970): 1–2. All translations are mine unless otherwise stated.

7. For an excellent overview of the history of Nietzsche reception in France, see Douglas Smith, *Transvaluations: Nietzsche in France, 1872–1972*.

8. Heidegger, *Nietzsche*, trans. Pierre Klossowski. For the German original see Martin Heidegger, *Gesamtausgabe*, vols. 45–48; English translation cited in this text is translated by Joan Stambaugh, David Farrell Krell, and Frank A. Kapuzzi. English and German editions hereafter respectively given as *N* and *GA*. All references to Heidegger in German throughout this study are to the *Gesamtausgabe* (unless otherwise stated).

9. Philippe Lacoue-Labarthe, "L'Oblitération"; reprinted in *Le Sujet de la philosophie*. *Le Sujet de la philosophie* gathers together in one volume a range of essays published by Lacoue-Labarthe throughout the 1970s, including many of the essays first published in *Poétique* (see below). All references to Lacoue-Labarthe's essays of the 1970s are to this collected edition.

10. Pierre Boudot et al., *Nietzsche aujourd'hui?* See in particular, Sylviane Agacinski, "Table Ronde," 191–233, and Derrida, "La Question du style," 235–99.

11. This point will be discussed further in the final section of this chapter, "The Persistence of the Subject," and in the third section of Chapter 2, "Heidegger and Existential Spatiality."

12. See "How the Real World Became Fable," in Friedrich Nietzsche, *Twilight of the Idols*, 50–51; for the original German see Nietzsche, *Kritische Studienausgabe*, 6:80–81.

13. "Nietzsche: Mais où sont les yeux pour le voir?" *Esprit* (March 1968): 482–503. Hereafter *E*.

14. Philippe Lacoue-Labarthe, "La Fable (philosophie et littérature)," *Poétique* 1 (1970): 51–63.

15. Ibid.; "Le Détour (Nietzsche et la rhétorique)"; and "L'Imprésentable." Jean-Luc Nancy, "Sur le trait d'esprit" and "Logodaedalus (Kant écrivain)." Their collaboration culminates in a joint presentation and commentary of texts by Anthony Shaftesbury, Franciscus Hemsterhuis, and Friedrich Schelling published in

the twenty-first issue of the journal, "Le Dialogue des genres," *Poétique* 21 (1975): 148–57. This issue was dedicated to the question of philosophy and literature, and also featured articles by Jacques Derrida, Sylviane Agacinski, and Sarah Kofman.

16. This point is discussed in further detail below in the discussion of *Logodaedalus*.

17. Nietzsche, *Twilight of the Idols*, 51; *Kritische Studienausgabe*, 6:81.

18. Lacoue-Labarthe immediately adds: "Is this possible? It would be necessary here to refer to the interpretation of Klossowski . . . " The importance of Pierre Klossowski's reading of Nietzsche for Lacoue-Labarthe is enormous, as he makes explicit at key points in his discussion. Klossowski's emphasis on the account of fable given in *Twilight of the Idols* is decisive, as is the way in which he reads Nietzsche's philosophy, and particularly the doctrine of the eternal return, as a form of parody or simulacrum. See Pierre Klossowski, "Nietzsche, le polythéime, et la parodie" (Nietzsche, Polytheism, and Parody), in *Un si funeste désir*, 187–228; and *Nietzsche et le cercle vicieux*. See also Ian James, "Simulacrum and the Play of Parody in the Writing of Pierre Klossowski," and *Pierre Klossowski: The Persistence of a Name*, in particular pages 84–97.

19. This recalls Heidegger's shift away from the motif of the "overcoming" (*Überwindung*) of metaphysics to the motif of "getting over" (*Verwindung*) metaphysics. See *Zur Seinsfrage/The Question of Being*, 86 ff.

20. *Critique of Pure Reason*, 123; from the preface to the 2nd ed. (*B*, xliv). Hereafter *CPR*. The equivalent page references to the first and second editions of the original German are also given (preceded by *A* and *B* respectively: *Kritik der reinen Vernunft*).

21. Examples of this in French would be terms such as *déconstruction, destruction, indécidable, disruption*, and *disjonction*.

22. In *L'Écriture et la différence* Derrida refers to the tendency found in "destructive discourses" since Nietzsche, Heidegger, and Freud, according to which such "destructive" thinkers move to "reciprocally destroy each other" (this is most clearly exemplified perhaps in Heidegger's Nietzsche lectures), and adds: "No other exercise is today more widespread" (*ED*, 413; *WD*, 282).

23. As Kant writes toward the beginning of the *Critique of Pure Reason*: "I call all cognition transcendental that is occupied not so much with objects but rather with our mode of cognition of objects insofar as this is to be possible *a priori*" (*CPR*, 149; *A*, 11–12).

24. Howard Caygill, *A Kant Dictionary*, 149.

25. Martin Heidegger, *Kant and the Problem of Metaphysics* (hereafter *KPM*). All references will be followed by the equivalent page reference in volume 3 of the *Gesamtausgabe* of Heidegger's works, *Kant und Das Problem der Metaphysik*. See also Gérard Granel, *L'Équivoque ontologique de la pensée kantienne*; Jacques Derrida, *Du Droit à la philosophie* and *Force de loi*; Geoffrey Bennington, *Frontières kan-*

*tiennes.* Bennington explicitly cites the influence, and underlines the importance, of Nancy's reading of Kant: *Frontières kantiennes,* 114, note 1.

26. Many of the responses to the *CPR* which have focused on this ontological dimension are also part of the antifoundationalist tradition detailed above (most notably Heidegger, Granel, and Nancy himself). This ontological dimension has been noted within the more analytic approaches to Kant of the Anglo-American tradition; see for instance, Paul Guyer, "The Transcendental Deduction of the Categories" in Guyer, ed., *The Cambridge Companion to Kant,* 123–60, 126.

27. Kant's conception of space thus has a complex relation to classical debates on this issue, the two sides of which are most clearly represented by the respective positions of Newton and Leibniz. For an illuminating account of the way Kant's critical philosophy as a whole develops in relation to these wider debates, see Alexis Philonenko, *L'Œuvre de Kant.* For a more detailed account of the classical philosophical debate around the question of space see Chapter 2, above, "Space: Classical and Phenomenological."

28. To this extent Kant's conception of space prefigures Husserl's phenomenological thinking of space, which is discussed at greater length in Chapter 2.

29. Here the issue of translation is potentially decisive. The French translation of the first *Critique* renders "a general but sufficient characterization" as "à l'aide de signes généraux mais suffisants," and emphasizes much more closely the role of verbal signs than does the English rendering with its more general term *characterization*; see *Critique de la raison pure,* 150. The original German reads, transcendental philosophy "muß zugleich die Bedingungen, unter welchen Gegenstände in Übereinstimmung mit jenen Begriffen gegeben werden können, *in allgemeinen aber hinreichenden Kennzeichen darlegen*" (emphasis added). The use of the term *Kennzeichen* suggests specific verbal characters rather than the more general "characterization." Nancy's reading, which, as will become clear, questions the fundamental role of the presentation *in language* of transcendental philosophy, appears much more plausible on the basis of the (arguably more accurate) French translation than it might in reference to the English translation, which slightly underplays Kant's emphasis on specific signs or characters (*Kennzeichen*).

30. For an illuminating and more detailed account of this process see J. M. Young, "Functions of Thought and the Synthesis of Intuitions," in Guyer, *The Cambridge Companion to Kant,* 101–22.

31. See Philonenko, *L'Œuvre de Kant,* 90.

32. Philonenko remarks that the categories give an overview of thinking about the scientific method to date, see ibid., 113–14; see also, Hermann Cohen, *Kants Theorie der Erfahrung,* 351 ff., "Logik der Reinen Erkenntnis."

33. As Eisler puts it, the schematism "constitutes . . . the only true condition of the signification of the concepts of understanding"; Rudolphe Eisler, *Kant-Lexicon,* 937.

34. Again, see Philonenko, who contests both the ontological status Heidegger ascribes to the pure power of the imagination and the reasons why Kant so rapidly elides his account of the schematism in favor of the categories; Philonenko, *L'Œuvre de Kant*, 172, 176.

35. To this extent Nancy's reading also owes a debt to Granel's earlier 1970 work *L'Équivoque ontologique de la pensée kantienne*; see in particular page 160.

36. Unsurprisingly Nancy cites Gödel's theorem in this context.

37. Jean-Luc Nancy, *Ego Sum*, 11; hereafter *ES*.

38. Nancy is not alone in this attempt to reveal a more "classical" subject at work in Lacan's discourse. The work of Mikkel Borch-Jacobsen, in particular, relates the Lacanian Subject to the Cartesian Cogito but also, via Kojève, to Hegel's conception. See Mikkel Borch-Jacobsen, *Le Maître absolu*, 18–35; *The Absolute Master*, 4–20, and "The Freudian Subject," in Peter Connor, Jean-Luc Nancy, and Eduardo Cadava, eds., *Who Comes After the Subject?*, 61–78, in particular page 63.

39. Malcolm Bowie, *Lacan*, 155.

40. Jean-Luc Nancy and Philippe Lacoue-Labarthe, *Le Titre de la lettre* (*The Title of the Letter*), 12 (in the French edition).

41. This point is echoed by Mikkel Borch-Jacobsen in his analysis of the Freudian subject. See "The Freudian Subject," in *Who Comes After the Subject?* 65.

42. Nancy's critical account of the Lacanian subject in *Le Titre de la lettre*, in *Ego Sum*, and elsewhere in his writing parallel that of his close friend Jacques Derrida in texts such as *Positions* and *La Carte postale*. For a lucid and helpful account of Derrida's relation to psychoanalysis see Christina Howells, *Derrida*, 96–121. See also Derrida's recent work, where he gives his fullest account of the complex relationship between psychoanalysis and deconstruction, *Résistences de la psychanalyse* (Resistances of Psychoanalysis).

43. To the extent that Nancy's philosophy does attempt to think in terms of "conditions of possibility" it remains, despite his antifoundationalist reading of the *Critique of Pure Reason*, within a post-Kantian tradition.

44. Heidegger's thinking of being or what in his later work he calls *Ereignis* (the giving of being or event of appropriation), Derrida's *différance*, and Nancy's attempt to figure a temporalizing/spatializing movement in excess of any subject or possibility of conscious thought offer similarities and differences in their respective structures. This question will be addressed more fully in the following chapter, in the context of the phenomenological account of space. The key point to retain at this stage is that all three imply some unfolding of temporality and spatiality which is irreducible to thought or representation and which precedes space and time, as traditionally conceived, as that which makes them possible.

45. Heidegger's conception of the tradition of European philosophy, and in particular his assertions on the total dominance of the subjective in the modern period, need to be viewed critically, since the history of the subject may be more

differentiated than he allows. See Simon Critchley, "Black Socrates? Questioning the Philosophical Tradition" and "Prolegomena to Any Post-Deconstructive Subjectivity"; see also Andrew Bowie, "Rethinking the History of the Subject."

46. Martin Heidegger, *Being and Time*, hereafter *BT*; see in particular division 2, chapter 4, "Temporality and Everydayness," 383–423; *GA*, 2:444–91.

47. Again, the thinking of *Ereignis* or "enowning" which permeates much of Heidegger's late thought will be dealt with in the next chapter. For an introductory overview of this later thinking in Heidegger's own words, see "Preview," in Martin Heidegger, *Contributions to Philosophy (From Enowning)*, 3–71; *Beiträge zur Philosophie (Vom Ereignis)*, in *GA*, 65:3–103; see also *On Time and Being*, published originally as *Zur Sache des Denkens*.

48. Christina Howells has remarked that the self-same, self-identical subject which Heidegger and others seek to displace has perhaps never existed in philosophical thinking (implying, as do Critchley and Bowie, cited above, that the construction of a monolithic canon is often misleading and serves far more the needs of the philosopher who constructs said canon in order then to deconstruct it). It should be noted, though, that Heidegger (and Nancy) are not talking about self-sameness or identity but about the subject which acts as *ground*, maintaining itself as such through all its divisions and alienations. While Heidegger is almost certainly overstating the dominance of a certain conception of the subjective within modernity, he may be right in his judgment that the "classical" or "metaphysical" subject implies a ground or grounding in this way. See Howells, *Derrida*, 135.

49. Jean-Luc Nancy, *The Inoperative Community*, 24; *La Communauté désœuvrée*, 62. Hereafter *IC* and *CD* respectively.

50. For an analysis of the "quasi-transcendental" in Derrida's work, see Geoffrey Bennington, *Jacques Derrida*, 248–63; and Marion Hobson, *Jacques Derrida: Opening Lines*, chapter 2, "Replications"; see in particular page 106.

51. *Discours de la méthode*, 35; *Discourse on Method*, 7.

52. *Discours de la méthode*, 34–35; *Discourse on Method*, 6.

53. The emphasis placed here on the figures of mask, on simulation and dissimulation, may recall the writing of Gilles Deleuze and his use of the term *simulacrum*. See Deleuze, *Difference and Repetition*, 66–67; *Différence et répétition*, 92. Nancy's emphasis on fable also recalls the writing of Pierre Klossowski (who influences Deleuze greatly throughout the 1960s and who from the 1950s onward emphasizes the subject as mask or fable); see Klossowski, *Un si funeste désir*, 187–228; see also Ian James, *Pierre Klossowski: The Persistence of a Name*, and "Simulacrum and the Play of Parody in the Writing of Pierre Klossowski."

54. Lacan, *Le Seminaire II*, 68; *The Second Seminar*, 52.

55. For a full account of Nancy's thinking of singularity, see in particular Nancy, *Être singulier pluriel*; this will discussed further in later chapters.

56. In this sense, since Nancy does seem to be making an ontological claim,

however paradoxical this may be, one could describe his writing, and the paradoxical logic of figuration which underpins it, as "quasi-transcendental ontology" (building on Derrida's notion of the quasi transcendental); see Derrida, *Le Toucher Jean-Luc Nancy*, 311, 317, 328.

57. See Nancy, *Une Pensée finie*, "L'Excrit," 55–64. *La bouche*, the speaking mouth, implies that Nancy is seeking to think the unthinkable giving of being in terms of an instance or site which would somehow be bodily (perhaps to reembody Derridean *différance*). See Nancy, *Corpus*.

CHAPTER 2: SPACE

1. *SM*, 238; *SW*, 157.

2. Derrida's thinking emerges, of course, within the context of a sustained critique of Husserl; see Derrida, *L'Origine de la géométrie de Husserl: Introduction et traduction* (English trans., *Edmund Husserl's Origin of Geometry: An Introduction*); and *La Voix et le phénomène*. In his recent work on Nancy, Derrida situates his thinking closely in relation to this philosophical tradition and in particular to the thought of Maurice Merleau-Ponty; see Derrida, *Le Toucher, Jean-Luc Nancy*. This work and Nancy's relation to Merleau-Ponty will be discussed in Chapter 3.

3. This point is made by Henri Lefèbvre in *La Production de l'espace*, 7.

4. For a full account the debate between substantivalism and relationalism and the polemic between Newton and Leibniz, see Barry Dainton, *Time and Space*; see in particular pages 1–12 and 151–68. Dainton also gives a comprehensive overview of philosophical and scientific accounts of time, as well as a full discussion of the ways in which the classical debate about space has evolved in modern scientific theories.

5. Ibid., 153–54; 162–63. As has been indicated, Descartes, whose understanding of space as extension might clearly position him as a substantivalist, in fact occupies an ambiguous and not always consistent position in relation to the two camps. Dainton highlights this in his presentation of Descartes and notes also that his ambivalence regarding this issue may have been, to a certain extent, a way of negotiating the theological sensibilities of his time and of avoiding the fate of Galileo; ibid., 159–62.

6. Kant's mature thinking of space and time can be found in the "Transcendental Aesthetic" of the *Critique of Pure Reason* (*CPR*, 155–92; A, 19–49, B, 33–73). For an earlier Kantian meditation on space see the 1768 essay "Concerning the Ultimate Foundation of the Differentiation of Regions in Space," in Kant, *Prolegomena to any Future Metaphysics*.

7. For a general introductory overview of phenomenological thought, see Dermot Moran, *Introduction to Phenomenology*.

8. Edmund Husserl, *Gesammelte Werke*, vols. 18 and 19, *Logische Untersuchun-*

*gen* (trans., *Logical Investigations*); *Ideen zu einer reinen Phänomeologie und phe-nomenologischen Philosophie*, vol. 3, *Husserliana* (trans., *General Introduction to a Pure Phenomenology*, vol. 1 of *Ideas Pertaining to a Pure Phenomenology and to a Phenomenological Philosophy*); *Ideen: Zweites Buch*, vol. 4, *Husserliana* (trans., *Studies in the Phenomenology of Constitution*, vol. 2 of *Ideas Pertaining to a Pure Phenomenology and to a Phenomenological Philosophy*); *Die Krisis der europäischen Wissenschaft und die transzendentale Phänomenologie*, vol. 6, *Husserliana* (trans., *The Crisis of European Sciences and Transcendental Phenomenology: An Introduction to Phenomenological Philosophy*); *Ding und Raum: Vorlesungen 1907*, vol. 16, *Husserliana* (trans., *Thing and Space: 1907 Lectures*, vol. 7 of *Collected Works*). References to the *Thing and Space* lectures will be to the English edition preceded with the abbreviation *TS* and followed by a reference to the original German. All references to Husserl in the original German will be to the collected works, abbreviated as *HUA*.

9. Nevertheless, Hermann Philipse has identified what he calls Husserl's "Platonic idealism," which, he argues, is distinctly different from, say, Kant's transcendental idealism as such. See Hermann Philipse, "Transcendental Idealism," in *The Cambridge Companion to Husserl*, 239–322; see in particular page 244.

10. This is a consistent point throughout Husserl's mature work and is best summed up by the following comment in *Ideas I*: "It must always be borne in mind here that *whatever physical things are*—the only physical things about which we can make statements, the only ones about the being, non-being, the being-thus or being-otherwise of which we can disagree and make rational decisions—*they are as experienceable physical things*. It is experience alone that prescribes their sense" (*Ideas I*, 106; *HUA*, 3:111).

11. Pierre Keller, *Husserl and Heidegger on Human Experience*, 50.

12. The importance of the notion of "flesh" in relation to Nancy and Maurice Merleau-Ponty will be discussed further in Chapter 3.

13. For an extended discussion of McTaggert's more traditional scientifically oriented theories of time, see Dainton, *Time and Space*, 13–26.

14. See *Being and Time* (*BT*, 122–34; *GA*, 2:89–101) and *Contributions to Philosophy* (*CP*, 262; *GA*, 65:376). See also "European Nihilism," *Nietzsche* (*N*, 4:96–138; *GA*, 48:181–249).

15. See Keller, *Husserl and Heidegger on Human Experience*, 111–31.

16. In this sense *Being and Time* retains a distinctly Kantian flavor insofar as its existentials can be considered to be conditions of possibility for experience.

17. For some introductory philosophical and biographical accounts of Heidegger's thinking, see Richard Polt, *Heidegger*; Rudiger Safranski, *Heidegger: Between Good and Evil*; and John van Buren, *The Young Heidegger*.

18. It is in this sense that Heidegger thinks the category of "truth" not as the adequation of meanings or concepts with given objects of experience but as an

originary unconcealment (*aletheia*) or unveiling of a world. See "On the Essence of Truth," in *Pathmarks*, 136–54; "Vom Wesen der Wahrheit" in *Wegmarken* (*GA*, 9:177–202).

19. For a useful introductory account of Heidegger's "turn" (*Kehre*) see Michael Inwood, *A Heidegger Dictionary*, 231–33.

20. See Derrida, *Marges de la philosophie*, "Les fins de l'homme," 156 (trans., *Margins of Philosophy*, 130); Philippe Lacoue-Labarthe, *La Fiction du politique*, 28; Jean-Luc Nancy, *La Pensée dérobée*, 99, 104. See also Miguel de Bestegui, *Heidegger and the Political*, 108.

21. This question of the "proper" or the *eigentlich* is already present in *Being and Time* in the motif of being-towards-death as the ownmost possibility of Dasein. Importantly, Derrida has remarked that the structure of the "proper" in Heidegger is an abyssal one according to which the appropriation of the truth of being in the event (*Ereignis*) is always the appropriation of an absence of ground and thus an appropriation without propriety (ownness) and in excess of any logic of identity to which any notion of the "own" or the "proper" would normally return. See Derrida, *Epérons*, 97–98. Nancy radicalizes this tendency in Heidegger, as will be argued in the discussion of the sense of space below.

22. Heidegger, *Zur Sache des Denkens*, 20; *On Time and Being*, 19.

23. Heidegger says of facticity (*Faktizität*) in *Being and Time*, "this implies that an entity 'within the world' has being-in-the-world in such a way that it can understand itself as bound up in its 'destiny' with the being of those entities which it encounters within its own world" (*BT*, 82; *GA*, 2:56).

24. For Heidegger our understanding of "being-in-the-world" and the originary giving of being which is world disclosure is pre-predicative. See "On the Essence of Ground," in *Pathmarks*, 97–135; "Vom Wesen des Grundes," in *Wegmarken*, *GA*, 9:177–202.

25. Pierre Keller argues that, in *Being and Time* at least, meaning and sense, that is to say intelligibility per se, are not necessarily functions of language but rather are that on the basis of which language can arise in the first instance. See Pierre Keller, *Husserl and Heidegger on Human Experience*, chapter 6, "Heidegger on the Nature of Significance"; see in particular page 138. It is interesting to note that Keller does not engage with Heidegger's later thinking, where, of course, language plays a much more fundamental disclosive role in the giving of being.

26. To this extent Nancy is rejecting the neo-Kantian residue of *Being and Time* (which views the existentials of being-in-the-world as a kind of condition of possibility), just has Heidegger will in his later thinking.

27. This point will be discussed in more detail in Chapter 3.

28. See in particular Viktor Farias, *Heidegger and Nazism*.

29. See Derrida, *De L'Esprit: Heidegger et la question*, and Lyotard, *Heidegger et "les juifs."*

30. Lyotard, *Heidegger et "les juifs,"* 93.

31. Lacoue-Labarthe, *La Fiction du politique,* 175.

32. Ibid., 59.

33. Ibid., 142. This gesture, he contends, also underpins the founding moment of any democratic polis, and he thus suggests, like many of his contemporaries on the philosophical left, that totalitarianism and democracy in some way have a common root within the deeper currents of European culture. This assertion will be discussed in more detail in Chapter 4.

34. The full scope of Lacoue-Labarthe's work cannot be discussed here. The question of his collaboration with Nancy concerning the thinking and the re-thinking of the relation of politics to philosophy will be discussed in Chapter 4.

CHAPTER 3: BODY

1. *C,* 12–13.

2. Michel Foucault's *Surveiller et punir* (1975) (*Discipline and Punish* [1977]) stands out as one of the most influential texts in this regard.

3. See for instance the entries under "Body" in some recent cultural theory glossaries: Peter Sedgwick, ed., *Key Concepts in Cultural Theory,* in particular page 47; and Peter Brooker, *Cultural Theory: A Glossary,* 22–23.

4. For instance Chris Shilling, in an essay entitled "The Body and Difference," has argued that, in its marginalization of material and biological aspects of embodiment, cultural theory lacks any satisfactory account of why the body should assume such central importance in the first instance. He goes on to argue that the body needs to be viewed as "a material and physical phenomenon irreducible to immediate social processes or classification," and adds: "Furthermore, our sense, knowledgeability and capability to act are integrally related to the fact that we are embodied beings"; "The Body and Difference," 65–103; see in particular page 81. See also Chris Shilling, *The Body and Social Theory.* As this chapter argues, Nancy's thinking of the body offers a philosophically rigorous way of responding to this demand to think embodiment, beyond the symbolic abstraction of cultural theory, in terms of its material situatedness.

5. There is another trajectory of thinking about the body in this context, one which might broadly be characterized as Nietzschean, and which emphasizes the body as a site of drives or forces, which, though intimately tied up with signifying processes, are also irreducible to them. In the 1960s and 1970s this strand of thought was most clearly present in the work of figures such as Pierre Klossowski, Gilles Deleuze, and Jean-François Lyotard. See, for instance, Pierre Klossowski, *Nietzsche et le cercle vicieux* (*Nietzsche and the Vicious Circle*); Gilles Deleuze, *Nietzsche et la philosophie* (*Nietzsche and Philosophy*); Gilles Deleuze with Félix Guattari, *L'Anti-Œdipe: Capitalisme et schizophrénie* (*Anti-Oedipus: Capital-*

*ism and Schizophrenia*); see also Jean-François Lyotard, *L'Economie libidinale.* This thinking of the body has made a significant impact on cultural theoretical approaches to the body in the anglophone context; see Bryan S. Turner, "The Secret History of the Body in Social Theory"; and Scott Lash, "Genealogy and the Body: Foucault/Deleuze/Nietzsche." See also Ian James, "Klossowski, Nietzsche, and the Fortuitous Body."

6. Although it is widely recognized that the rise of structuralism in France eclipsed the dominant position enjoyed by phenomenology (especially Sartian existentialism) during the immediate postwar years, the influence of Husserl's thought, particularly of the *Logical Investigations,* on seminal structuralists such as Roman Jakobson and, via Jakobson, on Claude Lévi-Strauss, is less acknowledged. Gutting gives a good account of the way in which structuralism displaced the dominance of subject-centered phenomenology in France; see Gary Gutting, *French Philosophy in the Twentieth Century,* in particular chapter 8, "The Structuralist Invasion," 215–57. François Dosse gives an important, although brief, account of the importance of Husserl on Roman Jakobson and of Jakobson's subsequent influence on Lévi-Strauss. See Dosse, *Histoire du structuralisme,* vol. 1 (*History of Structuralism,* vol. 1).

7. Michel Henry, *Incarnation,* in particular part 1, "Le Renversement de la phénoménologie," 61, 80, 89–94.

8. For an excellent introduction to Merleau-Ponty's thinking see Dermot Moran, *Introduction to Phenomenology,* 391–434. See also Stephen Priest, *Merleau-Ponty*; Monika M. Langer, *Merleau-Ponty's "Phenomenology of Perception": A Guide and Commentary*; Michael Dillon, *Merleau-Ponty's Ontology.*

9. On functionalist approaches to the body see Keller, *Husserl and Heidegger on Human Experience,* 24.

10. Moran, *Introduction to Phenomenology,* 425.

11. See Sean Dorrence Kelly, "Merleau-Ponty on the Body."

12. John 1:14.

13. Nancy, "La Déconstruction du christianisme."

14. Ibid., 504.

15. This foregrounding of Christian motifs is most evident in Nancy's invocation of the Eucharist in *Corpus,* but is also central to one of his most recent works, *Noli me tangere.*

16. Although this may seem a rather sweeping gesture it should be stressed that Nancy puts forward the linkage he makes between Christianity and the history of Western thought and culture in terms of a series of axiomatic judgments: (1) "The Christian is inseparable from the West," (2) "Dechristianization is not a vain word, but . . . what still ties us in many respects to the West are the very nerves of Christianity," and (3) "The West itself, occidentality, is that which is accomplished in the exposure of [*en mettant à nu*] a particular nerve of sense. . . . From here on,

to deconstruct Christianity is to accompany the West up to this limit"; *Études Philosophiques*, 506. As axiomatic judgments, then, these are not dogmatic statements but are offered in order to be thought in the light of, or tested against, the sweep of thought and culture of the West.

17. *Études Philosophiques*, 504. Pareysson's original phrase runs: "Christianity can only be contemporary/real if it contemplates the present possibility of its negation."

18. Nancy draws specifically upon the arguments of Marcel Gauchet in his 1985 work *Le Désenchantement du monde: Une Histoire politique de la religion.*

19. *Études Philosophiques*, 514.

20. Jean-Luc Nancy, "L'Extension de l'âme."

21. Descartes cited, *Po&sie* 99 (2002):77.

22. Ibid., 79.

23. Ibid., 80–81.

24. *Po&sie* 99 (2002): 83.

25. Hence Nancy's use of the words *soul* and *spirit* in place of sense his recent readings of Descartes and of the Resurrection in *Noli me tangere.*

26. *Études Philosophiques*, 519.

27. For Nancy's meditation on the intersection of embodiment and technology in the context of his heart transplant operation see *L'Intrus.*

28. "Agriculture is now a motorized food-industry—in essence, the same as the manufacture of corpses in gas chambers and extermination camps, the same as the blockading and starving of nations, the same as the manufacture of hydrogen bombs." Heidegger made this comment in a lecture given on December 1, 1949. It is cited in Wolfgang Schirmacher, *Technik und Gelassenheit*, from page 25 of a typescript of Heidegger's lecture. For the English translation see Thomas Sheehan, "Heidegger and the Nazis." This controversial comment is cut from the published version of the lecture; see "Die Frage nach der Technik," in Heidegger, *Die Technik und die Kehre*, 14–15 (trans. William Lovitt, "The Question Concerning Technology," in David Farrell Krell, ed., *Martin Heidegger: Basic Writings*, 296). This question is discussed in Miguel de Bestegui, *Heidegger and the Political*, 153, and 186, note 8. Nancy explicitly rejects Heidegger's monolithic understanding of technology as "enframing" (*das Gestell*); see *Une Pensée finie*, 45, note 1, 46.

29. This discussion of body began by highlighting the degree to which many contemporary cultural theoretical discourses on embodiment are rather abstract in the attention paid to an exclusively symbolic dimension; it also suggested that this tendency within the human sciences may have its roots in a complex genealogy which can be traced back through structuralism to Husserlian phenomenology. This genealogy might also account for the enormous gulf in basic understanding and methodology which separates many developments in cultural theory and those in the "hard" sciences. Nancy's thinking of ecotechnics, in moving beyond

the phenomenological "bracketing off" of the technical into the abstract sphere of science, addresses what may be at stake in the gulf separating much of the methodology of science and human science or cultural theory.

CHAPTER 4: COMMUNITY

1. Jean-Luc Nancy, *La Communauté affrontée*, 31–32.

2. These affairs were discussed in Chapter 2.

3. See Keith Ansell-Pearson, *An Introduction to Nietzsche as a Political Thinker*, and Simon Critchley, *Ethics—Politics—Subjectivity*. See also the useful Routledge series on the political dimension of a number of key thinkers in this area: Richard Beardsworth, *Derrida and the Political*; Miguel de Bestegui, *Heidegger and the Political*; Howard Caygill, *Levinas and the Political*; and Daniel Conway, *Nietzsche and the Political*.

4. Reprinted in English translation as "War, Law, Sovereignty—Techné," in *Rethinking Technologies*, ed. Verena Andermatt Conley, 28–58; 28.

5. Ibid., 28.

6. This essay cannot be discussed here. See, however, Hutchens, *Jean-Luc Nancy and the Future of Philosophy*, 144–55.

7. The proceedings of this colloquium are published in *Les Fins de l'homme: À partir du travail de Jacques Derrida*. It is interesting to note that not only Derrida but also Althusser was involved in offering the hospitality of the École Normale for the proceedings of the Center, although he never took part (*La Communauté affrontée*, 31, note 1).

8. Jacques Derrida, *Marges de la philosophie*, 131–64.

9. See Nancy Fraser, "The French Derrideans: Politicizing Deconstruction or Deconstructing the Political?"; Simon Critchley, "Retracing the Political: Politics and Community in the Works of Lacoue-Labarthe and Jean-Luc Nancy," a revised version of which is in Critchley, *The Ethics of Deconstruction*, 200–219; David Ingram, "The Retreat of the Political in the Modern Age: Jean-Luc Nancy on Totalitarianism and Community"; see also Simon Sparks, "Politica Ficta," in *RT*, xiv–xxviii. *RT* incorporates translations of texts by Nancy and Lacoue-Labarthe which relate to the work of the Center, and its origin in the Derrida colloquium is an invaluable source for readers in English in this context.

10. See also Derrida, *Positions*, 85; trans. *Positions*, 62–63.

11. See also Derrida, "*Ja*, ou le faux-bond II." This comment echoes and develops further the opening lines of the 1968 essay "Les Fins de l'homme," after which the colloquium of July 1980 takes its name: "Every philosophical colloquium necessarily has a political meaning" (*RT*, 89), See also Derrida, *Marges de la philosophie*, 131. This is a common theme of much avant-garde French philosophy in the wake of the events of May 1968. See, for example the discussion between Foucault and Deleuze printed in the edition of the review *Arc* devoted to Deleuze's work: "Les Intellectuels et le pouvoir"; see in particular pages 3–4.

12. This is discussed in Chapter 1.

13. This, of course, inherits from and largely repeats the Heideggerian understanding of metaphysics discussed in Chapter 1.

14. See *L'Expérience de la liberté*, "Le mal: La Décision," 157–81; and *Une pensée finie*, "La Décision d'existence," 107–45.

15. The question of invention, innovation, and the emergence of the new is arguably a central preoccupation of Derrida's writing as a whole. For a useful discussion of this see Marion Hobson, *Jacques Derrida: Opening Lines*, 147–86.

16. This is not to say, of course, that either believes that the identity of philosophy is straightforward or that the "proper" is not always already implicated in the improper, since this is precisely what has always been in question for both in their collaborative work throughout the 1970s (see Chapter 1).

17. It is here that their interrogation of the political in the work of the center is intimately related to their collaboration in the 1970s around the question of *Darstellung* and the relation of philosophy and literature (a point explicitly made in the text of the "Opening Address" [*RJ*, 20; *RT*, 114]).

18. Simon Sparks lucidly elaborates Nancy's and Lacoue-Labarthe's understanding in this respect in his introduction to *Retreating the Political*; see in particular *RT*, xxii and xxiv.

19. Nancy and Lacoue-Labarthe refer in this context to Sartre's famous comment, "Communism is the unsurpassable horizon of our time."

20. Nancy's most extended engagement with this logic can be found in his analysis of Hegel in "La Juridiction du monarque hégélien" (in *RJ*, 51–90), translated as "The Juridiction of the Hegelian Monarch," trans. Mary Ann Caws and Peter Caws (in *BP*, 110–42).

21. See Nancy and Lacoue-Labarthe, "La Panique politique" in *RT*, 1–31; for the original French see *Confrontations* 2 (1979): 35–57.

22. Nancy and Lacoue-Labarthe, "'Chers Amis': A Letter on the Closure of the Political," (*RT*, 143–47).

23. Claude Lefort, "La Question de la démocratie" (*RP*, 71–88), trans. David Macey as "The Question of Democracy"; Denis Kambouchner, "De la condition la plus générale de la philosophie politique" (*RP*, 113–58).

24. Fraser, "The French Derrideans," 148.

25. Ibid., 148.

26. Bill Readings remarks that Fraser "concludes lamely"; see Readings, "The Deconstruction of Politics," 243.

27. Simon Critchley, "Retracing the Political: Politics and Community in the Works of Lacoue-Labarthe and Jean-Luc Nancy."

28. Ibid., 78.

29. Ibid., 75.

30. Lefort, *Democracy and Political Theory*, 12–14. With thanks to Ruth Deyermond for her illuminating insights on the question of hegemony and totalitarianism.

31. Ibid., 17.

32. Critchley engages further on the issue of democracy in relation to Derrida's thought in *Ethics—Politics—Subjectivity*: see chapter 7, "On Derrida's *Specters of Marx*," 143–82; see in particular page 154.

33. David Campbell and Michael Dillon, eds., *The Political Subject of Violence*, 85.

34. This point will be returned to in more detail later in this discussion.

35. *CD*, 59; *IC*, 22.

36. Christopher Fynsk, however, provides an important qualification to this in his foreword to *The Inoperative Community* (*IC*, xvi).

37. An important context here is Nancy's collaboration with Jean-Christophe Bailly for the review *Aléa* starting in 1981. *Aléa* was an avant-garde publication whose project was deeply indebted to Bataille's thinking.

38. Nancy is writing, of course, in the mid-1980s, and he notes two exceptions to this absence of recognition: Denis Hollier's work *La Prise de la concorde*, together with his publication of the edited proceedings of the Collège de sociologie, and Francis Marmande, *Georges Bataille politique*. These works are now accepted as canonical texts in the wider academic reception of Bataille's work, as is the importance of its political dimension. See also Michel Surya, *Georges Bataille: La Mort à l'œuvre* (*Georges Bataille: An Intellectual Biography*); all references to this work will be to the English edition.

39. For an example of Bataille's attempt to marry his thinking of heterology with a thinking of revolution, see Georges Bataille, "La Valeur d'usage de D. A. F. de Sade," *Œuvres complètes*, 2:54–69; see in particular 68–69 (trans. in *Visions of Excess*, "The Use-Value of D. A. F. de Sade," 91–102; in particular 100–102). All subsequent references to Bataille in French will be to the complete works, with the abbreviation *OC*.

40. For a biographical account of Bataille's involvement with the Collège, see Surya, *Georges Bataille*, 261–70.

41. Again Surya gives some biographical information of Bataille's exposure to ethnography and ethnographic sources, principally via his friendship with Alfred Métraux and his reading of Marcel Mauss; see ibid., 55–56 and 173–74.

42. See Bataille, "La Notion de dépense," *Œuvres complètes*, 1:302–20 (trans., "The Notion of Expenditure," in *Visions of Excess*, 116–29).

43. Bataille draws this, of course, from Marcel Mauss's famous "Essai sur le don," in *Sociologie et Anthropologie* (trans., *The Gift: The Form and Reason for Exchange in Archaic Societies*).

44. See Surya, *Georges Bataille*, 235–53.

45. The reference here is to Hegel as mediated principally through Kojève, whose lectures on the *Phenomenology of Spirit* in the 1930s were attended by Bataille. See Alexandre Kojève, *Introduction à la lecture de Hegel*.

46. The term *désœuvrement* is used in the context of an interruption of Hegelian dialectical work in Blanchot's early essay "La Littérature et le droit à la mort," in *La Part du feu*, 303–45 (trans. in *The Work of Fire*, 300–344).

47. Nancy is probably correct in his assessment here. Surya warns against making overly reductive judgments about Bataille's intellectual itinerary and the impact of the events of 1940–45; he writes: "The war having ended it makes no sense to look for a different Bataille"; *Georges Bataille*, 395. Yet the Occupation sees Bataille begin a series of apparently more private or inward meditations (what will become his *Somme athéologique*), and his postwar writing career is most prominently marked by works which develop his interests in a more systematic or even systematized fashion and with a more detailed historical sweep, most notably his work on economy, *La Part Maudite* (*The Accursed Share*), and on unproductive sexuality *L'Erotisme* (translated as *Eroticism*). Not a different Bataille, then, but one who increasingly finds ways of engaging with his key concerns which are very different from those of the 1930s.

48. Bataille, *Œuvres complètes*, 7:257.

49. Ibid., 5:74.

50. Leslie Hill, *Blanchot: Extreme Contemporary*, 196–209, in particular page 200.

51. Ibid., 200–204.

52. This is not to say that Blanchot can always entirely be assimilated to a Levinasian position and that there are not important differences between the two. Again see ibid., 112–14. For an acute analysis of the complex relation between ethics and ontology in Levinas and the relation of this to political concerns, see Howard Caygill, *Levinas and the Political*, 94–97.

53. See Derrida, *Spectres de Marx* and *Politiques de l'amitié*. Derrida has explicitly signaled that this latter work marks a culmination in an engagement with the political which Nancy and Lacoue-Labarthe's work for the Center began in the early 1980s. He also calls into question Nancy's philosophical language, refusing the term *community* as far too burdened with the legacy of identitarian thinking.

54. Robert Antelme, *L'Espèce humaine*, might also figure in this context. See Martin Crowley, *Robert Antelme: Humanity, Community, Testimony*, 38–62.

55. Howard Caygill, for instance, argues that Nancy's ontological understanding fails to account properly for the nature of violence. See Caygill, "The Shared World: Philosophy, Violence, Freedom," in Darren Sheppard, Simon Sparks, and Colin Thomas, eds., *On Jean-Luc Nancy: The Sense of Philosophy*, 19–31, in particular 28–30.

56. Andrew Norris, "Jean-Luc Nancy and the Myth of the Common."

57. Ibid., 273.

58. Ibid., 286.

59. In this respect Nancy's reading and critique of Kant are particularly rele-

vant. See "Lapsus judicii," in *L'Impératif catégorique*, 33–60.

60. Nancy's reference to Blanchot here is clearly an attempt to align his think-ing of community with Blanchot's, and can be seen as a response to the critical as-pects of *La Communauté inavouable*.

61. On this basis Critchley's criticism in *The Ethics of Deconstruction* (discussed above) could be qualified further.

CHAPTER 5: ART

1. *LM*, 151; *TM*, 93.

2. These are mostly disparate and numerous pieces. For Nancy's collaborative work with Kiarostami, see *L'Évidence du film / Abba Kiarostami*.

3. G. W. F. Hegel, *Ästhetik*, vol. 1, *Vorlesungen*, 13–95; trans., *Hegels Introduc-tion to Aesthetics*; hereafter *As* and *LA* respectively.

4. For a brief but authoritative introductory account of Hegel's thinking of Spirit, see Michael Inwood, *A Hegel Dictionary*, 274–77.

5. This of course recalls Nancy's reading of Kant and questioning of *Darstel-lung* and *Dichtung* in *Logodaedalus*.

6. Hegel has no problem with these questions, since, as Nancy indicates, he is able to systematically deduce the rationality of the five senses and thus their ulti-mate unity and homogeneity (*LM*, 26; *TM*, 11).

7. On this point Nancy cites Aristotle's account of "common sensibles," the emphasis placed by modern physiology on the multiplicity of sense organs and re-ceptors, as well as the view taken by thinkers such as Merleau-Ponty and Deleuze that any one sense is always the result of an integration or synthesis of a plurality of sensations.

8. This recalls Nancy's treatment of technicity such as it was discussed in the final section of the Chapter 3.

9. Again this repeats thinking of spatiality and *Ereignis* as discussed in Chap-ter 2.

10. This recalls the Nietzschean theory of force such as it is read by Klos-sowski and Deleuze. See Gilles Deleuze, *Différence et répétition* (*Difference and Repetition*), and *Logique du sens* (*Logic of Sense*); Pierre Klossowski, *Nietzsche et le cercle vicieux* (*Nietzsche and the Vicious Circle*); see also Ian James, "Klossowski, Ni-etzsche, and the Fortuitous Body."

11. Maurice Blanchot, *L'Espace littéraire*, 28, 29; *The Space of Literature*, 32.

12. Ibid., 30, 33.

13. Such as one might find in the theories of the Russian formalists or in the poststructuralist literary theory of Barthes and Kristeva.

CONCLUSION

1. Nancy, *La Création du monde; ou, La Mondialisation*, 63.

2. This indicates that Nancy's use of the term *nothing* is different from that of Heidegger's use of the term in his famous essay "What Is Metaphysics?" Where Heidegger comes to view the nothing as the "origin of negation," that is, as that originary nihilating of the "nothing" which makes negation as such possible in the first instance, Nancy, as is here indicated, views the nothing as the origin of creation. See Martin Heidegger, "Was ist Metaphysik?" 103–21, in particular page 116; "What Is Metaphysics," in particular page 105.

3. In this respect Nancy's thinking opens up a way of reading and understanding the concepts of other thinkers closely associated with him in productive rather than negative terms. Nancy underlines this in relation to the Derridean concept of *différance*. "Différance must not be understood as a sort of permanent loss [*fuite*] of an asymptotic and unattainable 'self' . . . but rather as the generative structure proper to the *ex nihilo*" (*CM*, 97).

4. Specifically this issue has been raised in different but related ways by Nancy Fraser, Simon Critchley, and Andrew Norris; see Chapter 4.

5. In this respect Nancy's thinking in this essay is close to that of Derrida's account of the decisionism. See for example *Force de loi*, in particular pages 50–63. Derrida has pointed out that a decision *necessarily* implies the absence of specific criteria or established norms, for, if these are appealed to in order to dictate a certain outcome the decision ceases to become a decision and affirms itself rather as calculation or implementation of a rule; Derrida, *Force de loi*, 53.

6. See Jean-François Lyotard, *Le Différand*, 189–91, 193–97, 214–16. See also the collective volume of essays devoted to Lyotard entitled *La Faculté de juger*, in particular the essays by Nancy, "Dies Irae," 9–54; and Derrida, "Préjugés: Devant la loi," 87–139. Nancy first gives a sustained reading of this dimension of Kant's thought in *L'Impératif catégorique*. For an account of Kant's theory of reflective judgment from an Anglo-American perspective, see Paul Guyer, *Kant and the Claims of Taste*, 29–59.

7. Nancy emphasizes the extent to which the notion of an "inconstructible" (i.e., that which always exceeds structure and structuration) has been a constant concern within the thought of deconstruction. Deconstruction has always pointed to "that which is not constructed or constructible, but that which is withdrawn from structure, its 'case vide' and that which makes structure work or which traverses it" (*CM*, 71).

8. "Du droit à la justice," in Derrida, *Force de loi*, 13–63.

9. Ibid., 60–61.

# Bibliography

BOOKS BY JEAN-LUC NANCY, ORIGINAL FRENCH EDITIONS

*L'Absolu littéraire: Théorie de la littérature du romantisme allemand.* With Philippe Lacoue-Labarthe. Paris: Seuil, 1978.

*La Blessure.* With Ensemble Perceval. Paris: Les Petits Matins, 2004.

*Chroniques philosophiques.* Paris: Galilée, 2004.

*Au ciel la terre.* Paris: Bayard, 2004.

*Cœur ardent/Cuore ardente.* With Claudio Parmiggiani. Milan: Mazzotta, 2003.

*La Communauté affrontée.* Paris: Galilée, 2001.

*La Communauté désœuvrée.* Paris: Christian Bourgois, 1986.

*La Comparution.* With Jean-Christophe Bailly. Paris: Christian Bourgois, 1991.

*Corpus.* Paris: Métailé, 1992.

*La Création du monde; ou, La Mondialisation.* Paris: Galilée, 2002.

*La Déclosion: Déconstruction du christianisme, I.* Paris: Galilée, 2005.

*Dehors la danse.* With Mathilde Monnier. Lyon: Droz, 2001.

*A l'écoute.* Paris: Galilée, 2002.

*Ego Sum.* Paris: Flammarion, 1979.

*Être singulier pluriel.* Paris: Galilée, 1996.

*L'Évidence du film / Abbas Kiarostami.* Brussels: Yves Gevaert, 2001.

*L'Expérience de la liberté.* Paris: Galilée, 1988.

*58 Indices sur le corps et l'extension de l'âme.* Paris: Nota Bene, 2005.

*Au fond des images.* Paris: Galilée, 2003.

*Fortino Samano.* With Virginie Lalucq. Paris: Galilée, 2004.

*Hegel: L'Inquiétude du négatif.* Paris: Hachette, 1997.

*Hypnoses.* With Mikkel Borch-Jacobsen and Eric Michaud. Paris: Galilée, 1984.

*Iconographie de l'auteur.* With Federico Ferrari. Paris: Galilée, 2005.

*L' "Il y a" du rapport sexuel.* Paris: Galilée, 2001.

*L'Impératif catégorique.* Paris: Flammarion, 1983.

*L'Intrus.* Paris: Galilée, 2000.

*Un Jour, les dieux se retirent . . .* Bordeaux: William Blake, 2001.

*Des Lieux divins.* Mauvezin: Trans-Europ-Repress, 1987.

*Logodaedalus: Le Discours de la syncope.* Paris: Aubier-Flammarion, 1976.

*Mmmmmmm.* With Susanna Fritscher. Paris: Figuré, 2000.

*Les Muses.* Paris: Galilée, 1994. 2nd ed., 2001.

*Le Myth nazi.* With Philippe Lacoue-Labarthe. La Tour d'Aigue: De l'Aube, 1991.

*La Naissance des seins.* Valence: Erba, 1997.

*Nium.* With François Martin. Valence: Erba, 1994.

*Noli me tangere.* Paris: Bayard, 2003.

*Nus sommes.* With Federico Ferrari. Brussels: Yves Gevaert, 2002.

*L'Oubli de la philosophie.* Paris: Galilée, 1986.

*Le Partage des voix.* Paris: Galilée, 1982.

*La Pensée dérobée.* Paris: Galilée, 2001.

*Une Pensée finie.* Paris: Galilée, 1990.

*Le Poids d'une pensée.* Montréal-Grenoble: Le Griffon d'Argile—Presses Universitaires de Grenoble, 1991.

*Le Portrait (dans le décor). Les Cahiers-Philosophie de l'art,* no. 8. Villeurbanne: Institut d'art contemporain, 1999.

*Le Regard du portrait.* Paris: Galilée, 2000.

*Rejouer le politique.* Edited with Philippe Lacoue-Labarthe. Paris: Gallimard, 1981.

*La Remarque spéculative, un bon mot de Hegel.* Paris: Galilée, 1973.

*Résistance de la poésie.* Bordeaux: William Blake, 1997.

*Le Retrait du politique.* Edited with Philippe Lacoue-Labarthe. Paris: Gallimard, 1983.

*Le Sens du monde.* Paris: Galilée, 1993.

*Technique du présent: Essai sur On Kawara. Les Cahiers-Philosophie de l'art,* no. 6. Villeurbanne: Nouveau Musée, 1997.

*Le Titre de la lettre: Une Lecture de Lacan.* With Philippe Lacoue-Labarthe. Paris: Galilée, 1972.

*Transcription.* Ivry-sur-Seine: Crédac, 2002.

*La Ville au loin.* Paris: Mille et une nuits, 1999.

*Visitation (de la peinture chrétienne).* Paris: Galilée, 2001.

## JOURNAL ARTICLES BY NANCY CITED

"André Breton." *Esprit* (December 1966): 848–49.

"Catéchisme et persévérence." *Esprit* (October 1967): 368–81.

"Un Certain Silence." *Esprit* (April 1963): 555–62.

"La Déconstruction du christianisme." *Études Philosophiques* 4 (1998): 503–19.

"L'Extension de l'âme." *Po&sie* 99 (2002): 77–83.

"Logodaedalus (Kant écrivain)." *Poétique* 21 (1975): 21–52.

"Marx et la philosophie." *Esprit* (May 1966): 1074–87.

"Nietzsche: Mais où sont les yeux pour le voir." *Esprit* (May 1968): 482–503.

"La Panique politique." With Philippe Lacoue-Labarthe. *Confrontations* 2 (1979): 35–57.

"Sur le trait d'esprit." *Poétique* 15 (1973): 365–71.


WORKS BY JEAN-LUC NANCY IN ENGLISH TRANSLATION

*Being Singular Plural.* Trans. Anne E. O'Byrne and Robert D. Richardson. Stanford, Calif.: Stanford University Press, 2000.

*The Birth to Presence.* Trans. Brian Holmes et al. Stanford, Calif.: Stanford University Press, 1993.

"The Compearance." Trans. Tracy B. Strong. In *Political Theory* 20, no. 3. Newbury Park, Calif.: Sage, 1992.

*The Experience of Freedom.* Trans. Bridget McDonald. Stanford, Calif.: Stanford University Press, 1993.

*A Finite Thinking.* Trans. Simon Sparks. Stanford, Calif.: Stanford University Press, 2003.

"The Forgetting of Philosophy." In *The Gravity of Thought*, trans. François Raffoul and Gregory Recco, 7–71. Atlantic Highlands, N.J.: Humanities Press, 1997.

"The Gravity of Thought." In *The Gravity of Thought*, trans. François Raffoul and Gregory Recco, 75–84. Atlantic Highlands, N.J.: Humanities Press, 1997.

*The Gravity of Thought.* Trans. François Raffoul and Gregory Recco. Atlantic Highlands, N.J.: Humanities Press, 1997.

*Hegel: The Disquiet of the Negative.* Trans. Jason Smith and Steven Miller. Minneapolis: University of Minnesota Press, 2002.

*The Inoperative Community.* Ed. Peter Connor. Trans. Peter Connor et al. Foreword by Christopher Fynsk. Minneapolis: University of Minnesota Press, 1991.

*L'Intrus.* Trans. Susan Hanson. In *New Centennial Review* 2, no. 3. East Lansing: Michigan State University Press, 2002.

*The Literary Absolute: The Theory of Literature in German Romanticism.* With Philippe Lacoue-Labarthe. Trans. Philip Barnard and Cheryl Lester. Albany: State University of New York Press, 1988.

*The Muses.* Trans. Peggy Kamuf. Stanford, Calif.: Stanford University Press, 1996.

*Retreating the Political.* With Philippe Lacoue-Labarthe. Ed. Simon Sparks. Trans. Céline Surprenant, Richard Stamp, Leslie Hill, et al. London: Routledge, 1997.

*The Sense of the World.* Trans. Jeffrey S. Librett. Minneapolis: University of Minnesota Press, 1997.

"The Sharing of Voices." Trans. Gayle L. Ormiston. In *Transforming the Hermeneutic Context: From Nietzsche to Nancy,* ed. Gayle L. Ormiston and Alan D. Schrift, 211–59. Albany: State University of New York Press, 1990.

*The Speculative Remark.* Trans. Céline Surprenant. Stanford, Calif.: Stanford University Press, 2001.

*The Title of the Letter: A Reading of Lacan.* With Philippe Lacoue-Labarthe. Trans. François Raffoul and David Pettigrew. Albany: State University of New York Press, 1992.

SELECT BIBLIOGRAPHY OF BOOKS AND ESSAYS ON NANCY

Barnard, Philip, and Cheryl Lester. Foreword to *The Literary Absolute: The Theory of Literature in German Romanticism,* with Philippe Lacoue-Labarthe, trans. Philip Barnard and Cheryl Lester, vii–xx. Albany: State University of New York Press, 1988.

Collective. *Le Sens dans tous les sens: Autour des travaux de Jean-Luc Nancy.* Paris: Galilée, 2004.

Critchley, Simon. "Retracing the Political: Politics and Community in the Works of Lacoue-Labarthe and Jean-Luc Nancy." In *The Political Subject of Violence,* ed. David Campbell and Michael Dillon, 73–93. Manchester: Manchester University Press, 1993.

Deguy, Michel. "Un Corps de pensée." *Le Monde,* July 10, 1992.

Derrida, Jacques. "Interview with Jean-Luc Nancy." Trans. Peter Connor. *Topoi* 7 (1988): 113–21.

———. *Le Toucher, Jean-Luc Nancy.* Paris: Galilée, 2000.

Devish, Ignaas. "La 'Négativité sans emploi.'" *Symposium* 4, no. 2 (2000): 167–87.

Fraser, Nancy. "The French Derrideans: Politicizing Deconstruction or Deconstructing the Political?" *New German Critique* 33 (1984): 127–54.

Fynsk, Christopher. Foreword to *The Inoperative Community,* ed. Peter Connor, trans. Peter Connor et al., vii–xxxv. Minneapolis: University of Minnesota Press, 1991.

Gabaude, Jean-Marie. "Jean-Luc Nancy, *L'impératif catégorique.*" *Revue Internationale de Philosophie* (1982).

Gilbet-Walsh, James. "Broken Imperatives: The Ethical Dimension of Nancy's Thought." *Philosophy and Social Criticism* 26, no. 2 (2000): 29–50.

Guibal, Francis. "Venue, passage, partage: La Voix singulière de Jean-Luc Nancy." *Études* 10, no. 2 (1997): 357–71.

*At the Heart: Of Jean-Luc Nancy. New Centennial Review* 2, no. 3 (2002).

Hutchens, B. C. *Jean-Luc Nancy and the Future of Philosophy*. Chesham, U.K.: Acumen, 2005.

Ingram, David. "The Retreat of the Political in the Modern Age: Jean-Luc Nancy on Totalitarianism and Community." *Research in Phenomenology* 18 (1988): 93–124.

James, Ian. "The Persistence of the Subject: Jean-Luc Nancy." *Paragraph* 25, no. 1 (2002): 125–41.

Kamuf, Peggy, ed. *On the Work of Jean-Luc Nancy. Paragraph* 16, no. 2 (1993).

Kaplan, Louis. "Photography and the Exposure of Community: Sharing Nan Goldin and Jean-Luc Nancy." *Angelaki* 6, no. 3 (December 2001): 7–30.

Laus, Thierry. "La Fin du Christianisme: Désenchantement, deconstruction, et démocratie." *Revue de Théologie et de Philosophie* 133, no. 4 (2001): 475–85.

Librett, Jeffrey S. Preface to *The Sense of the World*, trans. Jeffrey S. Librett, vii–xxvi. Minneapolis: University of Minnesota Press, 1997.

Madou, Jean-Pol. "Jean-Luc Nancy, *Ego Sum*." *Nouvelle Revue Française*, no. 224 (November 1980): 139–43.

May, Todd. *Reconsidering Difference: Nancy, Derrida, Levinas, Deleuze*. University Park: Pennsylvania State University Press, 1997.

Melville, Peter. "Spectres of Schelling: Jean-Luc Nancy and the Limits of Freedom." *Arachne* 7, nos. 1–2 (2000): 62–75.

Naas, Michael. "In and Out of Touch: Derrida's *Le Toucher, Jean-Luc Nancy*." *Research in Phenomenology* 31 (2001): 258–65.

Norris, Andrew. "Jean-Luc Nancy and the Myth of the Common." *Constellations* 7, no. 2 (2000): 272–95.

Ormiston, Gayle L., and Alan D. Schrift. *Transforming the Hermeneutic Context: From Nietzsche to Nancy*. New York: State University of New York Press, 1990.

Raffoul, François. "The Logic of the With: On Nancy's *Être Singulier Pluriel*." *Studies in Practical Philosophy* 1, no. 1 (1999).

Readings, Bill. "The Deconstruction of Politics." In *De Man Reading de Man*, ed. Lindsay Waters and Wlad Godzich, 223–43. Minneapolis: University of Minnesota Press, 1989.

Sheppard, Darren, Simon Sparks, and Colin Thomas, eds. *On Jean-Luc Nancy: The Sense of Philosophy*. London: Routledge, 1997.

Sparks, Simon. "The Experience of Evil: Kant and Nancy." In *Theoretical Interpretations of the Holocaust*, ed. Dan Stone, 205–32. Amsterdam: Rodopi, 2001.

Spivak, Gayatri. "Response to Jean-Luc Nancy." In *Thinking Bodies*, ed. Juliet Flower MacCannell and Laura Zakarin, 32–51. Stanford, Calif.: Stanford University Press, 1994.

OTHER WORKS CITED

Ansell-Pearson, Keith. *An Introduction to Nietzsche as a Political Thinker*. London: Routledge, 1994.

Antelme, Robert. *L'Espèce humaine*. Paris: Gallimard, 1957.

Bataille, Georges. *The Accursed Share*. Trans. Robert Hurley. New York: Zone, 1988.

———. *Eroticism*. Trans. Mary Dalwood. London: Boyers, 1987.

———. *Inner Experience*. Trans. Lelsie Anne Boldt. Albany: State University of New York Press, 1988.

———. *Œuvres completes*. 12 vols. Paris: Gallimard, 1970–88.

———. *Visions of Excess*. Trans. Alan Stoekl. Manchester: Manchester University Press, 1985.

Beardsworth, Richard. *Derrida and the Political*. London: Routledge, 1996.

Bennington, Geoffrey. *Frontières kantiennes*. Paris: Galilée, 2000.

———. *Jacques Derrida*. Paris: Seuil, 1991.

Blanchot, Maurice. *La Communauté inavouable*. Paris: Minuit, 1983.

———. *L'Entretien infini*. Paris: Gallimard, 1969.

———. *L'Espace littéraire*. Paris: Gallimard, 1955.

———. *The Infinite Conversation*. Trans. Susan Hanson. Minneapolis: University of Minnesota Press, 1993.

———. *La Part du feu*. Paris: Gallimard, 1949.

———. *The Space of Literature*. Trans. Ann Smock. Lincoln: University of Nebraska Press, 1982.

———. *The Unavowable Community*. Trans. Pierre Joris. New York: Station Hill Press, 1988.

———. *The Work of Fire*. Trans. Charlotte Mandell. Stanford, Calif.: Stanford University Press, 1995.

Borch-Jacobsen, Mikkel. *The Absolute Master*. Trans. Douglas Brick. Stanford, Calif.: Stanford University Press, 1991.

———. *Le Maître absolu*. Paris: Flammarion, 1990.

Boudot, Pierre, et al. *Nietzsche aujourd'hui?* 2 vols. Paris: Union Générale d'Éditions, 1973.

Bowie, Andrew. "Rethinking the History of the Subject." In *Deconstructive Subjectivities*, ed. Simon Critchley and Peter Dews, 105–26. Albany: State University of New York Press, 1996.

Bowie, Malcolm. *Lacan*. London: Fontana, 1992.

Brooker, Peter. *Cultural Theory: A Glossary*. London: Arnold, 1999.

Caygill, Howard. *A Kant Dictionary*. Oxford: Blackwell, 1995.

———. *Levinas and the Political*. London: Routledge 2002.

Cohen, Hermann. *Kants Theorie der Erfahrung.* Berlin: B. Cassirer, 1918.

Conley, Verena Andermatt, ed. *Rethinking Technologies.* Minneapolis: University of Minnesota Press, 1993.

Connor, Peter, Jean-Luc Nancy, and Eduardo Cadava, eds. *Who Comes After the Subject?* London: Routledge, 1991.

Conway, Daniel. *Nietzsche and the Political.* London: Routledge, 1997.

Critchley, Simon. "Black Socrates? Questioning the Philosophical Tradition." In *Ethics—Politics—Subjectivity,* by Simon Critchley, 122–42. London: Verso, 1999.

———. *The Ethics of Deconstruction.* Edinburgh: Edinburgh University Press, 1992.

———. *Ethics—Politics—Subjectivity.* London: Verso, 1999.

———. "Prolegomena to Any Post-Deconstructive Subjectivity." In *Deconstructive Subjectivities,* ed. Simon Critchley and Peter Dews, 13–45. Albany: State University of New York Press, 1996.

Critchley, Simon, and Peter Dews, eds. *Deconstructive Subjectivities.* Albany: State University of New York Press, 1996.

Crowley, Martin. *Robert Antelme: Humanity, Community, Testimony.* Oxford: Legenda, 2003.

Dainton, Barry. *Time and Space.* Chesham, U.K.: Acumen, 2001.

de Bestegui, Miguel. *Heidegger and the Political.* London: Routledge, 1998.

Deleuze, Gilles. *Difference and Repetition.* Trans. Paul Patton. London: Athlone, 1994.

———. *Différence et répétition.* Paris: Presses Universitaires de France, 1968.

———. *The Logic of Sense.* trans. Mark Lester with Charles Stivale. New York: Columbia University Press, 1990.

———. *Logique du sens.* Paris: Minuit, 1969.

———. *Nietzsche et la philosophie.* Paris: Presses Universitaires de France, 1962.

———. *Nietzsche and Philosophy.* Trans. Hugh Tomlinson. New York: Columbia University Press, 1983.

Deleuze, Gilles, and Michel Foucault. "Les Intellectuels et le pouvoir." *Arc* 49 (1972): 3–10.

Deleuze, Gilles, and Félix Guattari. *L'Anti-Œdipe: Capitalisme et schizophrénie.* Paris: Minuit, 1972.

———. *Anti-Oedipus: Capitalism and Schizophrenia.* Trans. Robert Hurley, Mark Seem, and Helen R. Lane. Minneapolis: University of Minnesota Press, 1983.

Derrida, Jacques. *La Carte postale.* Paris: Flammarion, 1980.

———. *Du Droit à la philosophie.* Paris: Galilée, 1990.

———. *L'Écriture et la différence.* Paris: Seuil, 1967.

———. *Edmund Husserl's Origin of Geometry: An Introduction.* Trans. John P. Leavey, Jr., and David B. Allison. Sussex: Harvester Press, 1978.

———. *Epérons.* Paris: Flammarion, 1978.

———. *De L'Esprit: Heidegger et la question.* Paris: Galilée, 1987.

———. *Force de loi.* Paris: Minuit, 1994.

———. *De la grammatologie.* Paris: Minuit, 1967.

———. *Of Grammatology.* Trans. Gayatri Spivak. Baltimore: Johns Hopkins University Press, 1998.

———. "*Ja,* ou le faux-bond II." *Digraphe* 11 (1977).

———. *Marges de la philosophie.* Paris: Minuit, 1972.

———. *Margins of Philosophy.* Trans. Alan Bass. Chicago: Chicago University Press, 1982.

———. *L'Origine de la géométrie de Husserl: Introduction et traduction.* Paris: Epiméthée, 1962.

———. *Politiques de l'amitié.* Paris: Galilée, 1994.

———. *Positions.* Paris: Minuit, 1972.

———. *Positions.* Trans. Alan Bass. London: Athlone, 1987.

———. *Résistences de la psychanalyse.* Paris: Galilée, 1996.

———. *Le Toucher, Jean-Luc Nancy.* Paris: Galilée, 2000.

———. *La Voix et le phénomène.* Paris: Presses Universitaires de France, 1967.

———. *Writing and Difference.* Trans. Alan Bass. Chicago: University of Chicago Press, 1978.

Derrida, Jacques, Jean-Luc Nancy, et al. *La Faculté de juger.* Paris: Minuit, 1985.

Descartes, René. *Discours de la méthode.* Paris: Flammarion, 1966.

———. *Discourse on Method.* Trans. Desmond M. Clarke. Harmondsworth, U.K.: Penguin, 1999.

Dillon, Michael. *Merleau-Ponty's Ontology.* Bloomington: Indiana University Press, 1988.

Dosse, François. *Histoire du structuralisme.* 2 vols. Paris: Découverte, 1991–92.

———. *History of Structuralism.* 2 vols. Trans. Deborah Glassman. Minneapolis: University of Minnesota Press, 1997.

Eisler, Rudolphe. *Kant-Lexicon.* Paris: Gallimard, 1994.

Farias, Viktor. *Heidegger and Nazism.* Paris: Verdier, 1987.

Foucault, Michel. *Discipline and Punish: The Birth of the Prison.* Trans. Alan Sheridan. New York: Pantheon, 1977.

———. *Surveiller et punir: Naissance de la prison.* Paris: Gallimard, 1975.

Gauchet, Marcel. *Le Désenchantement du monde: Une Histoire politique de la religion.* Paris: Gallimard, 1985.

Glucksmann, André. *Les Maîtres penseurs.* Paris: Grasset, 1977.

Granel, Gérard. *L'Équivoque ontologique de la pensée kantienne*. Paris: Gallimard, 1970.

Gutting, Gary. *French Philosophy in the Twentieth Century*. Cambridge: Cambridge University Press, 2001.

Guyer, Paul. *Kant and the Claims of Taste*. 2nd ed. Cambridge: Cambridge University Press, 1998.

———, ed. *The Cambridge Companion to Kant*. Cambridge: Cambridge University Press, 1992.

Hegel, G. W. F. *Ästhetik*. 2 vols. Frankfurt: Europäische Verlagsanstalt.

———. *Hegel's Introduction to Aesthetics*. Trans. T. M. Knox. Oxford: Clarendon, 1979.

Heidegger, Martin. *Basic Writings*. Ed. David Farrell Krell. New York: Harper and Row, 1977.

———. *Being and Time*. Trans. John MacQuarrie. Oxford: Blackwell, 1962.

———. *Contributions to Philosophy (from Enowning)*. Trans. Parvis Emad and Kenneth Maly. Cambridge: Cambridge University Press, 1998.

———. *The End of Philosophy and the Task of Thinking*. Trans. Joan Stambaugh. Chicago: University of Chicago Press, 1973. Revised ed., 2003.

———. *Gesamtausgabe*. 102 vols. Frankfurt: Klostermann, 1975–.

———. *Kant and the Problem of Metaphysics*. Trans. Richard Taft. Bloomington: Indiana University Press, 1990.

———. *Nietzsche*. 4 vols. Trans. Joan Stambaugh, David Farrell Krell, and Frank A. Kapuzzi. San Francisco: Harper and Row, 1987.

———. *Nietzsche*. 2 vols. Trans. Pierre Klossowski. Paris: Gallimard, 1972.

———. *Pathmarks*. Cambridge: Cambridge University Press, 1998.

———. "What Is Metaphysics." In *Basic Writings*, ed. David Farrell Krell, 93–110. New York: Harper and Row, 1977.

———. *Zur Sache des Denkens*. Tübingen: Niemeyer, 1969.

———. *Zur Seinsfrage/The Question of Being*. Bilingual ed. Trans. William Kluback and Jean T. Wilde. London: Vision, 1959.

———. *Die Technik und die Kehre*. Neske: Pfullingen, 1962.

———. *On Time and Being*. Trans. John Stambaugh. New York: Harper and Row, 1972.

———. "Was ist Metaphysik?" In *Wegmarken*, by Martin Heidegger, 103–21. 2nd ed. Frankfurt: Klostermann, 1978.

———. *Wegmarken*. 2nd ed. Frankfurt: Klostermann, 1978.

Henri-Lévy, Bernard. *La Barbarie à visage humain*. Paris: Grasset, 1977.

Henry, Michel. *Incarnation*. Paris: Seuil, 2000.

Hill, Leslie. *Blanchot: Extreme Contemporary*. London: Routledge, 1996.

Hobson, Marion. *Jacques Derrida: Opening Lines*. London: Routledge 1998.

Hollier, Denis. *La Prise de la concorde*. Paris: Gallimard, 1974.

———, ed. *Collège de sociologie.* Paris: Gallimard, 1979.

Howells, Christina. *Derrida.* Cambridge: Polity, 1999.

Husserl, Edmund. *The Crisis of European Sciences and Transcendental Phenomenology: An Introduction to Phenomenological Philosophy.* Trans. David Carr. Evanston, Ill.: Northwestern University Press, 1970.

———. *General Introduction to a Pure Phenomenology.* Vol. 1 of *Ideas Pertaining to a Pure Phenomenology and to a Phenomenological Philosophy.* Trans. F. Kersten. The Hague: Nijhoff, 1982.

———. *Gesammelte Werke.* 38 vols. The Hague: Nijhoff, 1950–.

———. *Logical Investigations.* 2 vols. Trans. J. N. Findley. New York: Humanities Press, 1970.

———. *Studies in the Phenomenology of Constitution.* Vol. 2 of *Ideas Pertaining to a Pure Phenomenology and to a Phenomenological Philosophy.* Trans. Richard Rojcewicz and André Schuwer. Dordrecht: Kluwer, 1989.

———. *Thing and Space: 1907 Lectures.* Vol. 7 of *Collected Works.* Ed. and trans. Richard Rojcewicz. Dordrecht: Kluwer, 1997.

Inwood, Michael. *A Hegel Dictionary.* Oxford: Blackwell, 1992.

———. *A Heidegger Dictionary.* Oxford: Blackwell, 1999.

James, Ian. "Klossowski, Nietzsche, and the Fortuitous Body." *Romance Studies* 19, no. 1 (2001): 59–70.

———. *Pierre Klossowski: The Persistence of a Name.* Oxford: Legenda, 2000.

———. "Simulacrum and the Play of Parody in the Writing of Pierre Klossowski." *French Studies* 54, no. 2 (2000): 299–311.

Kant, Immanuel. *Critique de la raison pure.* Trans. A. Tremesaygues and B. Pacaud. Paris: Presses Universitaires de France, 1944.

———. *Critique of Pure Reason.* Trans. Paul Guyer and Alan W. Wood. Cambridge: Cambridge University Press, 1998.

———. *Kritik der reinen Vernunft.* 2 vols. 1781, 1789. Reprint, London: Routledge, 1994.

———. *Prolegomena to Any Future Metaphysics.* Ed. and trans. Gary Hartfield. London: Routledge, 1997.

Keller, Pierre. *Husserl and Heidegger on Human Experience.* Cambridge: Cambridge University Press, 1999.

Kelly, Sean Dorrence. "Merleau-Ponty on the Body." *Ratio* 15, no. 4 (2002): 376–91.

Klossowski, Pierre. *Nietzsche et le cercle vicieux.* Paris: Mercure de France, 1969.

———. *Nietzsche and the Vicious Circle.* Trans. Daniel W. Smith. Athlone, 1997.

———. *Un si funeste désir.* Paris: Gallimard, 1963.

Kojève, Alexandre. *Introduction à la lecture de Hegel.* Ed. Raymond Queneau. Paris: Gallimard, 1947.

Lacan, Jacques. *The Second Seminar.* Trans. Sylvana Tomaselli. Cambridge: Cambridge University Press, 1988.

——. *Le Seminaire II*. Paris: Seuil, 1978.

Lacoue-Labarthe, Philippe. "Le Détour (Nietzsche et la rhétorique)." *Poétique* 5 (1971): 53–76.

——. "La Fable (philosophie et littérature)." *Poétique* 1 (1970): 51–63.

——. *La Fiction du politique*. Paris: Christian Bourgois, 1987.

——. "L'Imprésentable." *Poétique* 21 (1975): 53–95.

——. "L'Oblitération." *Critique* 313 (1973): 487–513.

——. *Le Sujet de la philosophie*. Paris: Aubier-Flammarion, 1979.

Langer, Monika M. *Merleau-Ponty's "Phenomenology of Perception": A Guide and Commentary*. Tallahassee: Florida State University Press, 1989.

Lash, Scott. "Genealogy and the Body: Foucault / Deleuze / Nietzsche." In *The Body Social Processes and Cultural Theory*, ed. Bryan S. Turner, 256–80. London: Sage, 1991.

Lecourt, Domique. *Les Piètres penseurs*. Paris: Flammarion, 1999.

Lefèbvre, Henri. *La Production de l'espace*. Paris: Anthropos, 1974.

Lefort, Claude. *Democracy and Political Theory*. Trans. David Macey. Oxford: Polity, 1988.

——. "The Question of Democracy." Trans. David Macey. In *Democracy and Political Theory*, by Claude Lefort, trans. David Macey, pp. 9–20. Oxford: Polity, 1988.

Lyotard, Jean-François. *Le Différand*. Paris: Minuit, 1983.

——. *L'Economie libidinale*. Paris: Minuit, 1974.

——. *Heidegger et "les juifs."* Paris: Galilée, 1988.

Marmande, Francis. *Georges Bataille politique*. Lyon: Presses Universitaires de Lyon, 1985.

Mauss, Marcel. *The Gift: The Form and Reason for Exchange in Archaic Societies*. Trans. W. D. Halls. London: Routledge, 1990.

——. *Sociologie et Anthropologie*. Paris: Presses Universitaires de France, 1950.

Merleau-Ponty, Maurice. *Phénoménologie de la perception*. Paris: Gallimard, 1945.

——. *Phenomenology of Perception*. Trans. Colin Smith. London: Routledge and Kegan Paul, 1962.

——. *Le Visible et l'invisible*. Paris: Gallimard, 1964.

——. *The Visible and the Invisible*. Trans. Alphonso Lingis. Evanston, Ill.: Northwestern University Press, 1968.

Miami Theory Collective, ed. *Community at Loose Ends*. Minneapolis: University of Minnesota Press, 1991.

Moran, Dermot. *Introduction to Phenomenology*. London: Routledge, 2000.

Nietzsche, Friedrich. *Kritische Studienausgabe*. 15 vols. Ed. Giorgio Colli and Montinari Mazzino. Berlin: De Gruyter, 1967–77.

———. *Twilight of the Idols.* Trans. R. J. Hollingdale. Harmondsworth, U.K.: Penguin, 1990.

Philipse, Hermann. "Transcendental Idealism." In *The Cambridge Companion to Husserl,* ed. Barry Smith and David Woodruff-Smith, 239–322. Cambridge: Cambridge University Press, 1995.

Philonenko, Alexis. *L'Œuvre de Kant.* 5th ed. Paris: Vrin, 1996.

Polt, Richard. *Heidegger.* London: University College Press, 1999.

Priest, Stephen. *Merleau-Ponty.* London: Routledge, 1998.

Safranski, Rudiger. *Heidegger: Between Good and Evil.* Cambridge, Mass.: Harvard University Press, 1998.

Schirmacher, Wolfgang. *Technik und Gelassenheit.* Freiburg: Alber, 1983.

Sedgwick, Peter, ed. *Key Concepts in Cultural Theory.* London: Routledge, 1999.

Sheehan, Thomas. "Heidegger and the Nazis." *New York Review of Books,* June 16, 1988, 41–42.

Shilling, Chris. "The Body and Difference." In *Identity and Difference,* ed. Kathryn Woodward, 65–103. London: Sage, 1997.

———. *The Body and Social Theory.* London: Sage, 1993.

Smith, Barry, and David Woodruff-Smith, eds. *The Cambridge Companion to Husserl.* Cambridge: Cambridge University Press, 1995.

Smith, Douglas. *Transvaluations: Nietzsche in France, 1872–1972.* Oxford: Clarendon, 1997.

Sparks, Simon. "Politica Ficta." Introduction to *Retreating the Political,* by Jean-Luc Nancy. With Philippe Lacoue-Labarthe, ed. Simon Sparks, trans. Céline Surprenant, Richard Stamp, Leslie Hill, et al. London: Routledge, 1997.

Spivak, Gayatri, Christopher Fynsk et al. *Les Fins de l'homme: À partir du travail de Jacques Derrida.* Paris: Galilée, 1981.

Surya, Michel. *Georges Bataille: An Intellectual Biography.* Trans. Krzysztof Fijalkowski and Michael Richardson. London: Verso, 2002.

———. *Georges Bataille: La Mort à l'œuvre.* Paris: Gallimard, 1992.

Turner, Bryan S. "The Secret History of the Body in Social Theory." In *The Body Social Processes and Cultural Theory,* ed. Bryan S. Turner, 12–18. London: Sage, 1991.

———, ed. *The Body Social Processes and Cultural Theory.* London: Sage, 1991.

van Buren, John. *The Young Heidegger.* Bloomington: Indiana University Press, 1994.

Woodward, Kathryn, ed. *Identity and Difference.* London: Sage, 1997.

# Index

## DATE DUE

| | | | |
|---|---|---|---|
| OhioLINK | | | |
| | | | |
| MAR 14 REC'D | | | |
| | | | |
| | | | |
| | | | |
| | | | |
| | | | |
| | | | |
| | DISCARDED | | |
| | | | |
| | | | |
| | | | |
| | | | |
| | | | |
| | | | |
| GAYLORD | | | PRINTED IN U.S.A. |

B 2430 .N364 J36 2006

James, Ian

The fragmentary demand